Fanon & Education

Studies in the Postmodern Theory of Education

Joe L. Kincheloe and Shirley R. Steinberg
General Editors

Vol. 368

PETER LANG
New York • Washington, D.C./Baltimore • Bern
Frankfurt am Main • Berlin • Brussels • Vienna • Oxford

Fanon & Education

Thinking Through Pedagogical Possibilities

George J. Sefa Dei & Marlon Simmons, Editors

PETER LANG
New York • Washington, D.C./Baltimore • Bern
Frankfurt am Main • Berlin • Brussels • Vienna • Oxford

Library of Congress Cataloging-in-Publication Data

Fanon and education: thinking through pedagogical possibilities /
[edited by] George J. Sefa Dei, Marlon Simmons.
p. cm. — (Counterpoints: studies in the postmodern theory of education)
Includes bibliographical references.
1. Education—Philosophy. 2. Education and state—Philosophy.
3. Racism in education. 4. Fanon, Frantz, 1925–1961—Political and social views.
5. Fanon, Frantz, 1925–1961—Criticism and interpretation. 6. Colonialism.
7. Postcolonialism. I. Dei, George J. Sefa. II. Simmons, Marlon.
LB14.7.D45   370.1—dc22   2009036550
ISBN 978-1-4331-0642-2 (hardcover)
ISBN 978-1-4331-0641-5 (paperback)
ISSN 1058-1634

Bibliographic information published by **Die Deutsche Nationalbibliothek**.
Die Deutsche Nationalbibliothek lists this publication in the "Deutsche
Nationalbibliografie"; detailed bibliographic data is available
on the Internet at http://dnb.d-nb.de/.

© 2010 Peter Lang Publishing, Inc., New York
29 Broadway, 18th floor, New York, NY 10006
www.peterlang.com

All rights reserved.
Reprint or reproduction, even partially, in all forms such as microfilm,
xerography, microfiche, microcard, and offset strictly prohibited.

Table of Contents

Acknowledgments vii
Foreword
   Carl Grant ix
The Pedagogy of Fanon: An Introduction
   George J. Sefa Dei and Marlon Simmons xiii

Chapter 1. Rereading Fanon for His Pedagogy and Implications for
   Schooling and Education
   George J. Sefa Dei 1
Chapter 2. Body Politics and the Experience of Blackness within
   the Field of Education
   Camille Logan 29
Chapter 3. Rereading the Ontario *Review of the Roots of Youth Violence Report*:
   The Relevance of Fanon for a Critical Disability Studies Perspective
   Katie Aubrecht 55
Chapter 4. Resistance to Amputation: Discomforting Truth
   about Colonial Education in Ghana
   Paul Adjei 79
Chapter 5. The Fact of Blackness: A Critical Review of Bermuda's Colonial
   Education System
   Donna Outerbridge 105
Chapter 6. Reading Fanon in "Homosexual Territory": Towards the Queering
   of a Queer Pedagogy
   Rory Crath 123
Chapter 7. Strategic In/Visibility and Undocumented Migrants
   Francisco J. Villegas 147
Chapter 8. Concerning Modernity, the Caribbean Diaspora, and Embodied
   Alienation: Dialoguing with Fanon to Approach an Anticolonial Politic
   Marlon Simmons 171

Notes on Contributors 191

Acknowledgments

We would like to thank the students in George Dei's graduate course, SES 3999: Frantz Fanon and Education: Pedagogical Challenges, at the Ontario Institute for Studies in Education of the University of Toronto (OISE/UT), who provided the inspiration for putting together this much-needed collection. Our class discussions, which took a critical look at Fanon as a philosopher, pedagogue, and anticolonial practitioner, was a learning moment for all. As class discussions began to broach such issues as the contexts in which Fanon developed his ideas and thoughts, and how these developments subsequently came to shape anticolonial theory and practice, the limits and possibilities of political ideologies, as well as the theorization of imperialism and spiritual "dis-embodiment," particularly in Southern contexts, etc. we all began to feel that a book on Fanon and Education was much needed. We also want to acknowledge the assistance of Olga Williams of the Department of Sociology and Equity Studies at OISE/UT for assisting with editorial work on sections of the manuscript. We thank Shirley Steinberg and the late Joe Kincheloe of McGill University for believing in our abilities to undertake this work and to ensure that our ideas continue to reach a much wider audience. Marlon would like to thank Arnold Itwaru for his insightful conversations, for in many ways his thoughts influenced Marlon's growing understanding of Fanon. Finally, Marlon would like to voice his gratitude to George Dei for his unwavering support and critical comments contributed during the work and for the invitation to coedit.

Foreword

CARL GRANT

Fanon and Education: Thinking Through Pedagogical Possibilities, edited by George J. Sefa Dei and Marlon Simmons, is a much-needed piece of academic scholarship on pedagogy, schooling, and education. "Taking up Fanon's writing," as the editors argue, "should be a way to examine counter approaches to schooling and education to truly create a space for all students so that learning becomes meaningful" (p. xx). The book contains insightful ideas and scholarly commentary on the theory and practice of pedagogy at this time of heightened globalization, a theory and a practice that are influenced and accompanied by debates over human rights, social justice, colonialism, race and racism, and other prevailing issues surrounding diversity. However, before I continue, let me—like each contributor in the volume—discuss my prior relationship with Fanon's work and the ideas in this book.

I came upon Frantz Fanon's *Black Skin, White Masks* in a used book store in the early 1970s during my grad school days. The title immediately captured my attention, and the narrative therein was different from anything I was hearing in grad school: Fanon's ideas and related discussions received little if any attention there. Conversations about the impact of white colonialism and racism that happened both in an overt manner and as a nuanced, silent, and destructive discourse were not often discussed. As I read the book, I wondered, *Who* is this individual who is so insightful about much of what I am feeling and struggling to articulate? At the time, there was no search engine to "Google" him. Reading *Black Skin, White Masks* was illuminating and (would have been) very meaningful to the numerous controversial and racialized theses in education that were prominent at the time, such as James Coleman's theses that family matters more than schooling and that education spending is unrelated to achievement; Frank Reissman's theory of the culturally deprived child; Pat Moynihan's thesis about the traditional matriarchal black family structure; and Arthur Jensen's thesis that the races are unequal in regard to IQ. However, while I realized that Fanon's writing would have contributed to these conversations and controversies, what was I actually going to do with this discovery? The ideology and curriculum—theory and practice—of grad school (e.g., the nature of American schools, the foundations of education, teacher-centered v. student-centered instruction, the value of compensatory education programs like Headstart, etc.) were not seriously entertaining any of Fanon's views. Graduate school pedagogy lacked Fanon's comprehensive and intense interrogation of race and racism and his understanding of racial othering, internalized oppression, the personal aspects of living as a person of color every day, and the significance of the intersection and complexity of race, class, gender, and language.

I did not find that faculty or grad students were particularly interested in engaging in discussions of race and white colonialism. I was actually the one most at fault. I had not yet developed a scholarly voice in a department that was all white, with the exception of me and one other grad student. I lacked a voice to clearly and convincingly explain how white colonizers marginalized, subjugated, and stripped blacks of their culture, making them feel inferior and demanding that they emulate white culture and society. Here I am reminded of Fanon's statement that, "A man who has a language, consequently possesses the world expressed and implied by that language" and Foucault's coupling of knowledge and power. Both points resonate with personal meaning.

As I continued my graduate work into my current scholarship, I pursued the idea of multicultural education, much of which I believe both in theory and practice to be in keeping with Fanon's ideas. But Fanon as a scholar and active contributor to discussions of race, racism, colonial rule, anticolonialism, black consciousness and identity, and language as a rubric of power was not a reference point. Why, you might ask? This is a good question! Not because I did not find Fanon to be a scholarly and passionate voice to take action against race and racism in its varied and many forms, because I did. There is no satisfactory answer to why I did not return to Fanon's work, especially as two of his books are clearly visible on my shelf. At most I can say, "An excellent opportunity was missed," or, as I force myself to think back to this time, maybe I should say, "My choice of not including Fanon's work was a problem of Black scholarship not being recognized and accepted as a valuable theoretical discourse, and I wondered about the possible extent to which it would additionally influence my being further "othered."

Now, because of the assignment George and Marlon bestowed on me—that of writing this foreword—I have energetically renewed my interest in Fanon's work. These chapters were an excellent (re) introduction for me as they will be for any and all teacher educators, teachers, and graduate students to Fanon's work, especially *Black Skin, White Masks* and *The Wretched of the Earth*. What I have found most useful and powerful is the notion of "racial othering" in *Black Skin, White Masks*. Fanon poignantly and at times painfully demonstrates how the notion of blackness is constructed as inferior, less than, and outside of the colonizing norm of whiteness. I have come to realize that Fanon's observations about race and blackness offer a theoretical analysis and foundation to work concerned with issues of power, inequities, and social constructions of race, class gender, and sexuality. It is for these reasons that *Fanon and Education: Thinking Through Pedagogical Possibilities* is much needed and will serve as an inspiring expression of Fanon's ideas on anti-colonial, black consciousness, race, racism, power and privilege, all of which have great application for education and schooling. Work of this kind is long overdue.

Fanon and Education, as the editors note, addresses questions of "difference, diversity, and power, as defined through the lens of class, ethnicity, gender, disability, sexuality, religion, language and indigeneity" (p. xiv). The eight chapters, starting with George Dei's splendid opening chapter, deal with three key aspects of Fanon's writing for schooling and education: colonialism, violence, and decolonization, all of which give readers an excellent understanding of Fanon's central ideas. Each and every chapter in the book deals with troubling issues in education and society and gives readers who may come from various disciplines insights into how to deal with each issue. The book unapologetically wrestles with the personal and political struggles of identity and representation of black educators. It explains ablism and racism in the context of a critical disability discourse that takes into account and critiques language as found in policy and everyday life. It challenges heteronormative thinking and shows how Fanon's ideas may serve as an inspiration for rethinking sexuality and gender variance in a decolonized classroom space The text offers an insightful perspective about undocumented migrants and how Fanon's ideas of visibility and invisibility inform the "production of illegality." Two chapters, including one on education in Ghana, help readers to understand how educational "amputation" can be resisted with the use of Fanon's ideas. A chapter discusses how Bermuda as a former British colony still maintained a colonial system. Such chapters will illustrate Fanon's ideas about blackness and a new "humanism." The final chapter addresses Caribbean diasporic life and is framed by the colonial communicative practices, everyday artifacts, symbols and history and influenced by the socialization process of that diaspora. In addition this chapter addresses the importance of Fanon's ideas surrounding efforts to unshackle Diasporic peoples influenced by a colonizing socializing process.

As a multicultural and social justice (e.g., material equality, cultural recognition) teacher educator dealing with the influence of the paradoxes of globalization on children and teachers, I find that each chapter has particular significance for my research/scholarship, teaching, and service and to those whom I teach and mentor. The chapters collectively and individually argue that education includes not only schools but governmental agencies, public spaces in the community (e.g., museums, parks, libraries), and the media. The authors compel readers to think about systems of colonization, freedom in the context of people's minds, and the freedom for all people to take action for equity and social justice. Also during this time of numerous social and educational injustices, the contributors' interrogation of "knowledge, power, curriculum, and instruction and coming to know, act and engage the world" in order to "rupture historical 'master narratives'" is significant pedagogy for educators who are concerned about educational equality. Finally, the chapters' attention to sites and spaces of individuals and their collective resistance to the culture of dominance in educational settings provides a meaningful way to understand the faces and complexity of resistance. To re-connect to the ideas of Fanon in a book that is inspiring and very well written is exciting. Let me say to my colleagues and students, "You need to get and read *Fanon and Education: Thinking Through Pedagogical Possibilities* edited by George J. Sefa Dei and Marlon Simmons!"

Carl A. Grant
University of Wisconsin-Madison
June 2009

The Pedagogy of Fanon

An Introduction

GEORGE J. SEFA DEI AND MARLON SIMMONS

From the outset, we want to be clear on an important objective that has guided us through this work. We decided to engage Fanon out of a deep concern with the way Fanon is usually taken up as an intellectual exercise with a certain degree of discursive sophistication. Of course, criticisms of scholarly works should always be welcome because they push us to strive for excellence. However, we have been struck by the extent a few critics focus on perceived shortcomings of Fanon's work and brush aside with a sweeping broom his entire scholarly contributions. We know that a critical reader somewhere is asking us to give concrete examples of such critics. We will not take the bait. We are simply fascinated by the "high-level theorizing" of Fanon. In fact, our shared desire is to bring Fanon down to earth, to the basics, so to speak. We would engage Fanon in ways that aspects of his works speak to us in education, while mindful of the complexity, as well as the shortcomings of his writings. So, in taking up Fanon, we have a request. We want to be able to speak and write as we want. We make no false pretences to an "elaborate theoretical language" or claim to possess "big ideas" about Fanon. We do, however, believe we have something important to say about this scholar, and it is a form of knowledge valid in its own right from where we sit. The practice and limits of Eurocentricity have been a factor in the inadequate attention paid to Fanon's ideas and the pedagogical implications. Where and when Fanon is taken up, there is a form of "domestication of his writings," which is literally intellectualizing his ideas so as not to ruffle feathers, while the fundamental values and assumptions that undergird liberal democracies are not subverted. Thankfully, we have an emerging generation of scholars wanting to take up Fanon, breathing new energies into ways of thinking and interpretations of anticolonial knowledge informed by contemporary challenges of schooling and education.

Of course, we are fully aware that the examination of Fanon for his pedagogic implications is a huge and risky undertaking. This is because Fanon has been understood more outside the field of schooling and education and also that conventional understandings of education tend to be limited to schools. As Dei notes in his chapter critical feminist analysis of Fanon has pointed to his oversexualizing black women's bodies, a troubling engagement of hypermasculine and de-ableizing language, and perhaps, misreading the complicated experiences of black women's lives. Nonetheless, these critiques do not mean Fanon is irrelevant to contemporary discourses, and those who dismiss his works do so in the spirit of intellectual arrogance. In this project we challenge education to go beyond the formal processes of schooling and engage how we come to learn and know about everything in our worlds. We conceptualize education to include the workplace, homes and families, schools, media, museums, arts and the criminal justice system. Education is about everything—knowledge, power, curriculum, and instruction, a coming to know, act, and engage the world. Understanding education requires a holistic approach that extends beyond schools, to culture, media, law and justice, employment etc. Education is about the power to define oneself, to construct, validate, and legitimize knowledge and learn what is acceptable and not. It is about values, ideas, practices, as well as identities [race, class, gender, sexuality, disability, etc.] and how they link to knowledge production and social processes. Education is a power-saturated discussion. What we are arguing here is that there is more to inclusion than the dominant conception of education. This is often compounded by the failure to acknowledge difference as a significant site for education. That is, addressing questions of difference, diversity, and power, as defined through the lens of class, ethnicity, gender, disability, sexuality, religion, language, and indigeneity. It is such an expanded discussion that can help us respond to the possibility of creating a new vision of education that holds the promise and possibility of excellence for all.

Historically, education as it emerged through positivist epistemologies have come to be experienced through institutionalized spaces. What we are confronted with is a prism of knowledge as organized through particular procedures of standardization, through specific sociocultural technologies. Education denotes the capital of "Truth" systems, whereby the ensuing knowledge forms itself as the imperial sacrosanct within society. Education revealed itself through constitutive bodies of legitimation and hierarchical spaces. We need to understand education therefore as a process involving embodied knowledge. Knowledge is not void of the social, nor is it some absolute linear procedure, or some universal certainty. One of the challenges for pedagogy is how do we work with a process that cannot be measured? In other words, how do we come to recognize resident geographies of knowledge? We need continually to remember and remind ourselves of the protean ways colonial historic determinants come to be embedded in contemporary systems of education. We need to understand the orientation of Euro-Enlightenment neoliberal discourse immanent to conventional education. We query what knowledge governs institutionalized ways of knowing, and what are the ways in which Eurocentric idealized knowledge produces colonizing sites in everyday social interactive moments? We query how normative institutionalized geographies of education form the governing conditions of the neo-Euro modern subject. We ought to be cognizant of the danger wherein everyday colonizing sites come to "organize and inscribe" embodied knowledge that governs identity formations through particular communicative practices. This calls for thinking about different identities through race, class, gender, sexuality, abelism, and how identity is linked to knowledge production. The watershed here though, is the limitation of historical colonizing determinants, that which marks the procedure of possibility onto bodies of difference. We must give voice to the co-present bodies of knowledge immanent to different identities.

Critical education ought to rupture historical "master narratives" as deposited through the colonial will. In a sense then, education ought to instill pedagogic practices that subvert dominant Eurocentric paradigms. Pedagogues, as all learners, must recognize knowledge as nonarchived, as nonpartitioned. We must think of education as being communal. We cannot continue to talk about knowledge as neutral, objective, and of not being biased. Instead, we must confront our politics, implicate the self, identify different bodies, and push on to rupture hegemonic status quo spaces. We need to keep in mind the relationship of state and schooling and ask: What are the bodies and histories being centered and marginalized through state and schooling relations? Whose interests are sought through neutral locals of state and schooling allegiance? Education ought to centre the learner within the learning process. By centering the learner, sociocultural spaces are not operationalized tangentially but more so through multiple processes of meaning making. Education must consider the geohistorical local of all learners in relation to the attending pedagogies and curricula. We recognize that the notion of "revolution and liberation" has been contemporaneously reshaped, revealing itself, more through anticolonial and decolonizing sites. We cannot dismiss these moments given the popularized neoliberal humanitarian talk. In fact, even more now given the currency of neoliberal discourse do we need to engage with anticolonial and decolonizing methodologies. Anticolonial and decolonizing knowledge allows for the transformation of one's lived social existence. It allows one to recall experiential knowledge, that is, to draw from one's cultural resources to fertilize the meaning-making process. In the context of imperious knowledge systems, it allows the learner to reside through contrapuntal locals. Yet as the socializing mode of education gives us a commodified way of interacting with knowledge, we come to learn in particular ways, more as the passive body, eager, and willing to comply. Notably, scholars have spoken about education as a form of "epistemic violence" (see Spivak, 1988; Ladson-Billings, 2000). Fanon's question is still with us today, that of: "How do we extricate ourselves?" The challenge here lies with finding ways through which all learners can "develop" pedagogies that allow for the transformation of their geosocial spaces.

Historically, anticolonial knowledge has been disavowed from the corridors of education, the whisper being, anticolonial knowledge is not real knowledge. For the most part, anticolonial knowledge as governed through the expert Eurocentric epistemology has been reduced to superstition. What we have then is a particular colonizing procedure, in which one of the experiences of interest is, and as Fanon does well to speak about, a form of alienation for all learners. Like Fanon, we need to be concerned with the quality of humanism being formed through our day-to-day social interactions. We need to be alert not to be seduced by the ethical and moral register of colonialism. Ultimately, education as praxis ought to foster a climate of communal care.

Consequently, in this edited collection, authors explore the sites and spaces of individual and collective resistance to the culture of dominance in educational settings. The book will utilize a critical Fanonian discursive framework to understand the issues of colonialism, reorganized colonial relations in schooling, questions of identity, and representation in education. A critical Fanonian approach questions institutionalized power and privilege and the accompanying rationality for dominance. The approach draws on a critical analysis of the institutional structures within which the delivery of "social services and goods" takes place. The Fanonian discursive framework acknowledges the role of societal institutions in producing and reproducing social inequalities. A Fanonian analysis problematizes the marginalization of certain voices in the society, as well as the delegitimization of the knowledge and experience of subordinate groups. This framework views schools, families, workplaces, media, and the arts as part of the institutional structures sanctioned by society and the state to serve powerful material, political, and ideological interests. Thus, strategies designed to respond to issues of colonial representation and decolonization should address questions of systemic inequalities and explore viable and alternative forms of organizing a humane society.

The various contributions in the text broach such issues as the contexts in which Fanon developed his ideas and thoughts and how these developments subsequently came to shape anticolonial theory and practice, the limits and possibilities of political ideologies, as well as the theorization of imperialism and spiritual "dis-embodiment," particularly in Southern contexts. Specific subject matters include Fanon's understanding of violence, nationalism and politics of identity, national liberation, and resistance, the "dialectic of experience," the psychiatry of racism and the psychology of oppression, the limits of revolutionary class politics, and the power of "dramaturgical vocabulary," and how his ideas continue to make him a major scholarly figure.

The edited collection also aims at interrogating what Michael Sonnleitner (1987) identified as "the logic and liberation of Frantz Fanon and how this sheds light of a critical reading of terror and terrorism" of conventional forms of schooling and education; and also, Hussein Adam's (1997) exposition on "Frantz Fanon as a democratic theorist." We are interested in the reflections of Fanon's writings on political conflict, rebellion, and revolution in Africa and his thesis of violence for, particularly, schooling, education and development. We ask: How can Frantz Fanon's writings be understood in a contemporary perspective? And what are the insights for social change from working with the revolutionary thought of Frantz Fanon? How can we interpret and re-intepret the violence of schooling and education? What connections can be made of the colonizing experience and colonial discourses? How does Fanon help critical educators' subvert the imperial [dis]order of conventional schooling? How is Fanon relevant in engaging the pedagogies of identifications in schooling and education, and particularly the subjective agency, voice and struggles for liberation of the oppressed learner?

In one of his works Fanon made this well-known declaration: "Each generation must come out of its relative obscurity, discover its mission, fulfill it or betray it." (Fanon, 1963, p. 206). We see the project of decolonization as critical to our intellectual, political, mental and spiritual survival in the academy. The subverting of dominant knowledges in the Western academy is a project of decolonization and liberation. Fanon (1988) argues that there can be no authentic liberation without decolonization. This understanding is borne out of his conviction that we need to make a clear distinction between "liberation" and "decolonization." Liberation was foremost a political act for independence. Particularly in African and other colonized contexts, nationalist liberation struggles had an end in the goal of political independence from the colonizer. But such liberation can be fleeting given its preoccupation with political power. To Fanon, if such "liberation" left intact the broad macro structures of economic, political and material conditions that determined everyday existence, then it was a Pyrrhic victory. When liberation moves into the zone of transforming the sociopolitical, economic, and discursive mind-set of the oppressed/colonized and that of the colonizer/oppressor, then it becomes decolonization. Given the enormous nature of such struggle and transition, it is understandable to view decolonization as always ongoing and in process. Decolonization must be complete and must overcome exploitation, alienation and oppression, and dehumanization. Decolonization requires developing a national consciousness out of culture, politics, history, and identity. Such a victory will not come easy. It will be met with resistance and it will be costly to both parties in colonizing relations.

In other words, decolonization is not only a complete transformation but also has a double-sidedness to it as implicating both the colonized and colonizer. Decolonization is about unleashing the human resilience to triumph in the face of oppression, exploitation, alienation and inhumanity. Decolonization is violent and is a creative urgent necessity. Such violence has a cleansing force to rinse the oppressor detoxify the oppressed, and make both the oppressor and oppressed human again.

Fanon (1963) argues that, while hatred is disarmed by psychological windfalls, a war of liberation built upon achieving economic ends would be more lasting and successful. After all, colonialism has depersonalized the individual, as well as the collective sphere, on the level of social and political structures. This means a struggle to decolonize must be waged as more than a personal, spiritual cleansing. It must target and lead to social, economic, and political structural transformation. Among the major problems that colonized, oppressed and marginalized peoples have to deal with are the negations of historical experiences and collective and cultural memories; negation of our subjectivities; the invalidation of the embodiment of our knowing; a continuing struggle against our dehumanization and the "spirit injury" of perpetual resistance; and the oftentimes easy and seductive slippage into the form, logic, and implicit assumptions of the very things we are contesting. Fanon thus offers an opportunity to rethink transformative pedagogy and education by pointing to the areas of focus. We need to create a new humanity, and we must see the goal of education as helping all learners "become human."

The power of engaging in a dialogic process, in discussions over the project of decolonization and the anticolonial, struggles against all forms of oppression. As we begin to address these issues, it is equally important for us to resist the temptation of wearing a mask and not revealing our identity, positionality, and complicities in colonizing practices, as well as when engaging in decolonizing practices. Our subject location and personal identities shape the construction of particular knowledges and pursuit of politics. Our respective experiences as social beings are shaped by an embodiment that speaks to significant political and social relations that can be established with our bodies, minds and senses (see Titchkosky and Aubrecht, 2009).

In our pursuit of anticolonialism, we must continually confront the challenge of breaking away from colonial frames of reference with a renewed subjectivity, politics, and reclaiming of intellectual agencies. For the minoritized, this involves simultaneously speaking of personal acceptance and complicity in domination and colonizing relations, ways our bodies can be silenced through normalizing and colonizing gazes of the dominant, the risks and fears that we daily endure and the rage that calls on us, as minoritized and oppressed, to resist vigorously. As Fanon teaches us, colonialism and oppression are about the damage to the human psyche and the internalization of racism. This damage will endure in so far as the oppressed body of today is unwilling to challenge dominant definitions of success and continually seeks legitimization in the eyes of the oppressor.

When we look at educational change, we learn how racialized minoritized bodies have challenged "education models that valued assimilation, and in response educational policy-makers to acknowledge cultural diversity" (Simpson, 2006, p. 160). Educational change is about power and dominance. It is about who controls our learning institutions. It is about how issues of staff representation are [un]addressed, and how the representation of knowledge in curriculum and texts is understood and responded to. It is about how we utilize knowledge and power to challenge or maintain Eurocentric/Euro-American dominance (Simpson, 2006, p. 160).

In the pursuit of a decolonized education that addresses questions of oppression, exploitation and alienation, it is important to work with the knowledge that even as critical educators we have all not arrived yet. We are each at different learning stages. It is therefore important for us to acknowledge the limits of our knowing and the complexities of identity and subjectivity as embodied. We must reflect on how our own positionalities inform how we come to know or not know about colonialism, racism and other forms of social oppressions. This may in part assist us to avoid the familiar seductiveness of engaging in self-serving and self-aggrandizing rationales for doing anticolonial and decolonizing work.

This book is also intended to help us engage Fanon so as to ask and reflect on some pertinent questions: For example: (a) How can we become uncompromisingly self-reflexive in our anticolonial/decolonizing work and also ensure our own humility in knowing or not knowing about the colonial relations, colonialism, racism, sexism, ableism, and other oppressions? (b) What does it mean to critically disengage ourselves from positions of power, while simultaneously engaging power in order to exploit positions of influence in the service of the anticolonial and decolonizing struggles? (c) How do we reconcile the discourse of intersectionality of colonial and colonizing oppressions structured along lines of race, class, gender, sexuality, [dis]ability, language, religion, etc. and the salience of particular oppressions at a given time, place and moment? (d) Does intersectional analysis dilute or strengthen commitment to a broader anti colonial politics informed by Fanon? For example, as Levine-Rasky (2009) asks: "If race is salient and if blackness is also intersected by gender, sexuality, and class (for example), how can one be attentive to other axes of identity that affect the dynamics of racism and the way it is experienced?" (p. 1); (e) What are the possibilities of a transracial coalition praxis devoid of any symptoms of politics of identity? Is this possible/feasible or is this even desirable?

What would such politics look like? (f) How do we bring a critical anticolonial reading to power?

The papers in this collection engage these questions from different vantage points. The whole question of anticolonial theorizing of power is critical in order to fully push forward a Fanonian decolonial project of education. This project would see power as working simultaneously, insidiously, systemically, culturally, emotionally, and symbolically, as well as view power work top-down and through "interstices"/intersection as Foucault (1980, 1983) points out. But it also acknowledges there is a double-sidedness to power as exemplified in both Albert Memmi (1969) and Frantz Fanon's (1963, 1967) work—the "colonizer/colonized" and the Manichean divide. Power works "through" social structures and through social relations, as well as through cultural, symbolic, and political means. There is more to power than insisting that in power-saturated situations all the relations are in concert with each other and are co-productive of social effects. There are emotional, spiritual, and psychological [as well as material and political] attachments to power and privilege (e.g., whiteness and the attachments to purity, innocence, reason, objectivity and rationality). Power is not the same everywhere and as hooks (1992) noted, such "imposition of sameness is a provocation that terrorizes" (pp. 22–23). As it has been argued elsewhere (Dei, 2009), we can no longer pretend that we do not see a colonizer and colonized as distinct and yet connected. In every colonizing relation there is a clear oppressor and a clear oppressed. Saying that there are victims of oppression does not negate the resistance of the oppressor/victimized. Even as we articulate our shared complicities in maintaining oppressions and subordination we must not forget the severity of issues for certain bodies in our midst.

Contemporary education must involve genuine dialogue and critical discourse into everyday conversations about power in ways that recognize how power is understood and acted upon to access ethnicities, cultures, histories, and spaces. This can assist learners in their schooling engagement to promote liberation and decolonization. Schools have not served the needs of all students and many schooling processes, in fact, end up reproducing problems in inequity and alienation. There has not been a serious attempt to ensure that all students are included and/or have had the opportunity to have their voices heard. Many students feel a sense of disconnectedness in school (Dei, Mazzuca, McIsaac and Zine, 1997; King, 2005; hooks, 1994; Ogbu, 2002; Brathwaite and James, 1996; Grant and Sleeter, 2007). Schools continually reproduce preexisting hierarchy and expectations that only few can reach. Taking up Fanon's writings should be a way to examine counterapproaches to schooling and education to truly create a space for all students so that learning becomes meaningful. How do we critically reflect on our teaching practice so as to ensure that we are making a difference in terms of actual structural transformation? Today's educators must grapple with how we can expand our pedagogical frameworks for teaching the oppressions and colonial relations of schooling. We must find critical ways to speak and work with our own vulnerabilities and acknowledge the risk of "entering unfamiliar territory and bring teaching and learning full circle for everyone involved" (Simpson, 2006, p. 196).

To say that we cannot study social and educational change from a distance (see also Simpson, 2006, regarding race) is to bring an embodied connection to our teaching and instruction and acknowledge that the educator must be personally invested in her or his pedagogies, while becoming reflexive of how our own locations, identities and desires shape the production of knowledge and pursuit of political practice. Today we write and teach about equity in education. Given Fanon's interpretation of colonialism and colonial relations, perhaps we can ask: What do equality and equity mean in the context of a sustained history of colonialism, racism, oppression and unequal power relations?

SITUATING THE ESSAYS

All of the essays in the text are written by students of Fanon who are actively engaged in politics of educational change and social transformation at the broadest level. Each author engages their piece from particular experiences of coming to learn and know about Fanon. We share a desire to bring Fanon more closely to the field of education as broadly defined. As noted, there is a relative paucity of major works theorizing Fanon and the specific implications for schooling and education. It is our hope that the issues covered will have a broad appeal to readers who want to engage Fanon's ideas in the schooling and educational politics of change and transformation. We are sure that this book will be useful for students, teachers, educational practitioners, community activists and researchers working in schools, colleges, universities, arts and media, law and the justice system, as well as social service sectors, for the promotion of genuine educational change. We see a particular appeal for educators in teacher-training colleges, as well as for graduate instruction in university departments of education, social work and sociology.

George Dei's opening chapter on "Rereading Fanon for His Pedagogy and Implications for Schooling and Education" sets the tone for the discussions in this collection. He examines three key aspects of Fanon's writings for schooling and education: colonialism, violence and decolonization. He pays particular attention to the latter at three levels, namely, how we create decolonized spaces; the understanding of decolonization as discourse and discursive practice; and what decolonized education really is about. Dei places the discussion in the broad cultural politics of schooling and the power of race ideology, while briefly extending his analysis to look at other sites of difference: gender and sexuality and the decolonizing project of schooling. It is argued that, so far, attempts have been a mere tinkering within the box without any fundamental structural changes to make a difference in the lives of the minoritized, disadvantaged, and oppressed. What is needed is to "step outside the box," engage in a decolonized schooling and education, which holds the possibilities of creating a new vision of education that holds the promise and possibility of excellence for all.

Camille Logan, in her "Body Politics and the Experience of Blackness within the Field of Education," broaches the personal and political struggles of identity and representation for black educators as they seek to dismantle the institutional barriers within the educational system. She points to the psyche of the colonized subject and the link to the ways in which black educators experience the colonial encounter in schools, in order to understand the ways the structures of racism and white privilege embedded in Western society result in the misrepresentation of the black body such that it is mis/interpreted despite the individual's "accomplished" role of educator. She argues that these mis/interpreted moments result in a tension between identity and misrepresentation such as the black body in the role of educator must skillfully navigate the public school system and ultimately decide to engage in resistance work in their classroom and school districts. Through personal narratives and reflexivity, the author argues that resistance work, despite the numerous risks articulated in the article, is worth it. Logan concludes by visioning transformative education as consciousness-raising action, thus illuminating the decolonizing nature of resistance, which educators must seek to transform themselves in order to transform education.

Through a critical disability studies perspective, as informed by the work of anticolonial thinker and pedagogue Frantz Fanon, Katie Aubrecht seeks to understand how the Executive Summary of the Province of Ontario's *Review of the Roots of Youth Violence Report*, provides a blueprint for the reorganization of colonialism in contemporary Canadian society. The intention is to uncover how the racist and ableist assumptions, implicit in the civilizing language of the report, reference an imperial culture. Considered are the historical implications of representing youth violence as a symptom of the alienation of "disadvantaged neighborhoods and individuals," and as a sign of the need for an increased presence of mental health programs and administrators in marginalized communities. Aubrecht's hope is to bring the disabilities studies community to new awareness of the historical conditions of its emergence and assist disability scholars and activists in creating a different world for thinking with and through disability.

Paul Adjei, in thinking through antiracism and anticolonial readings, interrogates the writings of Frantz Fanon in the context of education in Ghana. In his "Resistance to Amputation: Discomforting Truth about Colonial Education in Ghana," he queries how Fanon's ideas can inform, shape, and encourage resistance to colonial and racist relations in knowledge production, validations and disseminations. Adjei challenges the disturbing "Truths" of colonial education. He speaks to the colonizing tendencies that *amputate* learners from the fecund cultural knowledges and experiences they bring to learning. Central to his argument is the concept of *resistance to amputation*, as determined through the personal and political struggles in challenging colonial and racist thinking in the current educational system.

In her essay "The Fact of Blackness: A Critical Review of Bermuda's Colonial Education System," Donna Outerbridge discusses the relevancy of Fanon's notion of blackness and how it speaks to the schooling and education system in Bermuda. Her inquiry is organized through questions such as: How does Fanon's conceptualization of a new humanism provide a means or rethinking and reconstructing a curriculum that centres and acknowledges black Bermudian students? And how can a reconceptualization of humanism, as it relates to blackness, be envisioned in order to eradicate structures that promote a lack of self-esteem and disrupt the sense of belonging and identity. As a decolonizing method, Outerbridge leaves us thinking of the concept of "loving blackness as ontological resistance."

Rory Crath, in his "Reading Fanon in 'Homosexual Territory': Towards the Queering of a Queer Pedagogy," has two overlapping goals: the first is to think about the ways in which the writings of Frantz Fanon might inspire a rethinking of how issues and experiences of sexuality and gender variance are understood and practised within the classroom space and also the decolonization practice that would involve the exposure and dismantling of colonialist mechanisms that operationalize universalizing Western sexual, gendered and cultural norms. To the first end, Crath employs the Toronto District School Board's Triangle Program, Canada's only high school program for "LGBTQ" youth as a test site. The author's second aspiration is to utilize the writings of Fanon in order to contribute to a growing body of literature referred to as "a renewed queer studies," to the "queers of color" activism in Toronto, and also to re-queer queer space and other spaces by interrogating the ways in which queer or LGBT(Q) practices might be contingently engaged or complicit with normalized aestheticised codifications of whiteness, gender and sexuality on the body.

Francisco Villegas, in "Strategic In/Visibility and Undocumented Migrants," examines the ways in which Fanon's concepts of visibility and invisibility relate to undocumented migrants in the United States. Importantly, Villegas engages the various ways in which undocumented migrants become invisibilized through the discursive and material "production of illegality," and also how migrants engage in resistance in their daily lives, including strategically visibilizing and/or invisibilizing their immigration status.

Marlon Simmons, in "Concerning Modernity, the Caribbean Diaspora and

Embodied Alienation: Dialoguing with Fanon to approach an Anticolonial Politic," wants to better understand how one comes to make meaning of diasporic life, in particular the communicative practices which endow the socialization process of the Diaspora. He is interested in how the diasporic self comes into the moment of recognizing the historical colonial experience of Euro-modernity. Some of the questions that frame his discussion are: How do everyday artifacts come to be revealed and shaped through the temporal discourse of Euro-modernity? What are the ways in which the colonizing paradigms of Euro-Enlightenment come to encode a particular form of knowledge onto the diasporic body of difference as it lives itself within the public sphere of modernity? Simmons draws on Fanon's diasporic experience within colonial territories, personal memory and speaks through an autobiographical voice as active vantage points, more so to "recall" the past into the present moment and to hone a communal dialogical spirit.

We do not presume to offer a sum of universalized thinking on Fanon. We do offer to share our experiences concerning how we come to understand these moments through reading Fanon from different discursive frameworks. Our intention with *Fanon and Education: Thinking through Pedagogical Possibilities* is to conjure different possibilities of humanism. We live in a time where social justice continues to be the central question. To this end, we hope to retrieve a holistic way of understanding our intertextualized realities.

REFERENCES

Adams, H. M. 1997. "Fanon as a Democratic Theorist" In Nigel Gibson (ed.), *Rethinking Fanon: A Critical Anthology on Aspects of Frantz Fanon's Thought*. Atlantic Highlands, NJ: Humanities Press, pp. 141–178.

Brathwaite, K., and James, C. (eds.) 1996. *Educating African Canadians*. Toronto: James Lorimer & Co.

Dei, G. J. S., Mazzuca, M., McIsaac, E., and Zine, J. 1997. *Reconstructing 'Drop-out': A Critical Ethnography of the Dynamics of Black Students' Disengagement from School*. Toronto: University of Toronto Press.

Dei, G. J. S. 2009. "Afterword. The Anti-Colonial Theory and the Question of Survival and Responsibility," In Arlo Kempf (ed.). *Breaching the Colonial Contract: Anti-Colonialism in the US and Canada*. New York: Springer Press.

Fanon, F. 1963. *The Wretched of the Earth*. New York: Grove Press.

Fanon, F. 1967. *Black Skin, White Masks*. New York: Grove Press.

Fanon, F. 1969. *Toward the African Revolution: Political Essays*. New York: Grove Press.

Fanon, F. 1988. *A Dying Colonialism*. New York: Grove Press.

Foucault, M. 1980. *Power/Knowledge: Selected Interviews 1972–77*. Edited by C. Gordon. Brighton: Harvester Press.

Foucault, M. 1983. "The Subject and Power." In H. Dreyfus and P. Rabinow (eds.), *Michel Foucault: Beyond Structuralism and Hermeneutics*. Chicago: University of Chicago Press, pp. 208–226.
Grant, C. A., and Sleeter, C. E. 2007. *Doing Multicultural Education for Achievement and Equity*. New York, London: Routledge.
hooks, b. 1994. *Teaching to Transgress: Education as the Practice of Freedom*. New York: Routledge.
hooks, b. 1992. *Black Looks: Race and Representation*. Boston: South End Press.
King, J. 2005 (ed.). *Black Education: A Transformative Research and Action Agenda for the New Century*. Mahwah, NJ: L. Erlbaum Associates.
Ladson-Billings, G. 2000. "Racialized Discourses and Ethnic Epistemologies." In N.K. Denzin and Y. S. Lincoln, (Second Ed) *Handbook of Qualitative Research*. Thousand Oaks, CA: Sage Publications, pp. 257–277.
Levine-Rasky, C. 2009. External Examiner's Comments on: "The Double-Edged Sword: A Critical Race Africology of Collaborations Between Blacks and Whites in Racial Equity Work." Ph D. dissertation, Philip S. Howard, OISE/UT.
Memmi, A. 1969. *The Colonizer and the Colonized*. Boston: Beacon Press.
Ogbu, J. U. 2002. *Black American Students in an Affluent Suburb: A Study of Academic Disengagement*. Mahwah, NJ: Lawrence Erlbaum Associates.
Simpson, J. 2006. "Racism Is Not a Theory: Racism Matters in the Classroom." In J. Simpson, *I Have Been Waiting: Race and US Higher Education*. Toronto: University of Toronto Press, pp. 155–196.
Sonnleitner, Michael W. 1987. "Of Logic and Liberation: Frantz Fanon on Terrorism," *Journal of Black Studies*, Vol. 17, No. 3, March. pp. 287–304.
Spivak, G. C. 1988. Can the Subaltern Speak? In *Marxism and the Interpretation of Culture*, edited by C. Nelson and L. Grossberg. Chicago, Urbana: University of Illinois Press, pp. 271-313.
Titchkosky, T., and Aubrecht, K.. 2009. "The Power of Anguish: Re-mapping Mental Diversity with an Anti-Colonial Compass." In Arlo Kempf (ed.). *Breaching the Colonial Contract: Anti-Colonialisms in the US and Canada*. New York: Springer Press.

CHAPTER ONE

Rereading Fanon for His Pedagogy and Implications for Schooling and Education

GEORGE J. SEFA DEI

I begin this chapter with an observation. I see myself as a pedagogue learning to work with "difficult knowledge." This observation cannot be read simply as an attempt to teach. It is just that, personally, I have been concerned with the "craze" to "overtheorize" Fanon works as sheer "academic exercise" and, as a consequence, the fear of students in engaging Fanon. I would venture so far to say that perhaps the "problem" with Fanon for the contemporary student is "language." That is, some students find his words impenetrable and have neither the training nor the will to sit and work through Fanon on their own. He is seen as being "too tough." Hence, for the educator there is a need to find an interpretation that is accessible to multiple readers and that captures Fanon's complexity. I see this project as an opportunity for me to continue on the decolonial/anticolonial intellectual journey in ways informed by Fanon's works as well as those of early anticolonial theorists. In this journey I am desirous to highlight my own African agency in the exploration of contemporary critical intellectual traditions articulating emancipatory discourses.

Undoubtedly, Fanon makes an impressive, ambitious, and provocative read. His writings are pedagogically relevant for the search for spaces of strategic engagement for subversion. He draws on a plethora of themes, based on social location, hybridity, cross-cultural communication, narratives of ideological climates and the mediations of culture, history, politics, and identity. His writings point to the ways dominant/colonizing knowledge "perniciously cemented resistance to any knowledge that challenges the privileged ethos of empirical and theoretical practices that reaffirm the dominance of racialized/coercive hierarchies of authority" (see Visano, 2008, writing in another context). Fanon's readings and arguments involve an engagement with various intersectionalities (antiracist, critical race and anticolonial, anti-imperialist, neocolonial perspectives), as well as a conceptualization of everyday political praxis.

Fanon also challenges us to ask ourselves: How are we complicit in Western hegemony? How does the search for knowledge create an ethical responsibility to give back to our communities? And pedagogically how do we teach about ethical responsibility to community? To Fanon (1967a, 1967b), the "Third World" (read the oppressed) knows its history by its scars and chains, an irrefutable evidence of colonialism. Racism has shed/shirked Europeans off/from their humanity. Europeans have attained a warped sense of humanity through a very racist humanism conducted through slavery, colonial thievery, a devaluation of other culture, traditions, and histories. Such racist humanism is leading Europe to its doom. This is the implicit text when Fanon notes that Europe has today reached a level of "atomic and spiritual disintegration" (Fanon, 1963, p. 311) and the "European spirit has strange roots" (Fanon, 1963, p. 313). Europe has "lost her sense of humanity. Her game has finally ended; and we the oppressed must find something different . . . not to imitate Europe . . . but search for . . . a new direction" (Fanon, 1963, pp. 312–313).

I agree with Taiwo on p. 26 (1996, p. 252) that Fanon's writings are about "description, explanation and prediction." It is equally important to note that there is a creative (artistic) and scientific side to Fanon. There is the poetics and the discourse interface that is often missing from a critical examination of the activist scholar's work. As Fontenot (1978) long ago noted, Fanon uses his personal firsthand experience and the account of history to theorize the colonial experience. But Fanon also writes with a prose and language that shows the depth of his artistic gifts and the individuality of his thoughts. Fanon's ideas are not solely based "on the historico-economic and political conditions . . . encountered in his own revolutionary activity" (Fontenot, 1978, p. 108). He theorized beyond his lived experience when engaging the dialectical process of "demystifying" the colonial operation. In fact, Fontenot (1978, p. 113) aptly summarizes the contributions of Fanon to contemporary scholarship, pointing bravely to his views on/about: (a) language as a means of communication; (b) the argument that the black man's destiny is to strive toward the "universal conception," which the white man was also striving for; (c) an acknowledgment of the power of the revolutionary consciousness and political force of the rural peasantry, women, and the lumpen proletariat; (d) a theory of violence as a cleansing force for the lumpen proletariat; (e) a notation and critique of the plight of the African intellectual in his/her colonial mimicry; and (f) upholding a vision of a new nation to be created from the ashes of the existing one.

In his vision of the triumph of the human collective spirit against the evil of colonialism, Fanon connected the "alienation of the self" to the "oppression of the collective." He saw culture and politics as "the vehicle of truth" in all matters concerning repression and rebellion (Sharawy, 2003, p. 2). He would argue that "modernization," politics, and liberation were prerequisites to the formation of a true "national culture," and that such national culture was evolving. It is "born out of the womb of the revolution and takes shape through self-awareness" (Sharawy, 2003, p. 3). This is a powerful rendition if we are to take the position that decolonization through critical education is an essential and necessary route to the acquisition of a true national culture. Fanon was adamant that colonialism was "indivisible" and "non-negotiable" and constituted a material, spiritual, and moral violence that can only be countered by true revolutionary violence (Sharawy, 2003, pp. 6–7). He placed colonialism squarely at the foot of European inhumanity. Colonialism creates a repressive presence that marks every European in the colonized space as a repressor (Sharawy, 2003, p. 6).

In his analysis of the effects of colonialism and colonial racism, Fanon focused on three areas: oppression, exploitation, and alienation. That is, oppression of the mind/psyche, is matched by the material exploitation of human's labour, and a concomitant spiritual, cultural, and mental alienation of the self that creates a sense of nihilism, despair, hopelessness, and living a dead-end existence among the brutally colonized. Of course, colonialism and resistance went hand in hand, but the fact is that there is a heavy mental, physical, emotional, and material cost. There are implications of such readings for social theory and the theorizing of everyday social movement politics. In fact, it is the poverty of theory in not responding to the mechanizations of the colonist and capitalist machine that is at the heart of human despair in bringing about social change. The task today is to use Fanon to articulate a social theory and progressive educational politics that help us to understand internalized oppression and the way it works on different bodies in schooling and education, as well as to understand the seduction of the "multicultural imperialism" and the denial of the consequences of the materiality of race and social oppressions. We must also use Fanon to identify educational sites where the struggle for human dignity and well-being is being waged in multiple and sometimes contesting and competing settings.

Fanon was all about a search to regain our lost humanity. To him, the development of an effective political strategy is a necessary precondition for social change. It is in this quest and the failure thereof that we can decry the lack of moral and intellectual leadership of the elite and the political vanguard. In rereading Fanon and his implications for schooling and education I have to ask: How then are educators and learners to nurture the "pedagogy of rage" to serve the broader cause of a "pedagogy of subversion?" Such pedagogies would have to work with rage, anger, humility of knowing, and politics in different ways to ensure social transformation. In the examination of Fanon in order to understand the power of individual and collective agency, I would recall the ontological primacy of interpretations, that is, how we make sense of our complex worlds. This is an important avenue of thinking about what forms and informs social interpretations of everyday experiences, especially in light of competing social narratives of identity, subjectivity, self, group, and history that shape the presses of schooling and educational delivery. Critical educational politics must continually pose some questions: How does interpretation influence the experience of multiple bodies and subjectivities of schooling? What are the respective resources for knowing in schools and other educational/learning sites? And how did Fanon come to know about his world?

It is well to note, as I point out later, that Fanon did not dismiss the significance of colour or class. However, he eschewed essentialist and reductivist orientations. To him, the concepts of colour, especially "whiteness" and "blackness," warrant refinement. He asks: How do we break through the compulsive and pervasive mediations of racist exchanges? To him, racism collaborates intertextually with other powerful configurations within the political economy (e.g., class and politics) (see Fanon, 1963, 1967b). In his chapter on "The Fact of Blackness" in the much-acclaimed *Black Skin, White Masks*, Fanon (1967a) points to the importance of "embodied knowing." There is a salience of showing up black in a white supremacist world. Generally, there is the salience of showing up as black in a visceral antiblack context. Fanon saw a "great white terror" in the oppression and the dehumanizing of the oppressed by the colonist/oppressor. He also saw the "great black mirage" in the Negro wanting to be white. To him, racism and the analysis of it was not an accidental discovery. He saw that racism as a pattern of "the exploitation of one group by men of another has a logical end ... to fight [for] the total liberation of the national territory" (Fanon, 1967b, p. viii).

I. FANON ON COLONIALISM, VIOLENCE, AND DECOLONIZATION

In *Toward the African Revolution*, Fanon gives a scientific account of the situation of the colonized. He had lived the colonial situation historically to be able offer such an intellectual account: There is a "common nature of the struggle of all the colonized" (Fanon, 1967b, p. ix). He argued that colonialism "was a perfectly logical, perfectly coherent whole in which all those who lived within it were inevitable accomplices" (Fanon, 1967b, p. ix). To Fanon, we must be aware of the complexities of what we are dealing with when we speak of colonialism. Colonization could not have succeeded without the crystallization of race prejudice. The colonizer arrives to impose his values through racial, economic and spirtual violence. In *A Dying Colonialism*, Fanon further reasons, "colonial domination distorts the very relations that the colonized maintains with his own culture" (Fanon, 1965, p. 130).

We cannot understand colonialism outside of the violence of the colonial encounter. But the violence of colonialism is unending inasmuch as colonial relations are continually being reproduced. It is here that perhaps Fanon is extremely relevant in reading the violence of contemporary communities and the educational project. For example, in contemporary educational contexts, there is the question of violence and colonial pathologies about oppressed communities. Any discussion of violence of particularly oppressed communities is thus a dangerous undertaking. Violence is often read in the lens of social pathologies and for communities so stigmatized that we must exercise caution when speaking of successes and failures.

Take schooling and the responsibility of local communities to ensure the educational needs of their youth. Usually in such discussions about "community responsibility for their youth's education," there is a blurring of the conceptual distinction between asking communities to take responsibility and naively blaming (pathologizing) families/communities for all the problems their children face in schooling. A Fanonian approach would interrogate the very notion of pathologization and its role in sustaining a set of power relations, based on the biologization and individualization of a society wherein resistance to oppression on the part of minoritized difference is viewed as deviance and thus a "problem" that must be cured, rehabilitated, treated, fixed, or removed from society—in other words, medicalized. Fanon teaches us to make visible this process of pathologization and medicalization in ways that remove the marking of a "problem" away from the minoritized, racialized individual and community to the space where it belongs, the systemic and the institutional. In schooling contexts, then, it is not the minoritized individual and/or community that is pathologized or pathological, it is the system, the institution; that is to say, it is the school and the educational system itself that constitute a "problem," and thus constitute violence.

As we learn from Fanon, violence is endemic to colonial and colonized societies. There are myriad manifestations of violence in our communities. There are many forms of violence—physical, economic, sexual, spiritual, and symbolic violence. These myriad forms of violence happen at multiple levels of our communities—homes, families, school, streets, workplaces, churches, and so on, and we must openly speak about these and the impact on all of us. The issue is which forms of violence the dominant chooses to focus on and whose violence is much decontextualized and discussed.

Many times, a colonized or oppressed community would reproduce and internalize such violence. By not confronting and/or resisting the violence we contribute to victimizing ourselves. The silence around the violence of schooling and education allows violence to be revisited upon communities. Part of this internalization also results from a feeling of hopelessness, that is, the feeling "there is nothing that can be done about the problem." It is out of control, out of our hands whether as families, individuals, or communities! It takes education and conscientization to rid oneself of the internalization of such violence. Violence is also about dehumanization of the self and the creation of a subhumanity. Violence is an act of self-destruction that dehumanizes both the perpetrator and the acted upon. Besides the economic and material impact, the effect on the human psyche and the spiritual well-being is profound. The ways in which the dominant uses violence to achieve his aims and goals of domination and subjugation show the power of privilege.

Violence can also be a form of resistance and a response to the perpetuation of the "inferiority complex" syndrome. In this context, the analysis of violence lies in understanding the dynamics and consequences of economic, material and sociopolitical exclusions and estrangement (e.g., unemployment, poverty, mis-education, alienation, marginalization) that fosters this sort of violence, that is, social and psychological ills). As Fanon (1963) points out, violence has a healing effect for the "spiritually wounded." Consequently, we need to understand the ways in which youth today view and use violence as a necessity, not just simply to win liberty and freedom but to cure the inferiority complex created by the dominant society. Fanon (1963) argued that "at the level of individuals, violence is a cleansing force. It frees the native from his inferiority complex and from despair and inaction" (p. 94). Fanon depicts "fratricidal" violence as violence that is turned inwards, as in Algerians unleashing their pent-up anger, frustrations, and anguish, not on the oppressor/colonizer but on themselves. Since violence is pursued by the colonizer to rid the oppressed of their humanity, the oppressed can unleash their pent-up anger, frustrations and anguish equally on the oppressor to reclaim a sense of dignity and self and collective worth. This level of violence of the colonized's subject is, in fact, "counterviolence." It is violence in reaction to systemic violence and social exclusion.

The intensity and pervasiveness of violence of education raises some concerns regarding the toll that violence takes on oppressed subjects. The pervasiveness of educational violence (e.g., racism and oppression in schooling, etc.) suggests that there is a problem for oppressed communities to deal with by way of reclaiming their self-worth and dignity. The fact of what the victims of such oppressions as racism, stereotyping, labeling, stigmatization, and so on have to go through in order to seek redress compounds the problem of violence on their bodies. Within the school system there is still a lack of sufficient safeguards and support mechanisms to help survivors of educational violence. The oppressed have to find their ways of resistance and violent decolonization becomes fundamental to their existence.

But decolonization can be pursued only when we come to understand the antecedents of violence. In acknowledging the powerful link between colonialism and racism, Fanon conceded there are different mechanizations of a racist psychology to be found among colonizers. All imperialist countries have acted on their racist potentialities to dehumanize others (Fanon, 1963). He enthused that decolonization (fighting against colonialism) can only be understood as a historical process that ultimately culminates in changing the social order. It is an initial violent encounter of two forces, " . . . opposed to each other by their very nature, which in fact results from and is nourished by the situation in the colonies" (p. 36). Fanon adds that decolonization is a calling into question of the whole colonial situation and its aftermath (Fanon, 1963, 1965, p. 130). Foremost, decolonization is a violent phenomenon. Decolonization can only be a subversive act. True liberation can only be achieved by force or through every means in the oppressed power. Decolonization is always successful, but only after hard-fought battles and struggles. As a subversive act, decolonization meets with resistance from the colonialists who institute very punitive measures for those who seek to decolonize (e.g., on the national scale we see capital take flight; pedagogically we see the ridiculing of oppositional intellectual discourses and politics, etc.). For the oppressed, there are other consequences for embarking on decolonization. For example, the elite who have been "whitewashed" take flight initially; there is a denigration of local culture, tradition, values and history. This is later followed by the stage of a "return to source," that is, a reclamation of culture, history, and tradition.

Decolonizing is invariably the search for true humanism. To Fanon, the search is about Indigenizing (Africanizing) the West (European). That is, humanizing the West as in the pursuit of interconnections, mutual interdependence and respect for shared/basic values of humanness. Decolonization is about ridding ourselves and the collective of its mental pathology, in that there is a particular mental pathology that comes with colonialism. This can be seen from the effects of colonial oppression and the consequences of the struggles for political liberation and freedom. Understanding this mental pathology cannot be approached as purely a "scientific work."

II. FANON AND IMPLICATIONS FOR SCHOOLING AND EDUCATION

If Fanon is relevant for schooling and education then we must ask: How does Fanon help us to conceptually and theoretically imagine the modern world? In what ways are recolonial racisms inspired by the material and physical exigencies of modern capital and capitalism? Fanon questioned colonialism and the racist imaginaries and cultural repositories that compel colonization in the first place. He showed how colonialism is a pathological process, firmly grounded in brutal repression and a denial of the link of the colonizer and colonized in a violent relation. To him, the colonizer's denial of the humanity of the colonized subject was subsequently a denial of the colonizer's own humanity. Colonialism is also in an interlocking relation given the ways it is produced and reproduced in the material, psychological and discursive levels. Colonialism can only be met with force and to Fanon (1967a), decolonization is a violent encounter that "never goes unnoticed" (p. 2).

Notwithstanding what is arguably a lack of a more in-depth critical analysis of the issues of femininity, queerness, and disability, as well as his problematic conception of madness, Fanon has a lot to offer pedagogy and education. There is relevance in the study of the symbolic representation of colonial texts and narrative. But it is also important to assess what Fanon truly offers by way of understanding contemporary victims of the violence of education. Within the Euro-American educational system, we can see the issues of minority youth disengagement, dropouts and "pushouts" as the direct products of a reorganized colonial relations of schooling. We can point to many sources of alienation in school systems for minority youth. Youth alienation can be related to particular sociopolitical arrangements of schooling. There is a normalization of the violence of education. What are the possibilities, then, as educators to help reopen students as subjects to society and to see a role for anticolonial educators to help and strengthen learners to question the established criteria of normality in schools? This calls for a transformed, decolonized education that assists today's learners with destabilizing the hegemonic practices of schooling.

Fanon's take on decolonization is critical in examining schooling and how educators' pedagogic, instructional, and communicative practices truly lead to decolonizing education. Decolonization as noted is an ongoing process that can lead to transformation. Decolonization requires working on the mind and intellect of learners and educators. We can broach decolonization and education from three aspects. First is the question of creating decolonized spaces in our classrooms. A decolonized classroom context must be strived for at all times. A decolonized space is not simply there for the taking. We struggle, fight and create such spaces. Like the notion of community "decolonized space" emerges from struggles and contestations to claim a voice, experience, history, and knowledge. Consequently, decolonization, that is a struggle for an anticolonial space, entails educators and learners working together to address questions of power, history, knowledge identity, and representation.

Creating a decolonizing learning space is about rewarding (rather than punishing) resistance. The process begins by asking new critical questions that acknowledge differential levels of safety and security for diverse learners. It is a process of affirming multiple knowledge (based on experience and affective relations) and having learners coming to claim a sense of ownership and responsibility for their own knowledges. It is about bringing to the fore subjugated voices, histories, and experiences. It is about legitimizing practice and experience as the contextual basis of knowing. The process of creating a decolonized classroom space also entails learners and educators being able to acknowledge the link of identity, schooling, and knowledge production. It is about negotiating around power and the asymmetrical power relations that structure schooling processes. It is about placing questions of responsibility and complicity on the table for discussion to see how we are each implicated in the process of creating conducive learning space for all.

The decolonized space is one where learners from disadvantaged backgrounds are able to construct and privilege their own intellectual, cultural, and political knowledge and agency. The decolonized space allows learners to be organically connected with their communities so as to make their learning meaningful in terms of its impact on the daily lives of communities. If, as Fanon instructs, there is a physical, cultural, and spiritual context of colonialism, racism, and oppression, then creating a decolonized space is also about dealing with the spiritual and emotional harm that schooling causes, particularly oppressed bodies. Decolonizing then becomes a process of healing and becoming healthy and whole again through affective learning. Sometimes, strategic separation from dominant spaces (as in racially minoritized bodies claiming "spaces of their own") becomes a matter of survival for the oppressed community. For racialized minoritized students, education should not simply be about getting the learner to think through the inherited prisms and concepts that have emerged from Western intellectual and philosophical traditions. More important, learners must be able to think outside of dominant and oppressive traditions and discard the Eurocentric and hegemonic ways of knowing and acting. For minoritised students, this is what Asante (2009) implies by asking students to search for their "own intellectual footing" in the Western academy. We can no longer be comfortable simply arguing that our grounds are "continually shifting." If our grounds are shifting, we should still be able to identify some grounds to firmly stand on and to resist the "Europeanization of our minds" (Asante, 2009).

The second is to see decolonization at the level of discourse. Many times, as oppressed peoples, the discourses we insert ourselves into are themselves colonizing of our experiences. The claims of presenting opposing hegemonic practices become hollow when they are presented through Eurocentric prisms. We may feel the "sensation of moving while standing still." But this is no change. It can be the seduction of an insert or coercion after easy slippage into the form, logic, and the implicit assumptions of the very things we seek to contest. Thus, we all continually have to look within our discursive practices to see if we are engaging or partaking in colonizing and imperial discourses and discussions. As a reference point, I want to briefly engage antiracism discourse and the extent we situate Indigenous knowings and counterknowledge in the antiracist practice. Specifically, I would use critical discourses linking race and colonization, and the project of antiracism as a learning moment. No discourse is immune to criticism. All knowledge evolves as they speak to the complexity of the human experience. In recent years there have been calls to "decolonize antiracism." In the Canadian context, Lawrence and Dua (2005) argued that "rather than challenging the ongoing colonization of Aboriginal peoples, Canadian antiracism is furthering contemporary colonial agendas" (p. 123). Such critique of an oppositional discourse and practice cannot be lightly dismissed. The authors point out that by ignoring "the ongoing colonization of Aboriginal peoples in the Americas" and failing "to integrate an understanding of Canada as a colonialist in antiracist frameworks" (p. 123) antiracism can be a colonizing project. I would agree that antiracism must affirm the Native Aboriginal/ First Nations existence, histories of colonization, through critical interrogations of "writings on the history of slavery," and further contest the ways that diasporic identities "are situated in multiple projects of colonization and settlement on Indigenous lands ... and cannot ... simply equate decolonization politics with antiracist politics" (p. 128).

But such critiques of antiracism also got me thinking about just how exactly we conceptualize a "decolonized project" and, in this case, antiracism and antiracist practice. For example, how is the centrality and saliency of race featured in a supposedly "antiracist scholarship"? How can we separate the discourse itself (i.e., principles and ideas of antiracism) from the actual questions/issues of scholarly gaze or research focus? How do we bring the multiple discourses of antiracism and the intersections with other forms of difference and indigenity in our work, mindful of not as prescribing a particular model of antiracism for all? Such intellectual posture of prescribing a particular model of antiracism I would argue is equally hegemonic. Critical antiracist work must engage the categories of race, ethnicity, gender, class, sexuality, disability, language, and other forms of difference in a relational way. An antiracist analysis must also affirm the saliency of race, as it seeks the imbrications of all differences. Such analysis must engage where people are speaking from and the particular experiences that speak to our discourses. As I have long argued (Dei, 1996), there is no one model of antiracism. Supposedly, critical approaches can themselves be hegemonic if they proscribe a particular approach to solidarity and antioppressive work. We pursue multiple politics, and we must read such politics in their respective contexts.

To see decolonization as an on-going/unfinished work requires bringing to the fore questions of complicity in producing hegemonic knowledges. It also means owning up to the knowledge we produce; that is, responsibility for the knowledge. A discourse purporting to be "transformative" and "anticolonial" must highlight how local knowledges have shaped the discourse at a particular moment. This is an important starting point from which to decolonize. Decolonization is building bridges and solidarities among oppressed groups (as well as oppositional discourses), not sowing the seeds of tension. By the nature of oppositional work, we ought to begin by affirming and validating local experiences and knowing. We can acknowledge that we maintain blind spots in our work and not be dismissive, a hallmark of the intellectual arrogance of knowing more than others. Thus, there is an implication of what we take to be antiracism, which sources of knowledge we fall on, and who is producing the knowledge that is deemed to be antiracist and by whom? The most important lesson about decolonization is that, unless we constantly watch our discursive engagements, we run the risk of falling into the trap and becoming complicit in the very things we are contesting.

In decolonizing antiracism, it is important for the discourse to acknowledge the ongoing colonization of Indigenous peoples everywhere and to uncover the ways that diasporic identities are implicated in multiple projects of colonization and settlement on Indigenous lands (see Dua, 2008, in the context of Canada). The link between state policies/practices and racist exclusions of groups and their experiences has been demonstrated. Historically, Western political systems have been founded upon the construction of racial hierarchies, with white bodies at the top. Such hierarchies have become the basis of distribution of rewards and punishments for different groups in society. Dominant bodies lay claim to a sense of entitlement, while communities of colour struggle daily to resist claims of their "illegitimacy," "degeneracy," and "unbelonging" (see also Fanon, 1963; 1967a; Goldberg, 2002; Said, 1994; Razack, 2002; Omi and Winant, 1994; Johal, 2009). Importantly, I will add that such claims of illegitimacy are not merely about our bodies or our mere physical "presence" or "absented presence" in certain spaces, but also about our indigenous/cultural resource knowings and how everyday lived experiences can be respected as part of the contextual basis of knowing. Unfortunately, within dominant contexts, the knowledges and social realities of the less powerful are dismissed, either because such knowledges do not conform to dominant expectations and experience, or that such knowledge dares to herald and insist on the epistemic saliency of the minoritized voices.

The third level of engaging decolonization is to pose the question: What is a decolonized education? I would argue that such education must be truly transformative. It must engage multiple knowledges as we seek to revision schooling in more ways than one. Such new ways call for breaking up power hierarchies and the merit badges that characterize schooling processes. It means engaging in new conversations about what constitutes success for the learner, and how such success cannot be accomplished without creating truly decolonized learning spaces. For example, let me focus on the idea of acknowledging multiple success and achievements. Schools, educators, and parents have a responsibility in exploring multiple assessment strategies in order to uncover hidden talents and skills of our students. We need to provide students with options and opportunities to display their brilliance, talents, and educational excellence. Both teachers' and parents' expectations of students and their children are critical to promoting brilliance in learners (see Sleeter and Grant, 1999). Currently there is "too much schooling, too little education" (Shujaa, 1994). Education is the broader perspective of learning and teaching and is concerned more with how students think and apply knowledge. Schooling, in today's neoliberal context, is increasingly being geared towards the "best," "brightest," "smart," "gifted." The downside to this trend is a very inimical youth learning in general. A whole generation of students is now characterized as "at risk," a "deficit model of education" rather than finding ways to uncover hidden brilliance/talents in all students (see Valencia, 1997; King, 2002, 2003; Levin, 2004; Kerr, 2005).

Schools are using examinations as the sole measure of uncovering a learner's "brilliance." But we know examinations are not a true measure of learners' abilities. Examinations are a snapshot of what students have learned. It does not measure issues about how students learned and the effects of such learning. It simply measures "what" students have learned. It is definitely one of the measures of abilities, but absolutely not the correct measure of students' abilities. Bad marks may indicate a poor day for the exams. They may reflect a student's inability to comprehend what is on the test, not necessarily what has been learned and applied. Students have multiple abilities and the marks race and the overemphasis on test scores can be detrimental.

All children are born with remarkable abilities of one form or another. One may also speak to the danger of such lines of questioning if the data supporting the "objective" determinations are measured by subjective educational measures. We need look no further than IQ tests, now widely recognized as culturally specific, to know that it is difficult to measure intelligence outside of a specific sociocultural context. Certain knowledges, abilities, and proclivities are obviously more celebrated than others in each educational context, so such designations seem difficult to make on purely empirical grounds, not to mention the positivist ideology that too often accompanies such claims.

We know of students who do well on test scores but unfortunately are "very lousy" when it comes to fulfilling their social responsibility to a larger citizenry. The "me generation" of success and high achievers does not necessarily bode well for building a community and a connection to a community. We also know there are restrictive socioeconomic conditions that stifle the abilities of children and impinge on their learning and performance. When we focus on simply the test, something may be missing. There is an equity question as well—the dialectic of the factual equality of the classroom situation to which we assume all the kids are exposed. The socioeconomic setting of the home does not reflect similar equality; therefore, their performance is bound to show difference. We know teachers sometimes teach to the test. What do students learn from teaching is a critical question. The facts that affect students' performance in schools include curriculum, teacher expectations, cultural discontinuities in schooling and education, and a host of socioenvironmental and political factors. Many times tests do not gauge these pressures. The very idea of a term like "at risk" to describe a host of educational and social situations and conditions is problematic to begin with. We might start by asking what people mean when they say students "at risk." This will produce a host of results and perhaps encourage us to investigate some of the assumptions that feed these misleading terms. Consequently, a divestment from such nomenclature is important.

Therefore, in decolonizing schooling and education, we may want to look at the question of examinations and insist that assessments have to be age, grade, and subject-specific. There are a host of opportunities for educators, including research projects, presentations, and hands-on kinetic learning activities—all of which can incorporate multiple media approaches. In Canadian contexts, generally, a host of evaluation strategies are suggested in the exemplars published by the Ministry of Education, and available to teachers and the public through Publications Ontario (Kempf, 2008).

In decolonizing schooling and education we may venture to ask: How do schooling processes enhance success in all learners? Critical debates about schooling can help us carve out the path for educational and social transformation. This is why in re-reading Fanon for his pedagogic, instructional, and communicative significance for schooling and education, we will need to move beyond the current intellectual preoccupation of Fanon studies. We will have to explore Fanon's relevance for colonial discourse, the psycho-existential contradictions of colonialism and the pedagogic implications for schooling (see also Robinson, 1993, p. 79). The notion of conventional schooling as a colonial and violent process is fundamental to the analysis. Also, the question of how to transform schools in the context of post- and antirevolutionary class, gender, race-specific initiatives is paramount. After all, colonialism and oppression are more than a racial discursive practice. They have deleterious material, physical, and mental consequences on different bodies.

The violence of education is real when one comes to think of the effects of miseducation of youth, the oppressive practices of racist, classist, sexist and homophobic texts, curricular and instructional materials, and the failure to engage critical questions of culture, identity, representation in the both cultural, as well as the macro-social politics of schooling. By "macro-social politics of education," I mean the cultural politics of schooling and broader macro-political processes and structures through which education is delivered (e.g., curriculum, social organization of knowledge, policy, history of education, etc.). Such politics speak to the contestations over knowledge, culture, values, and understandings, as well as the dynamics of everyday relations, and the interplay of school culture, social climate, and environment that shapes the construction of learners' identities. Macro-social politics of education acknowledge the ways in which schooling is a racially, socially, politically, and culturally mediated experience for learners. Furthermore, it contends that issues of responsibility and accountability are critical for transforming the educational system.

Within Euro-American schools, we continually witness risk takers among educators, parents, and students who challenge the oppressive practices of dominant and hegemonic education. There are progressive educators who care and are bent on producing success for all. These educators acknowledge and are troubled by the "achievement ideology" that links individual effort, merit, and hard work in school as determinants of one's educational attainment and, ultimately, social mobility, and status. They draw attention to success as collectively produced and as something that implicates the systems and structures of schooling and education (Dei, with Butler, Charania, Kola-Olusanya, Opini, Thomas, and Wagner, 2010). Critical educators challenge the dominant ideology of "success," one that equates success with the acquisition of status symbols (see also Sackeyfio, 2006, p. 100).

The "cult of individualism" in accounting for school/academic success avoids institutional responsibility for failure. In the prism of a Fanonian critique, one can argue that the "cult of individualism" offers indicators of academic success that basically allow youth to mimic dominant conceptions and values. Students are colonized to perform Whiteness for acceptance and legitimacy. Often these students become reactionary and likely to engage in Eurocentric dialogue, focussing on defining themselves in relation to Western standards. To critique such conceptions of success, we pose these key questions: How can we account for success in ways in which the success of some is not served up for consumption to explain the "failures" of other students and/or as punishment for others? How can we account for "success" as not just simply the flip side of "failure"? And, how can we bring a holistic reading to success and to theorize success broadly and in different ways to include academic and social success?

Moving beyond the discursive prism of race, gender, sexual, and class inequality, we can critically engage the ways that race, class, gender, sexuality, ability, oppression, and colonialism conflate to produce differential outcomes for different bodies in the school system. We can begin to examine the intricate ways in which schools both produce and help learners to resist the creation of a "pathological personality." So today we speak of a postmodern/postcolonial educational context. But is the "post" in postcolonialism wishful thinking? The denial of the ways race and difference impact schooling makes some claims of postcolonial education very dubious. There is the reorganized colonial and there are fragile boundaries to speak of, given ongoing relations of differentiation (see also Mercer, 1996, p. 129). The social and cultural organization of colonial domination operates within and beyond racial discourses.

Educational transformation will not come about simply through wishful thinking. Action on the part of educators, learners, and communities will be key. We need to develop critical learners and thinkers who have broken free from the entrapment of their minds in the vestiges of colonialism and colonial education. The power of the psychology of the mind also requires the development of a critical consciousness that informs and anchors a political ideology for social action and transformation. Critical consciousness is about continually questioning our intellectual stances, as well as discursive and political positions. In fact, Fanon (1967a) concluded *Black Skin, White Masks* with the following exhortation, "Oh my body, always make me a man who questions!" points to the power of opening oneself to questioning of entrenched positions. Fanon's exhortation is symptomatic of a social theorist who sees his intellectual and political project of decolonization as ongoing. When he asserted that violence teaches the oppressed to resist, it was not just physical resistance but mental and discursive resistance as well.

Given the violence of colonialism and Fanon's diagnosis of violence as a healing response to colonial oppression, it is equally fair to ask for the victims of violence of schooling where is the healing taking place? (See also Presbey, 1996.) The healing can only take place if learners and educators undertake the equally violent act of decolonizing education. The task is violent in terms of the toll it is going to take in doing the work for educational justice and social transformation in schools. We would have to subvert the place and power of dominant texts, official pedagogy, and classroom instruction, as well as schooling processes to do with the social organizational lives, culture and environment of schools as we know it. It is a call for imagining and working to create a new way of schooling that subverts hegemonic knowledge and practice, breaks down power barriers, builds solidarities across communities and spaces, and offers hope to all learners.

Fanon had a radical humanist utopian vision. His desire was to extend human dignity, freedom, love, care, and justice to all who are daily exploited. In the language of schooling this means ensuring that the dignity of all learners is restored. It is working for the utopianism as understood and articulated by Fanon in the context of a decolonized education. All around us, when we hear discussions about policies and practices to transform education these are often "knee-jerk reactions" to emerging problems, often limited responses and not far-reaching in their effects(see also Issahaku, 2010). A host of educational practices and policies are developed and/or couched in ways that constitute "stop-gap and recycling measures," without producing truly transformative effects. It is like running in circles. The more things change in schools the more they remain the same! Educational policies and practices currently in place in schools do not subvert Western hegemony. As part of the process of decolonization, Fanon urged all oppressed peoples to uphold their culture in the face of Western hegemony and colonial destruction. Those of us who seek educational transformation, and, in particular, want to pursue a decolonized educational context must search for ways to uphold the myriad cultures, identities, and knowledges of all learners in the face of the hegemonic exclusionary practices of schooling. It is a task to uproot the dominance of whiteness in schooling and education. But let us remember that such whiteness is not only embodied by white subjects but in the colonized (oppressed) learners as well, and it is this latter situation that we find the insidiousness of the violence of education, for the oppressed (as students) do not simply internalize whiteness and colonializing knowledge, they are force-fed such knowledge from their very first encounter with the classroom. Thus, the violence of education lies in the enforcement of a process that requires minoritized students (and indeed all students) to negate their embodied knowledges and the multiple layers of identity that form their sense of self, individually and collectively, and thus to see this identity as a lack, and as a deficit, that must be amputated from their bodies. The requirement of success in such contexts then is dependent on this process of amputation. A decolonizing educational process must therefore be the antithesis of amputation and must dedicate itself towards a "refusal" of amputation in all its forms.

III. RACE, IDEOLOGY, AND THE CULTURAL POLITICS OF SCHOOLING

In the context of Fanon's writings, it can be argued that the central role of ideology in creating political consciousness has been underestimated, understudied, or misunderstood. Race and ideology have been central themes in Fanon's theorizing. As Nursey-Bray (1980) observed, with Fanon "the restructuring of consciousness" is as vital as any other aspect of decolonization. Fanon saw the development of a decolonized ideology as a revolutionary transformation of consciousness (p. 141). Revolutionary struggles must proceed through a direct focus to the distorted consciousness of the colonized and racially oppressed. Understanding the consciousness of race is critical to pursuing a decolonized education. Such consciousness is about acknowledging the significance, centrality and relevance of race in the cultural politics of schooling. It is also about not side stepping race but confronting race and education head-on. It is about acknowledging and responding to the material and political consequences of race for racialized subjects. Such consciousness about race is also about acknowledging the fluidity, complexity and contextuality of race, and the fact that race can only be fully grasped in conjunction with gender, class, sexuality, language, and religion.

It is important to examine how race ideology fits in Fanon's theorizing. As already noted, Fanon did not abandon race and its significance for the oppressed and privilege subject. He acknowledged race in his discussion of the colonial psychology, the embodiment of identity and the pursuit of politics of resistance to colonial oppression. While according a central role to race in his earlier writings, it appears that Fanon, at a later point in his life formulated the race question subsidiary to class (see Fanon 1963, 1967a, 1976b). Moving away from the earlier Negritude philosophical position of race essentialism he saw race as a dependent variable. He would argue that racism is an ideology that justifies economic exploitation . . . and it is "impossible to enslave men without first making them inferior or sub-human" (Nursey-Bray, 1980, p. 136). Fanon also opined that a revolutionary struggle must reshape national consciousness and a direct intervention at the level of ideology is necessary (Nursey-Bray, 1980, p. 141). More important, as Nursey-Bray (1980) points out, the fact that the "emergence of a restructured consciousness [was] a necessary precondition for a genuinely 'new' society shows the importance [Fanon] ascribed to the ideological dimension" (p. 142). The ideology of colonialism rested on opaque notions of race and therefore to resist racist colonization and oppression in its myriad forms, the development of a national culture was imperative. Such national culture is forged by a people "in their day to day struggle as they confront and overcome the ideology of colonialism and 'reassume their own history'." (Nursey-Bray, 1980, p. 139).

As already noted, Fanon was concerned with the stable presentation of race in his "racial epidermal schema," which he steadfastly interpreted as the salience of showing up as black in a visceral antiblack context. Fanon's analysis was neither reductionist nor an essentialist take on race. According to Fanon, we must be aware of the inadequacy of academic discourse and analysis to fully comprehend the racial situation. Our academic understandings of race must be supplemented by experience in order to fully comprehend a given racial situation. Although he had an academic understanding of race, the racist discrimination he experienced when going to Algeria revealed to him that his intellectualized understanding of racism had not prepared him to deal with his experience of race in the flesh (i.e., subjective experience), hence a call for meshing the objective and subjective in the analysis of race. Fanon's ideas are helpful in pointing to the limits of simply intellectualizing transformative political projects (Estrada and McLaren, 1993). The black body (and the white body) is an epistemological, pedagogic and communicative site for comprehending race and racism, but in different ways. In Fanon (1967a), he worked with race as both subjective and objective knowing. This is so important in informing us that the "objective knowledge of race" is different from the experiencing of race and racism "in the flesh" (subjective knowledge about race). In Fanon's experience, then, the objective analysis of race and racism had woefully prepared him for the actual/lived engagement of racism. Thus, race as "embodied" is not to be read in terms of knowledge rooted in the biology of being/subject/body. Rather, it must be seen as knowledge arising from social experiences of the body/subject in a context where such knowledge about race is salient (i.e., everydayness of racism in a white supremacist society) (see also Howard, 2009).

To Fanon, race is more than representation or a social construction. It is lived, practiced, and experienced in the everyday world. The everydayness of racism means we must challenge any simplistic discursive representations of race. The experiences of racism continually create a tension and dissonance. There is the dehumanizing of the subject and the subsequent struggle of the subject to reclaim her or his humanity. Howard (2009) sees this process as a "historical racial schema." It is a process of self-discovery that sets in motion a politics of self-reclamation. The politics itself is the effect and consequences of inhabiting a black body in a white supremacist social context.

In his later years, Fanon become fully aware of the inherent dangers in a superficial understanding of race, and in the psychologizing of a problem that is deeply ingrained in socially constructed ideologies of race. The problem is rooted less in the individual psyche of people/racists. It is an ideology that underpins social formations and social organizational lives of communities as national cultures. We must recall Fanon's caution of the pitfalls of racial identification, arguing that "the unconditional affirmation of African culture has succeeded the unconditional affirmation of European culture" (Fanon, 1968, p. 212).

Perhaps it is Fanon's analysis of the power of racial identity that would prove to be his important contribution to race and antiracist knowledge. Racial identity as a possible site of colonizing relations is an element of analysis in its own right. There is a vital connection or relation between the colonized/colonizer; oppressed/oppressor; nonwhite colonial disadvantage and white privilege. The colonizer/oppressor needs the colonized/oppressed to understand their colonizing oppressive acts. The colonizer/oppressor cannot claim to know and understand about colonization/oppression any more than whites/ the dominant group can claim to know fully about whiteness and privilege. There are implications regarding how we come to know differently and why we must accord what I have called "epistemic saliency" (Dei, 1999) to the voice of the racially oppressed in understanding race and racism. As Howard (2009) rightly argues, the dominant's claim of "ignorance" of their privilege or that such privilege is "invisible" to them present some "key theoretical and methodological lapses" in the dominant's ability to understand privilege, whiteness and oppression. In effect, the colonizer cannot have deep intellectual insights into their oppressive and colonizing acts and relations. How do we deal with the questions of complicity, accountability and responsibility? The cancerous thought that oppression, colonialism and white racism is always perpetuated by someone else must be challenged, with exhortations to both the dominant and oppressed to acknowledge our differential complicities and responsibilities in the production, reproduction, and perpetuation of racism and oppressions. By not doing anything to challenge/resist racism and oppressions, one may inadvertently contribute to the sustaining racism and oppression. The difficulty of making such connections collective and differential implicated in relations of domination and subordination is a major obstacle to overcome in the struggle for social transformation. Fanon consequently asks us to understand self and collective implications, and to become self-critical and self-reflective of our actions of oppressions and resistance to oppressions.

In situating the question of racism, colonialism, and oppression within schooling contexts we may ask: How does racism affect the subjectivity of the colonized/oppressed and how does racism impact the learner's agency and resistance to the dominant culture of schooling? In looking at the effects of race/racism on culture, we must appreciate how racism and culture are connected in Fanon's thinking. In his work on *Toward the African Revolution,* Fanon (1967b) presents us with his insights into the culture of racism and the role ideology plays in shaping racist thoughts. To him, the "colonial country is a racist country" . . . and the "racist in a culture with racism is therefore normal. He has achieved a perfect harmony of economic relations and ideology" (p. 40). To Fanon, "racism is a cultural element" (p. 32) and that "the racist atmosphere impregnates all the elements of the social life" (p. 40). Fanon also saw that "racism as a social fabric has serious cultural ramifications" when he argued that "racism that aspires to be rational, individual, genotypically and phenotypically determined becomes transformed into cultural racism" (p. 32). He would go on to argue that racism impacts on every social existence and that "the object of racism is no longer the individual man but a certain form of existing" (p. 32). It is through a perverse "doctrine of cultural hierarchy" (p. 31) that Europeans established a false sense of superiority over non-Europeans. Such racism has become endemic to society such that it " . . . haunts and vitiates American culture (p. 36). But racism does not exist on its own. It is supported by other institutions of society such that " . . . military and economic oppression generally precedes, makes possible, and legitimizes racism" (p. 38). A decolonized space is not a racist space. In fact, he would emphatically claim that a "people that undertakes a struggle for liberation rarely legitimizes race prejudice" (p. 43).

In what ways does this race, culture and ideology connection implicate the subjectivities and agency of learners? Fanon (1967a) argues that the relationship of the black subject with his compatriot is different than with the white man. The "mask" is about assimilation to the colonizer's institutions (e.g., education, media, communication, politics, etc.), which only ensures that the colonized "can only express himself in terms that renders him as an object" (Wright, 2004, p. 115). The mask gives a semblance of "subject status," which is simply about mimicking the white subject, his institutions and values. Yet, even in this case, the black "Other" never assumes the "identity of the white subject." Thus in Fanon's thoughts, connecting race and ideology is significant. To him, the creation of black-white binary/duality itself points to the paradoxes and contradictions of oppressions. The struggles to "perform a negation of the negation" (Wright, 2004, p. 119) points to the paradoxes of resisting oppressions (e.g., every action produces a reaction), and sometimes in the process there is slippage into the form, logic, and implicit assumptions of the very things the oppressed is contesting. While the colonizer has his own space [the metropolis] there is also the "colonial and colonized space" (the margins), which is dictated and shaped by the colonizer. In the eyes of the white subject, the black functions in the collective as there is an ambivalence in a lack of individuality, being indistinguishable from the collective, ensuring that the white subject only enunciates the black subject as the "Other."

Fanon insisted that "colonial racism is no different from any other racism (1967a, p. 88), and that "European civilization and its best representatives are responsible for colonial racism" (p. 90). Colonial education and what it accomplishes are the doings/machinations of the colonial oppressor. If minority learners are devalued and some students develop an inferiority complex of their existence, colonial education and racism are responsible. Like a black female student, who told me one time in responding to conventional misinformed knowledge that black students lack self-esteem, "Sir, we have self-esteem but we are trying to keep it at school!" The inferiority complex of the colonized does not predate colonization. Fanon (1967a) provided that "the feeling of inferiority of the colonized is the correlative to the European feeling of superiority" (p. 93). In other words, it is the racist who creates the inferiority of the colonized. Minority learners in educational contexts which inferiorize their identities, histories, and cultures can develop a complex which ensures that in the company of whites the black/minority learner experiences his being through the eyes of the white learner. This does not mean that the black learner cannot exercise his or her agency. It is rather that, not only must the black (subject/learner) be black; she/he must be black in relation to the white learner (Fanon, 1967a, p. 110). Consequently, "the Black [learner] has no ontological resistance in the eyes of the white man" (Fanon, 1967, p. 110). The learner has to deal with the problem of "cultural imposition." After having been a slave of the white man, the black (learner) enslaves herself or himself (see Fanon, 1967a, p. 192). Among his minority peers, the black learner may try to assert himself/herself by insisting "that attention be paid not to the color of his [her] skin but to the force of his [her] intellect" (Fanon, 1967a, p. 193). The black learner "expects his or her skin 'color' to be forgotten" (Fanon, 1967a, p. 193).

It has been suggested that Fanon might have precluded the possibility of the black subject. In other words, the question is: Is there a space in schools or elsewhere where black subjects/learners can achieve their subjectivity, agency, politics and resistance on their own terms? The answer to the question is yes. But it has to be through violent decolonization. We can pursue endless debates as to whether Fanon's analysis was from a materialist, subjectivist or idealist orientation. It is clear that Fanon offered a complex relationship of materialist and idealist dialectics (e.g., he saw the Algerian veil—as a site of liberation, resistance, and claiming black female subjectivity; see Fanon, 1967b). The veil was an embodiment of action while the white mask was the effect of colonialism and colonial practices on the black subject. The veil is an attempt by Fanon to offer a Marxist critique of idealist dialectic (see also Wright, 2004). Also it is important for us to note that Fanon did not offer an essentialist reading of black and blackness. In fact, he himself acknowledged his analysis will be different for black subjects, depending where they are located.

IV. THE GENDERED AND SEXUAL POLITICS OF SCHOOLING: WHAT HAS FANON GOT TO DO WITH THIS?

I would like now to touch on the question of gender and sexual identities in Fanon's work and how this may inform a rethinking of education. In raising issues of gender and sexuality in Fanon, I acknowledge that there has been thought provoking critical feminist analysis of Fanon highlighting the problematic of his oversexualizing black women's bodies, his use of hypermasculine language, and general misunderstanding of the complicated experiences of black women's lives (see also Wane 2010). But, as stated in our introductory chapter, these critiques do not serve to dismiss the relevance of Fanon. To think otherwise is simply to engage in exactly what Fanon was opposed to—an arrogance of knowing. The critiques by Wright (2004) inform the formulation of some pertinent questions: Did Fanon acknowledge the possibilities of the gendered (in this case, black female) subject? To what extent is Fanon's analysis of the black "Other" devoid of gender and female subjectivity (that is, contributions of black women to discussions of race, nation, and citizenship and the black diaspora)? Is Fanon's analysis of white(ness) and black(ness), despite pretensions to the contrary, still caught in the oppressive effects of the colonialist binary modes of thought? How do we come to consciousness about subjectivities? How does the black subject move from the margins (void) to the centre to achieve subjectivity?

As we have argued elsewhere, we may be forced to play the game but perhaps we can play by our own terms and conditions (Dei, Karumanchery, and Karumanchery-Luik, 2004). Is it important for the black "Other" to be recognized by the white subject in order for the former to become a subject? How is such "recognition" to be achieved? (Note that to Fanon this is not possible or accomplished through language but by action.) Pedagogically, how do we combine/work with essentialist, antiessentialist, materialist and idealist interpretations of "blackness and subjectivity"?

Despite pretensions to the contrary, Fanon wrote a bit about sexuality and sexual politics. In fact, in reading Mercer (1996), one confronts some critical questions: How do we liberate the subjectivity of the colonizer and colonized from an oppressive system and universe? How sexuality and sexual politics help unsettle questions and de-center narratives of national identity? How does Fanon help us challenge the racialist construct that blacks are "somehow intrinsically more homophobic by virtue of being supposedly closer to nature and hence less civilized"? (Mercer, 1996, p. 121). While Fanon may enthuse that psychoanalysis and the preoccupation with sexuality offer "an explanatory paradigm of the Black problem," there is more to sexuality. Questions of gender and sexuality linger in decolonizing projects of the oppressed and colonized. Sexuality is a key component in identities. Fanon is relevant when engaging the issues of identity and sexual politics within and among colonized and oppressed communities. Fanon has been taken to task for his weak and problematic treatment of sexuality. Mercer (1996) has long noted that homosexuality "is a powerful source of anxiety within Fanon's theorizing" (p. 125), and further opines that homosexuality is a key issue in black sexual politics" (p. 128). We need to pay attention to the role of sexuality and, particularly, sexual politics among oppressed groups in furthering resistance struggles. Fanon might not have embarked upon a critical analysis of sexuality and the connections with politics and liberation struggles. But today we are keenly aware of the important connections of sexuality and politics. Mercer (1996) calls for an acknowledgment of the ways the gay and lesbian space and presence, along with black feminisms, have altered "the public face of Black politics" (p. 128). Mercer (1996) also speaks of the "political disaggregation of Blackness" in the contemporary era in ways that bring to the fore the complications of race, sexuality, and politics.

In a similar vein, anticolonial studies inform us about the construction of masculinities and the politics of colonization and decolonization. The anticolonial framework allows for a critique of psychiatric studies and how the "discipline" has informed a particular construction of dominant masculinities. In rethinking schooling and education in light of Fanon, we can examine the implications of a new decolonized masculinity and the implications for addressing sexual repression. The political discourse of masculinity in black anticolonial and liberationist practice offers guides to retheorize Fanon. For example, the ways women are generally excluded from positions of power and authority in liberation struggles parallel the ways school systems reproduce patriarchal systems of authority favouring straight white males. Schools utilize gendered tropes to create new reorganized relations of ruling based on the allocation of power and resource. As we note from Fanon, the colonizer and the colonized mutually constitute each other's identity. Males subordinate females in order to lay claim to resources. Another underexplored point in Fanon theorizing is the link between homophobia and misogyny. If it is the violence of history that has shaped fears and anxieties about sexuality then we must focus on Fanon's analysis of colonial, colonialism, and psycho-sexuality, as well as integrating sexual politics and black and the oppressed people's liberation. We must be able to link sexuality to the political project of decolonization as one of the political strategies to de-center what has been called "the outmoded notion of the essential Black subject" (Mercer, 1996, p. 122) that schools continually reproduce.

V. FANON AND THE PAST: LOOKING TO THE FUTURE

In concluding this chapter, I turn now to examine how the past, present, and the future inform each other in Fanonian thought. How do we think of and take up the past and history? Fanon offers a critical reading regarding the evocation of the past that has relevance in the ways we can imagine the future. While the idea of moving beyond the "fruitless nostalgia of the past" (see also Robinson, 1993, p. 83) is helping, it is important for social theory to also invoke and reclaim that past, which cannot be suffocating. Speaking about Africa and the creation of a national culture in communities, Fanon asserts that the search for a culture should not take us back to the values of precolonial Africa since the treasures culled from the past cannot lead us to an authentic national culture. In other words, such national culture is not found in the past, but forged by a people "in their day to day struggle as they confront and overcome the ideology of colonialism and 'reassume their own history.'" (Nursey-Bray, 1980, p. 139).

In arguing that "the body of history does not determine a single one of my actions" and that the living cannot be burdened with the past, Fanon is not repudiating the past. As noted by many others, we live in the past and are haunted by the past when we fail to confront it (Morrison, cited in Verges, 1996, p. 63). While it is acknowledged that we are continually transformed by the past and its history of oppression and colonialism, such past must be acknowledged as constitutive of our subjectivities, and as a necessary exercise in decolonization. The past cannot simply be buried. It weighs continually on the present and the future. When we choose to live repressed histories, we lose part of our humanity. The project of reclaiming the past is an exercise in the restoration of what may be lacking in the present. History is relevant for the present. As Verges (1996) notes, "history is always ambivalent for the place it gives to the past is equally a means to open the way to the future" (p. 64). The implication here is that societal institutions such as the school need to teach about learners' pasts and to see history as a totality of a people's lived experiences. The past cannot be subjected to selected (mis-)capturing or misreading. The failure to engage learners' pasts and their histories leads to the creation of an educated subject who is not actually a whole being, but instead constitutes someone living a fragment of human existence. It is this mis-education that creates the learner who is lost and is devoid of any grounding in culture, history, and community. The ensuing result is a learner unable to claim any self-pride, self-worth, or sense of purpose. The whole project of educating the oppressed soul then must be to help learners not necessarily to "receive" an education but to reclaim education that is about their past, history, sense of self-worth, and pride (see also Rich, 1979). This is a major exercise of decolonization, an enduring lesson of Frantz Fanon.

ACKNOWLEDGMENTS

I would like to thank the students in my advanced-level graduate course, *SES3999:* "Frantz Fanon and Education: Pedagogical Possibilities" (Fall 2008) for their comments, insights, and critiques that helped sharpen my thoughts for this chapter. I also acknowledge the assistance of Stan Doyle-Wood of the Department of Sociology and Equity Studies of the University of Toronto for commenting on a draft of the paper, and Olga Williams for editing the paper.

REFERENCES

Anderson, B. 1991. *Imagined Communities: Reflections on the Origin and Spread of Nationalism.* London: Verso.
Asante, M. K. 2010. *Maulana Karenga: An Intellectual Portrait of an Activist Scholar.* Cambridge: Polity Press.
Dei, G. J. S. 1996. *Anti Racism Education: Theory and Practice.* Halifax, Nova Scotia: Fernwood.
Dei, G. J. S. 1999. "The Denial of Difference: Reframing Anti-Racist Praxis," *Race, Ethnicity and Education* 2(1): 17–38.
Dei, G. J. S. 2005 "Critical Issues in Anti-Racist Research Methodologies: An Introduction." In G. Dei and G. Johal (eds.). *Critical Issues in Anti-Racist Research Methodologies.* New York: Peter Lang, pp. 1–28.

Dei, G. J. S., L. Karumanchery and N. Karumanchery-Luik. 2004. *Playing the Race Card: Exposing White Power and Privilege.* New York: Peter Lang.

Dei, G. J. S., with A. Butler, G. Charania, A. Kola-Olusanya, B. Opini, R. Thomas, and A. Wagner. (2010). *Learning to Succeed: The Challenges and Possibilities of Educational Development for All.* New York: Teneo Press. [in press].

Dua, E. 2008. "Thinking Through Anti-racism and Indigeneity in Canada." *Ardent Review,* 1(1), 31–35.

Estrada, K., and P. McLaren. 1993. "A Dialogue on Multiculturalism and Democratic Culture." *Educational Researcher,* 22(3): 27–33.

Fanon, F. 1963. *The Wretched of the Earth.* New York: Grove Press.

Fanon F. 1965: *A Dying Colonialism.* New York: Grove Press.

Fanon F. 1967a: *Black Skin, White Masks* New York: Grove Press.

Fanon, F. 1967b. *Towards the African Revolution: Political Essays.* New York: Monthly Review Press.

Fontenot, C. J. 1978. "Fanon and the Devourers". *Journal of Black Studies* 9 (1): 93–114.

Foucault, M. 1990 *The History of Sexuality,* vol. 1. New York: Vintage Books.

Foucault, M. 1977. "Two Lectures." In Colin Gordon, (ed.). *Power/Knowledge: Selected Interviews and Other Writings 1972–1977,* New York: Pantheon Books.

Goldberg, D. T. 1996. "In/Visibility and Super/Vision: Fanon on Race, Veils, and Discourses of Resistance." In Lewis R. Gordon, T. Denean Sharpley-Whiting and Renee T. White, (eds.). *Fanon: A Critical Reader.* Oxford: Blackwell Critical Readers Series. pp. 179–202.

Goldberg, D. T. 2002. *The Racial State.* Malden, MA: Blackwell Publishers.

Howard, P. 2009. The Double-Edged Sword: A Critical Race Africology of Collaborations Between Blacks and Whites in Racial Equity Work. Unpublished Ph.D. dissertation, Department of Sociology and Equity Studies, Ontario Institute for Studies in Education of the University of Toronto, OISE/UT, Toronto, Ontario.

Issahaku, P. A. (2010) "Decolonizing the Euro-American Public Education System: A Transgressive Revisiting of Fanon" In G. J. S. Dei, (ed.). *Fanon and the Counterinsurgency of Education.* Rotterdam: Sense Publishers (Forthcoming).

Johal, G. 2009. Colonialism, Modernity and the Racist State. Unpublished Ph.D. Comprehensive Exam Paper. OISE, University of Toronto.

Kempf, A. 2005. *Personal Communication.* Department of Sociology and Equity Studies, Ontario Institute for Studies in Education of the University of Toronto, OISE/UT, Toronto, Ontario.

Kempf, A. 2008. *Personal Communication:* Comments on Bernadette Tynan's Video: 'Making Your Child Brilliant." Toronto.

Kerr, L. 2005. *Personal communication.* Department of Sociology and Equity Studies, Ontario Institute for Studies in Education of the University of Toronto, OISE/UT, Toronto, Ontario.

King, A. 2002. Double cohort study: Phase 2. http://www.edu.gov.on.ca/eng/document/reports/dcohortp2.html.

King, A. 2003. Double cohort study: Phase 3. http://www.edu.gov.on.ca/eng/document/report/phase3/.

Lawrence, B., and E. Dua. 2005. "Decolonizing Antiracism." *Social Justice, 32*(4), 120–143.

Levin, B. 2004. Students at Risk: A Review of Research Prepared for Toronto Learning Partnership. http://www.thelearningpartnership.ca.

McClintock, Anne. 1995. *Imperial Leather*. London: Routledge.
McCready, L. 2008. Personal Communication. Department of Sociology and Equity Studies, Ontario Institute for Studies in Education of the University of Toronto, OISE/UT, Toronto, Ontario.
Mercer, K. 1996. "Decolonization and Disappointment: Reading Fanon's Sexual Politics." In Alan Reed, (ed.), *The Fact of Blackness: Fanon and Visual Representation*. Seattle: Bay Press. pp. 114–131.
Mills, C. *Blackness Visible: Essays on Philosophy and Race*. Ithaca, NY: Cornell University Press, 1998.
Nursey-Bray, P. 1980. "Race and Nation: Ideology in the Thought of Frantz Fanon." *Journal of Modern African Studies*. 18(1): 135–142.
Omi, M., and H. Winant. 1994. *Racial Formation in the United States from the 1960s to the 1980s*. New York: Routledge.
Presbey, G. M. 1996. "Fanon on the Role of Violence in Liberation: A Comparison with Gandhi and Mandela." In Lewis R. Gordon, T. Denean Sharpley-Whiting and Renee T. White, (eds.). *Fanon: A Critical Reader*. Oxford: Blackwell Critical Readers Series. pp. 283–296.
Razack, S. H. 2002. *Race, Space and the Law: Unmapping a White Settler Society*. Toronto: Between the Lines.
Rich, A. 1979. "Claiming an Education." In *On Lies, Secrets and Silence*. New York: W.W. Norton & Co.
Robinson, C. 1993. "The Appropriation of Frantz Fanon." *Race & Class* 35(1): 79–91.
Sackeyfio, C. 2005 on p. 14. Hip-Hop Cultural Identities: A Review of the Literature and Its Implications for the Schooling of African-Canadian Youth. Unpublished MA thesis. Ontario Institute for Studies in Education of the University of Toronto (OISE/UT).
Said, E. 1994. *Culture and Imperialism*. New York: Vintage Books.
Sharawy, H. 2003 (September). "Frantz Fanon and the African Revolution, Revisited at a Time of Globalization." http://www.codesria.org/Links/conferences/accra/sharawi.pdf.
Shujaa, M. 1994. *Too Much Schooling, Too Little Education*. Trenton, NJ: Africa World Press.
Sleeter, C. E., and Grant, C. A. 1999. *Making Choices for Multicultural Education: Five Approaches to Race, Class, and Gender*. New York: John Wiley & Sons, Inc.
Stoler, A. L. 1995. *Race and the Education of Desire: Foucault's History of Sexuality and the Colonial Order of Things*. Durham, NC, and London: Duke University Press.
Taiwo, O. 1996. "On the Misadventures of National Consciousness: A Retrospect on Frantz Fanon's Gift to Prophecy." In Lewis R. Gordon, T. Denean Sharpley-Whiting and Renee T. White, (eds.), *Fanon: A Critical Reader*. Oxford: Blackwell Critical Readers Series. pp. 255–272.
Titchkosky, T. 2007. "Pausing at the Intersections of Difference." A reprint from the book: *Reading and Writing Disability Differently: The Textured Life of Embodiment*. Toronto: University of Toronto Press.
Valencia, R. 1997. (ed.). *The Evolution of Deficit Thinking: Educational Thought and Practice*. Washington, DC: The Falmer Press.
Verges, F. 1996. "Chains of Madness, Chains of Colonialism: Fanon and Freedom." In Alan Reed, (ed.), *The Fact of Blackness: Fanon and Visual Representation*. Seattle: Bay Press. pp. 46–75.

Visano, L. 2008. Personal communication; Comments on Meredith Lordan's Ph.D dissertation: "Education as a Human Right: A Critical Study of Accessible Education as Political Discourse and Practice at the United Nations." Department of Sociology and Equity Studies, Ontario Institute for Studies in Education of the University of Toronto, OISE/UT, Toronto, Ontario.

Wane, N. 2010 "Reading Fanon Differently: Black Canadian Feminist Prespectives." In G. J. S. Dei, (ed.). *Fanon and the Counterinsurgency of Education.* Rotterdam: Sense Publishers (Forthcoming).

Wright, M. 2004. "Some Women Disappear: Frantz Fanon's Legacy in Black Nationalist Thought and the Black Male Subject." In *Becoming Black, Creating Identity in the African Diaspora.* Durham, NC, and London: Duke University Press. pp. 111–135.

CHAPTER TWO

Body Politics and the Experience of Blackness within the Field of Education

CAMILLE LOGAN

Schools across the country are experiencing growing diversity within the population of students who make up the Canadian classroom of today. With the increasing ethnocultural and racial makeup of those who live in Canada, the bodies leading in Canadian classrooms must mirror the diversity that is reflective of those the system currently serves. Despite the growing number of racialized teachers entering the field of education, Brown and Rushowy of the *Toronto Star* reported that in the Toronto District School Board over 70% of their students in grades seven to twelve were non-white, yet over 77% of their teachers were white (2007). These stats continue to be a concern for those who hold the system accountable, as numerous reports reveal that large numbers of black and racialized students fail to graduate and/or drop out of school, clearly demonstrating the system's failure to meet the needs of all its learners.

Within educational research, numerous theorists identify probable causes for the continued failure of racialized students to successfully achieve within the system. In a relatively recent Ontario Ministry of Education report entitled *Early School Leavers*, " . . . visible minority youth identified difficulties with a particular teacher or school principal and negative school climate, as key factors that affected their learning and/or subsequent early school leaving" (Ontario Ministry of Education, 2005). Thus, lack of representation and role models are often cited as a foundation for student disengagement and lack of success. Despite the slight increase in racialized teachers within education, the system continues to fail these students.

Consequently, the expectation that racialized bodies placed within the existing structure of schooling as a solution to the system's failure is not only problematic, but also quite unrealistic. The complexities of systemic racism are so deeply embedded within the cultural norms, values and institutional structures of our society that multifaceted, critical approaches to educational transformation such as antiracism and anticolonialism are a necessity. Approaches that interrogate the system and use strategies for identifying and naming race and racism are integral to challenging white racism— an invisible, unidentified, often unnamed remnant of colonialism today.

Despite the incremental gains in education addressing issues pertaining to the equity agenda, the "colonial encounter," as articulated in Frantz Fanon's revolutionary book *Black Skin, White Masks,* still exists! His compelling personal narrative examines the impact of colonialism on the black psyche, identity and the development of one's consciousness, theorizes the black experience in a white society. Through Fanon's critical examination of French/European society, he reveals the structures of racism and white privilege embedded in Western society and identifies them as insidious parts of our social fabric as remnants of our colonial past. Thus, the colonial encounter and its effect on the racialized body prevails within the current system of education, as it is articulated through the ways in which those within the system continue to read, interpret and treat bodies of colour.

As a black woman, in the field of education, I and many of my colleagues who are black or racialized have been confronted with the challenge of engaging in work that specifically addresses issues of inequity pertaining to race and racism. In *Black Skin, White Masks,* Fanon takes up representation and identity as "embodied knowing" of the black body and speaks specifically to the experience of "the black." As a black educator, I strongly believe that those of us who are racialized and working within the field of public education must strive to actively ensure that the colonizing aspects of the school system do not go unchallenged. Nevertheless, this is not an easy declaration to make. There are serious professional risks to engaging in work that challenges the existing norms and structures within the current education system that work to privilege whiteness while de-privileging other bodies of colour. It has also been my experience that when racialized bodies enter the space of teacher and/or school administrator; not withstanding their performances, their skin speaks another story. As a result, many black educators continue to ask questions such as, how does one create a space for oneself within the current system of education? How does one disrupt the mis/representations of black identity within the school system? What is the role and responsibility of a racialized school leader/educator to challenge race mis/representation within the status quo? How does a black educator position his or her politics within the education system; especially, when there are personal, material, and spiritual repercussions for speaking back to power? Although

I do not intend to speak for all black teachers and/or school administrators, I do believe that my experiences are not unusual and may serve to interconnect with the thoughts and reflections of other black educators within the field.

For the purpose of this paper I will discuss Fanon's analysis of colonialism and its impact on the psyche of the colonized subjects and how this can be linked to the ways in which the colonial encounter is experienced for black educators in schools. Through Fanon's analysis of black identity, I will explore the politics of identity and how black bodies in the role of educator navigate the public school system. In this essay, my exploration of the experience of "blackness" within the field of education focuses on educators, who like me work in schools located within the Greater Toronto Area, a very diverse area within the province of Ontario. Although past explorations on this topic have often focused on racialized students (see Dei et al., 1997, 2000; Solomon, 1997), in this chapter, I redirect the discussion to the experience of black educators. Using Fanon's analysis of black identity, the discussion is guided by these questions: How does the colonized mind become conscious of the existing mechanisms that are inherent within a system that works to privilege whiteness? How does this consciousness lead to the engagement of activist work in some, while not in others? What are the risks of engaging in antiracism/anticolonial work in education?

My analysis is informed and shaped by an antiracism framework. As a critical framework, antiracism education is critical of the current structures of teaching, learning, and administering education; especially, the role of schooling in producing and reproducing inequalities that are based on race, class, gender, and religious beliefs (Dei and Asgharzadeh, 2001). This framework is useful for the essay as it helps readers understand how the colonial remnants within the education system can be challenged and restructured to address institutionalized and systemic violence.

SEARCHING FOR A CRITICAL DISCOURSE: ANTIRACISM EDUCATION AS A DISCURSIVE FRAMEWORK

Race is not everything, but it is about everything.

Antiracism education, according to Dei (1996, p. 25), is a critical discourse of race and racism in society and the continuous categorization of social groups for differential and unequal treatment. Antiracism education explicitly names issues of race and social difference as issues of power and equity rather than matters of cultural and ethnic variety. The historical construction of race in North America and Europe was not a simple act to differentiate between groups of human beings. Rather, race was constructed to organize human groups into a series of hierarchies (Moore, 1994; Montague, 1974; Stepan, 1982; Goldberg, 2002) to impose white power and privilege. As Rigney Lester-Irabinna (1997) argues concerning Aboriginal people of Australia:

> *My people were not racialized in order to satisfy scientific curiosity about our place in a nonindigenous classificatory system. Racializing discourses of difference, like all discourse of difference, are located as significant sites of power. We were racialized in order to exert power over us. (1997, p. 112)*

Similarly, through the social construction of race in Canada, whiteness is positioned to secure control and power. Antiracism education sees the struggle against racism as not a simple task against a few racist lunatics on the fringe, but rather a struggle to de-racialize micro-and macro-social formations left to us through slavery and colonization, which continue to affect and shape the lives of racialized bodies in North America and Europe (Adjei, 2008).

McIntosh (1990), Thomas (1994), Sleeter (1994), Dines (1994), Ahmed (2004), and Dei (1996) believe that whiteness and the privilege of white skin is often taken for granted by many white people. In fact, Gail Dines argues that the "power of whiteness as a social identity [is mostly] rendered invisible by privileges" (1994, p. 28). Antiracist education acknowledges that racism exists and operates in the forms of the individual, (overt and covert), within institutions, and is embedded in societal norms and systems. These different forms of racism work to fabricate social norms to those that are of whiteness. This serves to script meanings to "Otherness," and provide racial boundaries that police other bodies outside the circle of whiteness or what Stanfield (1985, p. 389) refers to as "a privileged subset of the population." Therefore, there are two competing interests operating within the field of education: those who benefit from racial categorization and those who do not.

Antiracism education, therefore, acknowledges the pedagogic need to confront the challenge of diversity and difference in Canadian society (Dei, 1996). The framework recognizes the need for inclusive school practices that are capable of responding to the needs and concerns of marginalized learners and teachers. Finally, antiracism education advocates for representation in schools. The issue of representation could be discussed in two folds. The first representation is in the need for knowledge, cultures, values, and history of racialized students to be included in the curriculum. The second part of representation speaks to question of hiring racialized teachers and administrators in schools. Sometimes, the liberal readings suggest that schools search for whom they deem best to teach and that race should not be a factor. However, in the work of Solomon et al. (2005), research has shown that we often see excellence when it looks, thinks, and sounds like us, therefore race does matter!

Today, legitimate questions are being asked concerning the day when our school staffs will be reflective of the diversity that is representative of the students and the communities they serve (Dei, 1996). Numerous reports have acknowledged that black and other racialized students identify a need to see themselves reflected in the schools they attend each day and that they see a lack of role models as a significant failure of the system (see Dei et al., 1997). Inclusive school practices demand that not only should absences of racialized knowledges be questioned, but they also hold the system accountable for the absent presence of racialized bodies in schools as teachers and/or administrators.

Thus, antiracism education serves as an appropriate framework for the following discussion as it places race at the centre while interrogating existing structures of power and privilege. Through the work of Fanon and this framework, the personal and political struggles of representation for the black educator will be explored in relation to this question: how do we as educators of colour break the barriers and move beyond the boundaries as defined by the legacy of colonialism?

SEARCHING FOR THE CENTRE: PERSONAL LOCATION

Before I begin the discussion, I believe it is important to provide my social location and the context for my analysis. I am a black woman, born in Canada to parents of Caribbean heritage. I grew up in a predominantly white middle-class suburb located just outside of Toronto, Ontario. Although the town in which I lived was beginning to experience some elements of racial and/or ethnocultural diversity, I was often the only child of colour in my class, on my soccer team, at swimming and skating lessons, and even at birthday parties. Although as a child I had many friends, it was clear that on numerous occasions that there is a time and a place when race counts!

Thankfully, my parents were not afraid to ensure that I was aware of these moments and clearly identified when race and racism came into play. They instilled within me a level of consciousness that helped me to develop a positive identity despite the barrage of negative images, low expectations, and stereotypical messaging about who I was and what I could be as a person of African descent in this society. The deconstruction of these social experiences provided me with tools to resist some elements of colonialism and the internalization of the way the world sees me, which ensured a positive development of my self-identity. This also created an awareness and understanding that illuminated the reality of social inequity for me as a young adult. Later as a public school educator, I began to see the ways one can actively challenge discriminatory behaviour, actions, and attitudes. As I continued to learn more about antiracism education, I began to deepen my understanding of equitable and inclusive practices. I became cognizant of the importance of championing all oppression through which I became conscious of my own biases and complicities.

As a young teacher, one of my goals was to ensure that my students were able to negotiate and understand difference. In my classroom, I worked to consistently implement antiracism principles, as this was the foundation for my professional practice and the lens through which I viewed the curriculum. I looked for opportunities to include the diverse knowledge and experiences various learners bring into the classroom to ensure that my students became aware of the ways power is distributed inequitably in society. Although social injustice may be a reality, I taught my students that we all have a responsibility as citizens to challenge the status quo and empowered my students to confront discrimination, which at times got me into trouble! Nevertheless, I felt strongly that it was my responsibility as a black female educator to challenge the constructed images within education that served to affirm Eurocentric notions of a white supremacist patriarchal culture (hooks, 1992).

Later in my career as a school principal, I looked for similar opportunities to challenge the systemic educational norms and values that continue to marginalize certain groups of students. My first principalship was in a school community that was predominantly white. Although this community was beginning to experience some racial and cultural diversity, many nonracialized members in the community perceived this negatively. Many teachers and parents from the community felt that "they" were becoming "outnumbered." As a result, these new families were not welcomed and subsequently, these parents were not engaged, resulting in a silencing of these voices in the decision-making processes. I felt my role as a new administrator was to ensure that all parents were welcomed, to ensure that all parents were well received in addition to being strongly encouraged and supported to become engaged in various aspects of the school: in a sense then, to have a voice! Thus, changes were made to certain long-standing traditions at the school that were not inclusive. As part of these new initiatives, I worked specifically with staff to make certain they understood that difference matters! Unfortunately, some believed that the differential education outcomes of certain groups of students were the result of students' ability or their circumstance rather than investigating the structural inequity within the system. As a result, I worked with my school staff to challenge many of the white, middle-class taken-for-granted assumptions that continue to be foundational beliefs for the majority of teachers about student achievement, as they allow for the institutionalized barriers within the system to go unseen and unchallenged (Dei, 2002; Solomon, 2003).

As a classroom teacher and currently as a school administrator, I truly believe that all educators (regardless of their role) must be engaged in the struggle to demand that the system has effective policies and practices in place that truly ensure equity of achievement for all students. Both dominant and marginalized educators must champion anticolonial/antiracism practices and principles. We must all be prepared to disrupt the liberal humanist agenda that posits change, yet seeks to maintain the existing structures of power and privilege. Although we must work together, "oppressor and the oppressed," the voices of the marginalized must be at the centre of the space where decisions, educational policy, and practice are developed. Consequently, for those of us who are racialized and/or black, how our bodies are read in educational contexts makes this an incredibly difficult undertaking. We are often challenged by the ways in which our bodies are marked, tainting the way our voices are heard and how we are seen and perceived.

Through personal narratives, I will provide a context for my thinking around identity and representation pertaining to black/racialized bodies in the education system. In the discussion I will highlight Fanon's concept of the "epidermal schema," in addition to his analysis of identity and consciousness. Through Fanon's concept of consciousness and his analysis of the dialect between visibility and invisibility, I will also argue the importance of educators who are racialized using these experiences as consciousness-raising moments to challenge the system and engage in transformative education.

THE EPIDERMAL SCHEMA: THE BLACK BODY, REPRESENTATION, AND CONSCIOUSNESS

Dirty nigger! or simply, Look a Negro!

I came into the world imbued with the will to find a meaning in things, my spirit filled with the desire to attain to the source of the world, and then I found that I was an object in the midst of other objects. (Fanon 1967, p. 109)

As indicated in this famous quote by Frantz Fanon, the colonial encounter is one that many of us who are racialized can identify with. In locating myself, I discussed how as a child, student, adult, and educator, I have often been the only racialized body in spaces that were/are predominantly occupied by white bodies. This passage exemplifies the colonial encounter as it relates to the experience of those who are racialized and how the black body is read in certain spaces and/or contexts. Through the experiences shared previously, it is clear race visibility can overshadow all other aspects of one's identity such as one's role and responsibility within a school and/or a school district.

As a classroom teacher, I can recall a disturbing instance pertaining to class placements where race and racism clearly came into play. The practice of class placements is the process of placing students into a particular teacher's class. This process usually occurs at the conclusion of the school year in preparation for following year. Parents are notified of their child's new classroom teacher at the end of the school year on the June report card.

I can specifically recall an instance when a student who appeared on my class list in June was mysteriously moved to another class before the school year began in September. This was a very rare occasion and was not done unless there was a parent request regarding a class change. When I questioned this occurrence, the school principal responded with insignificant answers to my query and was not able to clearly articulate the concern of the parent. This in itself was unusual. Should there be a concern about your teaching or a complaint made by a parent, administration would share the concern or issue with you in order to have it addressed and/or resolved. I began to question this further when it happened again without reason. It was not until I became an administrator that I had the opportunity to learn about the ways parent requests for class changes was managed. I then discovered a potential reason for this incident and similar ones that followed. Principal colleagues shared that at times they receive requests from parents wanting to remove their children from classrooms of some black and/or racialized teachers. Although not all parents openly state race as a reason, principals can often "read between the lines." Nevertheless, these requests are sometimes granted. Upon reflection, I surmised that race and racism were highly plausible reasons for these incidents. It was apparent that despite my certification and positive reputation in the school and community, there were some parents who did not see me simply as a teacher; they saw me as "the black teacher" and assumed that I was "not good enough" to teach their child.

Speaking on the fact of blackness in *Black Skin, White Masks,* Frantz Fanon contends that racialized bodies are often prejudged based on appearance. "I am given no chance. I am overdetermined from without. I am a slave not of the 'idea' others have of me, but my own appearance" (Fanon, 1967, p. 116). For Fanon, in the white world, the bodies of racialized subjects remain a text that produce images and knowledge of oneself even before one sets a foot into any space. In the world of law, one is to be presumed 'innocent' until proven otherwise. However, in the field of education, non-white bodies are often misread and predetermined as incompetent, less capable, less qualified and less intelligent, until she or he has proven otherwise. Unlike our white counterparts, we must often work harder to prove that we are worthy of the role and/or position that we have earned within this field. Consequently, we are often mis/read, mis/defined, and sometimes mis/treated based by virtue of colour.

Frantz Fanon insists that the misrepresentation and misinterpretation of Blackness is rooted in the legacy of colonialism that continues to permeate many facets of today's society. I now realize that in many contexts within the field of education, in the eyes of dominant (and in some cases, non-dominant) group members, I was "a black woman" and the reading of my body as such, came well before my role/position as educator (teacher, school administrator, or otherwise). In today's context, it is clearly understood that one has to have a certain level of education and training in order to earn a teaching degree and/or to attain the position of teacher or principal within a school, yet my qualifications were often questioned. This became more apparent when I entered the realm of school leadership. It was a regular occurrence for me to be asked questions such as, "How long have you been teaching?" (I could not have been teaching long enough); "When did you complete your Master's degree?" (I could not have been educated enough); "When did you complete your Principals' qualifications program?" (I could not have been qualified enough); and people even asked me my age (I could not have been old enough). The question they really wanted to ask was: "How could you, a young black woman, be a principal?" Yet, the real issue behind many of the questions was that I did not fit the visual representation of the role I am performing. Essentially, they assumed that I could not be qualified for the position, which was probably obtained through a district equity policy designed to target and unfairly promote educators for the role. When I share my experiences in conversation with colleagues who are young white males and particularly white females, it does not appear that they are subjected to this degree of interrogation. George Dei was right in his assertion that " . . . when Blackness makes itself so visible, the dominant psyche cannot stand it! It also affirmed [an] earlier assertion that certain bodies are read in very limiting ways . . ." (Dei, 2008, p. xiv).

Thus, the credentials for those of us who are racialized in the system are often questioned and/or scrutinized by others. The colonial gaze on black bodies in education continuously negates our qualifications and achievements. In educational circles where administrators are present and I am in this space, I am prepared for this inquisition. Interestingly enough, the myth of meritocracy is not upheld in support of racialized bodies, particularly when they enter spaces that are perceived as white strongholds.

During my tenure as a school administrator, I hired the first black teacher at my school. I can recall the look of surprise by some parents in the community regarding this new staff member. The uproar in the community to this new teacher was quite disturbing in that groups of parents actually had meetings at their homes regarding ways to "get rid" of this teacher (and probably me as the school administrator as well)! Yet, this teacher was highly skilled, well qualified, compassionate, and came with several years of experience. What more could a school community want? However, once I hired a black male teacher, suddenly my hiring practices came into question. Unfortunately, the panic was intensified because this black male teacher was assigned to a primary division classroom and was going to be working with six- and seven-year-old children who in this particular school community were predominantly white!

Although this was a highly qualified, experienced black male teacher, his body was marked. For some parents who were of the dominant group, he did not represent their notion of a teacher. I believe that the ways the black male body is negatively portrayed in society as something associated with violence and to be feared, created this apprehension on the part of the parents who felt they needed to 'protect' their young child(ren). Consequently, their fears were so intense that they worked collectively to remove this teacher from the school. Frantz Fanon articulates the perception of the ways in which the dominant group can read the black body in the following quote:

> ... the little white boy throws himself into his mother's arms: Mama, the nigger's going to eat me up. All round me the white man, above the sky tears at its navel, the earth rasps under my feet, and there is a white song, a while song. All this whiteness that burns me ... I sit down at the fires and I become aware of my uniform, I had not seen it. It is indeed ugly ... (Fanon, 1967, p. 114)

This quote exemplifies the ways the black body, and in particular the black male body, is read and interpreted by those of the dominant group as something to be feared and detested. This representation of the black male body contradicts the role of the primary school teacher as someone who is well educated, skilled, nurturing and supportive of their students. I believe that the tension between the reality (who the teacher was) and representation (the black male body) resulted in this racist response by these parents.

Albeit that the aforementioned quote from Fanon may be an exaggerated connection to this scenario presented, the epidermal schema of the black man as violent, inferior and something to fear results from what Fanon refers to as the "corporeal schema," which because of the nature and design of colonialism has been encrypted into the psyche of Western societies. This schema provides a framework for the ways the black male is defined. This may sound like an absurdity in the twenty-first century, particularly in an Ontario context; however, I began to wonder if there is a primal dialogue that takes place at the level of unconsciousness for dominant group members that surfaces when there is tension between what they know and understand in regards to racial inequity today and the imprinted messaging about representations of race that stem from colonialism?

Fanon's conception of the epidermal schema presented in *Black Skin, White Masks* identifies a level of consciousness or knowing about the ways in which the black body is read within the context of Western societies. Thus, the structure of colonialism provided the schema in which members of the colony were to view the world. This essentially became the lens of the dominant; a lens that served to negate and/or reject all that is not white. For Fanon, this schema is such that the black man is seen only in relation to the white man. It is such that is " . . . a definitive structuring of the self and of the world—definitive because it creates a real dialectic between my body and the world" (Fanon, 1967, p. 111).

As I reflect on my past and continue to read about anticolonial thinkers such as Dei, hooks, Wane, Fanon, and Memmi, I am now able to comprehend the degree to which the colonial encounter and the "white gaze" was a consistent element of my childhood experiences and is still a regular occurrence as an adult, particularly in my work and within social settings. Over time, I have developed a greater critical consciousness of the ways in which inappropriate comments, odious glances, and perturbed stares regarding my occupation within certain spaces is clearly questioning my presence and creating an indication that I do not belong. As I continue to gain new knowledge resulting from reading antiracist, anticolonial, and critical race theorists, I am now able to attribute these experiences and others as remnants of our colonial past that continue to plague our society and the current system of education today.

I have used and continue to use this knowledge to inform my antiracism and equity work as an educator and currently as a school leader. The "white gaze" is one that I know all too well. As I continue to work with colleagues who are committed to equity in education, I challenge this incredibly significant element that is present in the curriculum and cultural norms of the organization that reproduce the "hegemonic modes of seeing, thinking, and being that block our capacity to see ourselves oppositionally, to imagine and invent ourselves in ways that are liberatory" (hooks, 1992, p. 2).

Thus, the individual identity that a black person may create for him/herself outside of this schema is refuted by the colonial way of seeing and knowing "blackness," which in many ways is strongly evident within the institutions and systems of today: "in the white world the man of colour encounters difficulties in the development of his bodily schema. Consciousness of the body is solely a negating activity" (Fanon, 1967, p. 110).

In *Black Skin, White Masks,* Fanon articulates how this consciousness is raised as a result of his personal experiences: "As long as the Black man is among his own, he will have no occasion, except in minor internal conflicts to experience his being through others" (Fanon, 1967, p. 109). Thus, Fanon identified that amongst other black individuals, his identity was different from that of the identity imposed upon him when in the presence of whites. In *The Fact of Blackness,* Stuart Hall explores racial identity as "the inscription of race on the skin" as defined by colonial "cultural and discursive" notions and ideas as opposed to a "physiological, genetic" reality, thus creating Fanon's "dialectic of experience," as the negative, inferior notions of what it is to be black imprinted on the psyche of "the Black" (cited in Reed, 1996).

I subjected myself to an objective examination, I discovered my blackness, my ethnic characteristics, and I was battered down by tom-toms, cannibalism, intellectual deficiency, racial defects, slave ships and above all else, above all: "Sho' good eatin." (Fanon, 1967, p. 112)

This dialectic is articulated throughout *Black Skin, White Masks* as expressed in the previous quote. Here the Epidermal Schema has defined Fanon to the point where he feel as though he must discover himself, and consequently does so through the lens of the colonizer.

ONTOLOGICAL RESISTANCE AND THE RISKS OF ENGAGEMENT

In much of Fanon's work, he analyzes the shifting between identities and representation that is a result of the gaze and or lens through which one is viewed. R.A.T. Judy in "Fanon's Body of Black Experience" identifies this as " . . . the process of consciousness becoming in-itself and for itself and for others" (Judy, 1996, p. 55). The "look" from the place of "other" is the exercise of power through the dialect of the look. The self is the self-defined by the other as a result of the structure of racism as defined by colonialism. This dialectic results in the "othering" of the black identity at the level of self-consciousness of the black. The systemic denial of self-identification of the black results in the denial of humanity. This dynamic created through colonialism is one that results in this concept as established by Fanon.

In *Black Skin, White Masks,* Fanon speaks of ontology and attributes the ontology of the black as a result of this dialectic.

> Ontology—once it is finally admitted as leaving existence by the wayside—it does not permit us to understand the being of the black man. For not only must the black man be black; he must be black in relation to the white man. . . . The black man has no ontological resistance in the eyes of the white man. (Fanon, 1967, p. 110)

Here Fanon speaks to the development of one's consciousness; in particular, black consciousness in relation to the "white gaze" (hooks, 1992; Razack, 1998). Fanon speaks to the realization that in the eyes of and the presence of the dominant, that the black man exists only within these specifically, narrowly, prescribed ways. According to Fanon, blackness or black identity as determined or developed by the individual is negated by what has been created by the "white man" through colonialism (Fanon, 1967). Although the degree to which this experience as conveyed in *Black Skin, White Masks* is part of the metaphorical, contextual style of Fanon's writing, it highlights a significant aspect of representation such that blackness, through this lens, becomes the narrative of the black body. Fanon's analysis of ontology as it pertains to blacks is often a site of criticism as his critics question the perception that blacks must and can only be seen in relation to white.

Being black opposite (as vis-a-vis) or in front of (as in the presence of the white is to be something black for the white that is not the black in-itself and for itself. Denigration draws our attention to where Fanon wants it on the process of becoming that is the consciousness of the black. But this consciousness has no ontological status in the perception of the white. Nor should it. (Judy, 1996, p. 56)

Nevertheless, the tension between my identity and the body politics of colonialism, (which has imposed a societal representation of who I am), is a regular experience for me in a field of work that is predominantly white. I believe that my colleagues who are black or racialized may have similar experiences in this regard and may also experience these internal and external struggles as we wrestle with the ways in which we can and cannot respond to the racism that is a daily reality in our work or work places. The colour of my skin and how this is read amongst the dominant often negates the identity I have created and continually questions my place in education, my actions and my intentions. I can recall instances as a school principal when certain staff members and even parents questioned me on issues pertaining to routine board initiatives. I began to realize that in some of the occurrences where I was challenged, that this had more to do with me being a black, female school administrator, than the actual issue at hand. As a result, I began to learn how to anticipate the ways in which certain staff members and parents would position things that served to question not only my decision making, but ultimately my knowledge, skills and essentially my right to be in this role.

This consistent challenging from within and outside of the organization was at times quite daunting and emotionally draining. Both Fanon and hooks speak to this emotional and psychological tension as "damage to one's psyche." "A normal Negro child, having grown up within a normal family, will become abnormal on the slightest contact with the white world" (1967, p. 143). hooks also speaks to this phenomenon in her book *Black Looks:* "A culture of domination demands of all its citizens self-negation, the more marginalized, the more intense the demand" (1992, p. 19). As identified by both Fanon and hooks, this damage, whether conscious, acknowledged or denied, has an impact on how blacks are able to respond to racism, not only in its blatant overt forms, but more importantly, to those forms that are insidious and embedded neatly and invisibly into systems that are part of the tacit norms of our institutions.

In *Black Looks,* hooks discusses the damage to the black psyche as an internalization of white supremacist thoughts and values on black bodies in relation to and in significance of resistance.

> *Without ongoing resistance struggle and progressive black liberation movements for self-determination, masses of black people (and everyone else) have no alternative worldview that affirms and celebrates blackness.... As long as black folks are taught that the only way we can gain any degree of economic self sufficiency or to be materially privileged is by first rejecting blackness, our history and culture, then there will always be a crisis in black identity. Internalized racism will continue to erode the collective struggle for self-determination. (hooks, 1992, p. 18)*

In this quote, hooks highlights the internal struggle that some blacks may experience in relation to their identity and the body politic. In the field of education there are those who feel empowered (similarl to those who engaged in the black liberation movements), to take up the cause in education through antiracism, anticolonial and equity work. Whereas there are also many black or racialized teachers and administrators who do not actively engage in the politics of resistance. My question has always been, why? How can those of us who are marginalized both in and outside of the system not actively partake in work to challenge the system? If we as black or racialized bodies in the field are not willing to hold the system accountable for the repeated inequitable outcomes for racialized and marginalized students, who will?

In the following section of this chapter, I attempt to respond to these specific questions through the work of Fanon and hooks, as both theorists examine and discuss individual and collective responses to racist encounters. In *Killing Rage,* hooks learns from Fanon to develop the conceptualization of "Black Rage." Like Fanon, hooks sees violence as one type of response to the colonial encounter. Both hooks and Fanon posit theories that address the questions that I have posed in response to the tensions around race and representation that may act upon black educators within their schools and/or school districts. In the subsequent discussion, I will connect these theories by exploring the differing responses observed by black and racialized colleagues to everyday racism that is embedded in the system and culture of education: (1) acceptance and complicity; seeing the everyday racism as a lived reality of the black, (2) resistance; the black gaze and black rage, (3) the silencing of the black gaze and rage; all of which illuminate (4) the risks and fears that black educators face when engaging in antiracism, anticolonial, equity and social justice work in schools. These various types of engagement or disengagement by these theorists and others will be discussed in the context of the role of education and black or racialized educators in the system.

ACCEPTANCE AND COMPLICITY

When one considers the insidious nature of racism in our society, those who are racialized may feel overwhelmed and/or powerless, such that they believe that the daily onslaught of racist actions upon them as coined by Fanon is the *"lived experience of the black"* (1967, p. 111). As hooks states, they have "accepted this as one of the social conditions of our life while in white supremacist patriarchy that we cannot change. This acceptance is a form of complicity" (1995, p. 10). When reflecting upon these two theorists, I believe that for some black educators the thought of responding to racism in its more covert forms is daunting, disheartening and demoralizing. Some black educators may feel that working to challenge the numerous ways that the legacy of colonialism impacts upon them through the repeated assaults of everyday racism, is the lived reality of being racialized in a society dominated by whites. Thus, some black or racialized individuals may believe that we must work within the means of this society as opposed to resisting. This may be amplified by the fact that not all people who are racialized feel they have the "tools" to articulate and/or respond effectively to the vastness of racism that is the *"lived experience of the black."* According to hooks, they have " . . . [bought] into liberal individualism and see our individual fate as black people in no way linked to the collective fate" (1995, p. 17). However, as she continues to state " . . . it is that link that sustains full awareness of the daily impact of racism on [B]lack people, particularly its hostile and brutal assaults" (1995, p. 17).

As previously discussed, much of Fanon's work speaks to the damage done to the black psyche and the internalization of racism. The colonial legacy that permeates society within our system of education in conjunction with the various forms of mass media serves to normalize whiteness. As Fanon states, "Black men want to prove to white men, at all costs, the richness of their thought, the equal value of their intellect. . . . For the Black man there is only one destiny. And that is white" (1967, p. 10). Fanon articulates the significance of the oppressed internalizing the *"tropes of the oppressor and oppression itself."* The Negro, he states, " . . . *is not a creature of biology but of oppression."* As a result, the internalization, and desire to be human as defined by the colonial power, results in some black individuals negating their "blackness" in favour of the dominant in order to "gain their humanity." They may feel they have acquired the status of normalcy, success, and achievement as defined by whiteness. As they strive to achieve their "humanity," they become complicit and are therefore, implicated in the very forms of oppression used against him/her that are designed to reproduce the existing social structures of power and privilege. As hooks argues: "By demanding that black people repress our rage to assimilate, to reap the benefits of material privilege in white supremacist capitalist patriarchal culture, white folks urge us to remain complicit with their efforts to colonize, express and exploit" (1995, p. 16).

Fanon speaks of this complicity in relation to his critique of the Negritude movement. Fanon's criticism pertained specifically to the idea that the movement itself did not challenge or seek to disrupt the social structures of power and privilege in colonial society in regards to race. Therefore, leaving dominant systems intact as opposed to challenging them in their various forms. Negritude had a way of socializing and aculturizing in particular, the black bourgeoisie intellectuals within the current structure of white universal humanism. Negritude attempted to secure space for colonized bodies through negotiations with the colonizer. I believe that this perception continues to prevail with some black educators. Like those who bought into the Negritude movement, some black educators today actively acknowledge and celebrate their blackness. They collectively work toward achievement and success; however, this is defined by the white patriarchal structures within society that go unchallenged, unquestioned and maintained. These educators do not choose to "trouble" the Eurocentric space that has defined this notion of success. These educators may also perceive that they have "made it" despite the many inequitable aspects of the system that work to subvert the achievement and success of those who are racialized. As a result, some believe that they have obtained and achieved success as a result of their "hard work" (i.e., ensuring that they had excellent qualifications and in many cases additional credentials for their role/position). They may buy into the belief that despite the fact that they had to develop the skills and knowledge to overcome obstacles and navigate through the system, that all other black and or racialized individuals should work to do the same. Consequently, this ignores the fact that they have had to exceed and go beyond the accomplishments and achievements of their white counterparts, and in doing so they buy into the *"myth of meritocracy."*

As hooks states:

> *As individual Black people increase their class power, live in comfort, with money mediating the viciousness of racist assault, we can come to see both the society and white people differently. We experience the world as infinitely less hostile to blackness than it actually is. (1995, p. 17)*

The concept of *"lift as you climb"* is not one that is necessarily understood by all those who have managed to achieve despite the barriers embedded within the system. Often the assistance that is provided to black or racialized individuals by others who are racialized comes in the form of mentoring. Although this support is necessary to navigate the system, it may not be interpreted as such. At times, those who receive this support may fail to acknowledge and appreciate those who have come before them, not recognizing that they laid the foundation for their current success. As a result, some black educators may not see the importance of responsibility beyond oneself once achievement has finally been secured. It is important to note that simply by virtue of being black or racialized does not equate to an innate sense of responsibility to challenge the system. It is often a committed few who seek opportunities to contest the normative structures that serve to prevent racialized 'others' from particular positions of power. As Fanon and hooks attest, the individual must have a certain level of consciousness that permits him/her to question the status quo and work actively to dismantle the conventional structures of privilege (Fanon, 1967; Fanon, 1963; hooks, 1995; Dei, 2008).

Thus, acceptance and complicity ultimately serve to keep those few who do take agency, contained in marginalized spaces. The fact remains that in many regards, we are all called upon to participate in the building of empire and to produce capital, which serves to reproduce the production of knowledge that affirms the supremacy of the dominant. *To some degree we are all implicated!* Nevertheless, the complicity of the dominant can in no way be compared to complicity of the oppressed. The neglect in questioning inequitable structures and functions in society, through the inactivity acceptance and complicity, simply serves to reproduce existing structures of power and privilege. As critiqued by Fanon, those of the Negritude movement failed to see themselves implicated in the reproduction of colonial interests. Thus, in today's context acceptance and complicity simply serve to maintain the liberal humanist agenda (Wane, 2006; hooks, 1995; Dei, 2006).

SILENCING OF THE BLACK GAZE AND RAGE

An effective strategy of white supremacist terror and dehumanization during slavery centred around white control of the black gaze. "Black slaves could be brutally punished for looking or appearing to observe the whites they were serving, as only a subject can observe, or see." To be fully an object then was to lack the capacity to see or recognize reality. (hooks, 1995, p. 35)

Fanon speaks to this through the dialect of visibility and invisibility. Through colonialism the dominant group worked to control the gaze of its black subjects, which served as an apparatus of control to objectify, subject and oppress the black body. Thus, the control of the "black gaze" that hooks identifies, is one aspect of this construct as *"Race hides those it is projected to mark"* (Ahmed, 2006). Control of the "black gaze" essentially permitted whites not to "see" blacks, therefore objectifying the individual and group as items or objects to be oppressed and controlled. Through colonialism, this mechanism served to justify social constructs of power and privilege of the dominant group, such that whites "saw" blacks only in certain circumstances. Therefore, issues regarding racial oppression and inequity, despite the reality of the day, were permitted to remain invisible. This "lack of vision" served to conceal the structures within colonial society and its institutions that served as a mechanism of control and oppression of the colonized. The legacy of this construct continues to be embedded in the tacit cultural norms of institutions, such that barriers to blacks and other racialized groups continue to remain invisible to the dominant and society at large, as they are part of our institutional norms and values.

When reflecting upon my days as a classroom teacher, I can recall the consistent use of various instructional strategies to explicitly identify the ways in which power and privilege along racial, gender and class structures were made visible to my students. As a result, I was called into my principal's office to discuss a complaint from a parent. At this particular point in time I had been working with my class on the identification of stereotypical images in the media. One of my students had become so fascinated by this that he began to do a critical analysis of all commercials, television shows and news broadcasts while watching television with his family. Unfortunately, his parents did not appreciate his new learning; nor did the principal who directly instructed me to *'tone it down.'* The examination of power and privilege works through the recognition and understanding that in order for one to be advantaged the other must be disadvantaged. However, the dominant fail to question this construct, and when it is revealed it is silenced as it is to remain unquestioned, unseen and unknown. The convenient "lack of vision" in regards to what is and is not visible often comes into play when barriers and inequitable structures within systems become revealed. Often the response of the dominant group is to silence those who raise these issues. Silencing those who question and reveal whiteness and white privilege continues to be an apparatus of control today, particularly for those of us who use anticolonial and antiracism frameworks as the foundation for our work in our classrooms and schools (Fanon, 1967; hooks, 1992, 1995; Goldberg, 1996).

RESISTANCE: RISKS AND FEARS

Fanon is well known for his "diagnosis of violence" as a condition of colonialism. One of the many misconceptions of Fanon's work is that he endorses and actively promotes violence. As Fanon states, "The violence of the colonial regime and the counter-violence of the colonized balance each other and respond to each other in an extraordinary reciprocal homogeneity" (1963, p. 46). Upon further examination of Fanon's views on violence, one can conclude that he posits violence as a particular response due to the tensions that arise from everyday racism as described throughout this paper. Fanon and hooks both explicitly connect rage and violence as forms of resistance to the colonizing structures within our society.

> *The origins of violence lie in a presumptive "false guilt," which the colonized has to assume because of his powerless position; but it is a guilt that he does not accept or interiorize—"He is made to feel inferior, but by no means convinced of his inferiority." The eruption of violence*

is a manifestation of this anxious act of masking, from which the colonized merges as a guerilla in camouflage waiting for the colonist to let down his guard so that he might jump. (Fanon, 1963, p. 16)

In *The Wretched of the Earth* and *Black Skin, White Masks*, Fanon sees colonialism as a violent process as it is an act of subjugation designed to break the spirit, heart and soul of the colonized. Through hook's collection of essays, she shares the anger she experiences in relation to several racist encounters that give rise to her to feeling of rage and violent thoughts. As mentioned in the previous section on silencing of the black gaze and rage, hooks takes up the ways in which blacks have been socialized to suppress this rage that is a result of the various forms of everyday racism. However for hooks and Fanon, this rage and subsequent acts of violence are forms of resistance that should be considered liberating and seen as ways of healing (hooks, 1997). In *The Wretched of the Earth*, Fanon writes:

For the colonized, this violence represents the absolute praxis.... Violence can thus be understood to be the perfect mediation. The colonized man liberates himself in and through violence. This praxis enlightens the militant because it shows him the means to an end. (1963, p. 44)

Antiracism, anticolonial, and equity work designed to ensure equitable and inclusive approaches to education must be seen as resistance work. As discussed previously there are many plausible reasons why some black and racialized educators do and do not engage in work that sees education as a transformative site for change. Although there may be some notions of acceptance and complicity and limited understanding of the need for change and to challenge the existing structures of power and privilege, the fears associated with engagement are probably the more compelling reasons for disengagement.

Education continues to be a profession that is predominantly occupied by whites (Brown and Rushowy, 2007) and is perceived as a "race privileged profession [that is] protect[ed] from the other" (Solomon and Levine-Rasky, 2003). As a result, in the Canadian context, many black or racialized educators are few in numbers in their schools, amongst their colleagues and when sitting at boardroom tables. Consequently, when one seeks to question and challenge long-standing traditions, policies and processes that can be deemed inequitable, doing this alone is "risky business" as we are often the sole voice of divergence. Through the work of Patrick Solomon, researchers found that white educators responded to the challenge of diversity and confronting racism in three different ways: (1) *ideological incongruence:* a challenge to one's belief system or lived reality that creates a sense of discomfort, dissonance and/or guilt that sidetracks the exploration and acknowledgement of racial inequity; (2) *negating white capital:* denial of white privilege and unearned capital; and (3) *liberalist notions of individualism and meritocracy:* the notion that if one works hard enough he can overcome barriers. These responses identify the types of limitations regarding the knowledge of some white educators in dealing with issues of discrimination, prejudice and racism. The taken-for-granted assumptions of these educators that are illuminated, explored and critiqued through antiracism, anticolonial and equity work, can leave black educators who are actively engaged in this work as open targets for reprisal from colleagues and/or their superiors. (Solomon et al., 2005)

In reframing Fanon for today and current conceptions of "whiteness," these taken-for-granted assumptions of white privilege are in relation to the dialectic of visibility and invisibility conceptualized in his work. As discussed earlier, not only does this dialectic serve to make the black body "invisible" through control of the "black gaze and rage" and objectification of the black body, it also simultaneously renders the black body visible to the white body, as this body now goes unmarked and unseen. Sara Ahmed calls this the *"phenomenology of whiteness."* "The power of whiteness is that we don't see those bodies as white bodies. We just see them as bodies." "But of course whiteness is only invisible to those who inhabit it" (2004, p. 3). In this circumstance, whiteness in our society continues to be the unmarked, the unseen, and the invisible. It is the visible, yet invisible marker of what it is to be human. Whiteness retains its invisibility by projecting race onto others, maintaining the invisibility of power and racial privilege. Thus, the desire of the black "individual" to gain one's humanity that Fanon sites as "the Black man desiring to be white," is the black individual wishing to be seen as a human, rather than based on the societal misrepresentations of what it means to be black. For Sherene Razack (1998), the refusal to be complicit, to illuminate issues of race and racism, and place them at the forefront of discussions regarding student achievement, education policy and practice can be seen as "looking white people in the eyes"—challenging racism at the source.

Nevertheless, there is huge discomfort for everyone in naming race, racism and illuminating white privilege, especially for whites. Consequently, promotion and/or advancement in the workplace despite popular mythology, it is not solely about merit. It is about gaining and building alliances in addition to negotiating the politics of the institutional culture that defines the profession. Therefore, individuals who challenge those in power are obviously less likely to achieve the same upward mobility as those who remain silent. As hooks states:

> *By demanding that black people repress and annihilate our rage to assimilate, to reap the benefits of material privilege in white supremacist capitalist patriarchal culture. White folks urge us to remain "complicit" with their efforts to colonize, oppress and exploit. Those of us black people who have the opportunity to further our economic status willingly surrender our rage. (hooks, 1995, p. 16)*

The fear of losing one's socioeconomic/material gains and associated privileges is but one of the many possible fears. For others, it may be in relation to the achievement of perceived "success" in an area that is traditionally held by whites. This may be perceived as self-affirming and in relation to Fanon's work: having one's "humanity" finally acknowledged. The internalized racism that affects some black people as they "buy into" the societal representations of themselves as inferior, may also serve to fuel these fears. hooks speaks to this as the colonial legacy has created a notion for blacks that the only way to gain "economic self-sufficiency or to be materially privileged is to reject our blackness, our history and culture" (hooks, 1992, p. 18). Thus, achievement within certain spaces that are typically attributed to whites could also be perceived as a loss. Loss of a particular "position" or "role" for some may be considered a loss of the "attempt to regain their humanity." Nevertheless, it is important to go back to Fanon's work which recognizes that these fears are all predicated as a result of a particular level of consciousness and the damage to the psyche that has left some blacks not able to recognize their worth outside of white cultural norms as designed by colonial structures within society amplifying the fears and risks of engagement that ultimately serve the colonial agenda.

CONCLUDING THOUGHTS

Throughout the discussion, I have explored the politics of identity for the racialized body and the colonial encounter that oppressed bodies are faced with when they enter the colonized space of educational settings. Through the use of Fanon's analysis of identity and consciousness, I have explored a number of issues that black educators may face, particularly with regard to engaging in antiracism and anticolonial work while highlighting the risks and fears of this engagement. The timelessness of Fanon's work is evident in the current relevance of his conceptual framework regarding the tension that exists between development of the black identity and societal mis/representation of "blackness." Fanon's work in relation to the identity and representation can help us to understand the ways in which black educators negotiate their role within educational institutions, as we are challenged with both external and internal contestations in regards to our places of work in education along with the emotional struggle of facing and managing everyday racism. Therefore, Fanon's deconstruction of race and racism in society, and how this is translated into the everyday racism enacted upon black and/or racialized bodies, helps us to understand and interpret the various ways in which these bodies respond.

The impact of everyday racism on the human psyche is an unfortunate consequence of our colonial past. Although I have primarily focused on the fears of engagement that may preclude some educators from engaging in antiracism and anticolonial work, I believe that it is imperative that one move beyond them. Therefore, I would like to conclude this chapter with the acknowledgment of my personal beliefs regarding the significant impact that I experienced while engaging in this work, as I believe that anticolonial and antiracism education is worth the risks!

Despite the multifaceted reasons that may preclude one from engaging in anticolonialism and antiracism work as a result of the damage done to our psyche resulting from our colonial past, I believe that the fears must outweigh the possibilities. There is a necessity, and it is our responsibility to be engaged. As previously stated, I do not suppose that it is the responsibility of the racialized educator to solve the problems associated with race and racism in education in isolation. This would be unjust and would not ensure that the dominant members of our society take responsibility for their implication and role in reproducing and protecting their own power and privilege. I do wish to join the ranks of writers on this topic who inadequately analyze white privilege and position the responsibility of agency on the black or racialized body therefore, relinquishing white bodies of any accountability and playing a role in decolonization.

Nevertheless, I do believe that marginalized voices must be at the forefront of these conversations and should lead the way. Therefore, it is incumbent upon all educators to become conscious of the politics of identity, particularly those attributed to race in education. Fanon as a philosopher and anticolonial practitioner spoke consistently to the point of agency. Fanon was a strong advocate of taking action in response to one's responsibility. In *Black Skin, White Masks,* Fanon's analysis of the colonial experience leads to the conception of a "new humanism," and therefore to a quest for change. Fanon's criticisms of Negritude are an example of his belief in disrupting the inequitable structures in our society that seek to maintain existing structures of power and privilege. Fanon as an anticolonial thinker helps us to see the residual affects of the colonizing relations in our history that continue to plague our system in addition to exploring how these relations can impact black and/or racialized educators in the field.

Regardless, the call to act is clear! All educators must seek to interrogate the existing structures within education that seek to reproduce forms of knowledge, power and privilege that reinforce notions of white supremacy. Fanon refers to this in his work as *collective catharsis,* which speaks to the decolonizing nature of resistance that occurs when we resist as a united committed group. bell hooks and other anticolonial thinkers also articulate the power of resistance as one that serves to reclaim the lost souls of the colonized (hooks, 1995; Fanon, 1967):

> ... *self-recovery is ultimately about learning to see clearly. The political process of decolonization is also a way for us to learn to see clearly. It is the way to freedom for both the colonized and the colonizer. The mutuality of a subject to subject encounter between those individuals who decolonized their minds makes it possible for black rage to be heard to be used constructively. (hooks, 1995, p. 37)*

As an educator, the "development of a critical consciousness," which informs and anchors a political ideology for social action and transformation, has been a liberating experience for me (Wane, 2006; hooks, 1995). Antiracism and anticolonial work in education provides one with the sense that "something can be done." When I think back to my experiences as a student, teacher, and administrator, and reflect upon the ways in which race had an impact on the way I was treated or the way an issue was resolved, it is empowering to know that this circumstance could have and should have been different. With wisdom comes power:

> *At the individual level, violence is a cleansing force. It rids the colonized of their inferiority complex, of their passive and despairing attitude. It emboldens them, and restores their self-confidence. Even if the armed struggle has been symbolic, and even if they have been demobilized by rapid decolonization, the people have time to realize that liberation was the achievement of each and everyone. (Fanon, 1963, p. 51)*

The complexities of racism and the legacy of colonialism in our society can make the thought of transforming education overwhelming, and at times the work in this field appears to move at an incredibly slow pace and can be extremely frustrating. Nevertheless, as indicated in this quote, we can all be liberated—the colonized and the colonizer, the oppressed and the oppressor—through the decolonizing nature of resistance work as we are all negatively impacted by the lies that racism tells. Hence my eternal optimism and personal belief that at some point in time, enough educators will truly embrace antiracism/anticolonial practices such that these principles will be fully in place to hold the system accountable for its on-going failure to effectively and equitably serve certain groups of students.

As a collective, we must seek to engage in this work to first and foremost transform ourselves in order to truly transform the education system. Decolonizing our colleagues, and ourselves will ensure that the "ideological and political undercurrents that effectively demonstrated the systemic" nature of racism and racist practices deeply embedded in education today are revealed and ultimately eliminated from the system. (Solomon and Levine-Rasky, 2003) Regardless of current terminology, antiracism, anticolonial, culturally relevant, culturally proficient, equitable, and inclusive approaches to education, must be embraced such that transformation is seen as the responsibility of all educators:

> *The Negro is not. Any more than the white man. Both must turn their backs on the inhuman voices which were those of their respective ancestors in order that authentic communication be possible. Before it can adopt a positive voice, freedom requires an effort at dis-alienation. . . . It is through the effort to recapture the self and to scrutinize the self, it is through the lasting tension of their freedom that men will be able to create the ideal conditions of existence for a human world. Superiority? Inferiority? Why not the quite simple attempt to touch the other to feel the other to explain the other to myself. (Fanon, 1967, p. 231)*

Equity, anticolonialism, and antiracism education advocates committed to this work must remember that transformative and social justice education is centred on the premise of hope, freedom, and justice, for all those who are exploited, oppressed, and disenfranchised. Therefore, those who are engaged in this work can make a significant contribution in the field of education, in the learning of students and in the lives of many:

> *I believe that antiracist education is good education for all because it seeks to foster a diversity of relationships among subjects bent on changing the current status quo. (Dei, 2008, p. 146)*

REFERENCES

Adjei, Paul B. "Unmapping the Tapestry of *Crash.*" In *Crash politics and antiracism: Interrogations of liberal race discourse,* edited by Philip Howard and George S.F. Dei, 111–130. New York: Peter Lang, 2008.

Ahmed, Sara. Declarations of Whiteness: The Non-performativity of Antiracism. "*Borderlines e-journal 3:2,*" 2004.

Brown, Louise and Kristine Rushowy. "Teach us about us; Students." *Toronto Star,* November 28, 2007.

Dei, George J. S. "Challenges for AntiRacist Educators in Ontario Today." *Anti-Racism Practices and Inclusive Schooling.* 33:3, 2–5. 2003.

Dei, George J. S., Irma Marcia James, Leeno Luke Karumanchery, Sonia James-Wilson & Jasmine Zine, *Removing the margins: The challenges and possibilities of inclusive schooling.* Toronto: Canadian Scholars Press. 2000.

Dei, George J. S., Josephine Mazzuca, Elizabeth McIsaac, and Jasmine Zine. *Reconstructing 'drop-out': A critical ethnography of the dynamics of black students' disengagement from schools.* Toronto, Buffalo, London: University of Toronto Press. 1997.

Dei, George J. S., and Ali Asgharzadeh. The power of social theory: The anticolonial discursive Framework. *"Journal of Educational Thought,"* 35(3), 297–323, 2001.

Dei, George J. S. *Theory and practice: Antiracism education:* Halifax: Fernwood Publishing 1996.

Dei, George J. S., Sonia James-Wilson, and Jasmine Zine. *Inclusive schooling: A teacher's companion to removing the margins.* Toronto: Canadian Scholar's Press, 2002.

Dei, George J. S., and Arlo Kempf. *Anticolonialism and education: The politics of resistance.* Rotterdam: Sense Publishers, 2006.

Delpit, Lisa. *The skin that we speak: Thoughts on language and culture in the classroom.* New York: New Press, 2002.

Dines, Gail. "What's left of multiculturalism? Race, class, gender in the classroom." *Race, Sex and class,* 1(2), 23–34, 1994.

Fanon, Frantz. *Black skin, white masks.* C. L. Markmann (Trans.) New York: Grove Press. 1967 (Original work published in 1952, Paris: Editions du Suil).

Fanon, Frantz. *Wretched of the earth.* R. Philcox (Trans.) New York: Grove Press, 1963 (Original work published in 1961, Paris: F. Maspero).

Gibson, Nigel C. *Rethinking Fanon: The continuing dialogue.* New York: Humanity Books, 1999.

Goldberg, David Theo. *The racial state.* Malden, Mass., Oxford: Blackwell Publishers, 2002.

Goldberg, David Theo. "In/Visibility and super/Vision: Fanon on race, veils, and discourses of resistance." In L. R. Gordon, T. D. Sharpley-Whiting and R. T. White (eds.), *Fanon: A critical reader.* Oxford: Blackwell Critical Readers Series. pp.179–202. 1996.

hooks, b. *Killing rage: Ending racism.* New York: Henry Holt and Co., 1995.

hooks, b. *Black looks: Race and representation.* Boston, Mass.: South End Press, 1992.

Judy, R. A. T. "Fanon's body of black experience." In L. R. Gordon, T. D. Sharpley-Whiting and R. T. White (eds.), *Fanon: A critical reader.* Oxford: Blackwell Critical Readers Series. pp. 53–73, 1996.

Lester-Irabinna, R. "Internationalisation of an indigenous anticolonial cultural critique of research methodologies: A guide to indigenist research methodology and its principles." *Journal for Native American Studies,* 4(2), 109–125, 1997.

McIntosh, Peggy. "White privilege: Unpacking the (invisible) knapsack." *Independent School Winter,* 31–36, 1990.

Montague, A. *Man's most dangerous myth: The fallacy of race.* New York: Oxford University Press, 1974.

Moore, B. Resisting racism through religion education. *Religious Educational Journal of Australia,* 10(2). 1994.

Ontario Ministry of Education and Training. *Early School Leavers: Understanding the Lived Reality of Student Disengagement from Secondary School.* Special Education Branch. Toronto Canada, 2005.

Onwuanibe, R. *A critique of revolutionary humanism: Frantz Fanon.* St. Louis, Mo.: Warren H. Green, Inc. 1983.

Razack, S. *Looking white people in the eye: Gender, race, and culture in courtrooms and classrooms.* Toronto: University of Toronto Press. 1998.

Reed, A. *The fact of blackness: Fanon and visual representation.* Seattle: Bay Press. 1996.

Sleeter, C. *Teaching culturally different students: Political assumptions of the educational researcher.* Paper presented at the annual meeting of the American Educational Research Association, San Francisco, April 18–22, 1995.

Solomon, Patrick R., and Cynthia Levine-Rasky. *Teaching for equity and diversity: Research to Practice.* Toronto: Canadian Scholar's Press. 2003.

Solomon, Patrick R., "Race Modelling and representation in teacher education and teaching." *Canadian Journal of Education,* 22(4), 395–410, 1997.

Solomon, Patrick R., John P. Portelli, J. P., Beverley Jean Daniel, and Arlene Campbell. "The discourse of denial: How white teacher candidates construct race, racism and 'white privilege.'" *Race, Ethnicity and Education 82*:147–169, 2005.

Stanfield, John. "The ethnocentric basis of social science knowledge production." *Review of Research in Education, 12,* 387–415, 1985.

Stepan, Nancy. *The idea of race in science: Great Britain, 1800–1960.* Hamden, Conn.: Archon Books, 1982.

Thomas, B. The politics of being white. "In Carl E. James and Adrienne Shadd" (eds.), *Encounters.* Toronto: Between the Lines, 1994.

Trifonas, Peter. "Monstrous Lesson: The Educational Legacy of Imperialism." *Discourse Studies in the Cultural Politics of Education,* Vol. 22, No. 1, 105–114, 2001.

Wane, Njoki N. "Is Decolonization possible?" In George J.S. Dei, and Arlo Kempf. *Anti-Colonialism and Education: The Politics of Resistance* (pp. 87–108) Rotterdam: Sense Publishers, 2006.

CHAPTER THREE

Rereading the Ontario Review of the Roots of Youth Violence Report
The Relevance of Fanon for a Critical Disability Studies Perspective

KATIE AUBRECHT

Colonialism, read as domination and imposition, did not end with the return of sovereignty to colonized peoples or nation states. Colonialism is not dead. Indeed colonialism and reorganizing projects today manifest themselves in variegated ways ... (Dei, 2006, p. 2)

We have seen this violence throughout the colonial period, although constantly on edge, runs empty. We have seen it channeled through the emotional release of dance or possession. We have seen it exhaust itself in fratricidal struggles. The challenge now is to seize this violence as it realigns itself. Whereas it once reveled in myths and contrived ways to commit collective suicide, a fresh set of circumstances will now enable it to change directions. (Fanon, 1963/2004, p. 21)

Using a critical disability studies perspective informed by the work of anticolonial thinker and pedagogue Frantz Fanon, this chapter examines how the Executive Summary of the Canadian province of Ontario's *Review of the Roots of Youth Violence Report* provides a blueprint for the reorganization of colonialism in contemporary North American society. It considers the historical implications of representing youth violence as a symptom of the alienation of "disadvantaged neighborhoods and individuals," and a sign of the need for an increased presence of mental health programs and administrators in marginalized communities. Following Fanon's instruction, this chapter aims to uncover how the racist and ableist assumptions implicit in the civilizing language of the report reference an imperial culture. Rather than accept the report's assertion that violence is a sign of the need for more "integrated governance structures," it turns to Fanon's conception of violence as a unifying force for colonized peoples. Reading these two conceptions of violence against one another makes it possible to interrogate the historical context that gives meaning to the report and its recommendations for a more "coordinated" and "collaborative" approach to economic, social, and political governance by present-day colonial authorities and administrations.

Given that cultural assumptions about disability are mobilized to marginalize and oppress colonized peoples, we are now faced with the challenge of representing the interests of the disability community in a way that recognizes that disability is also a social and political identity forged out of struggle against colonial regimes. This chapter thus also aims to show how the teaching and writing of Fanon can bring the disability studies community to new awareness of the historical conditions of its own emergence, assisting disability scholars and activists in creating a new world for thinking with and through disability.

THE REPORT

The *Review of the Roots of Youth Violence Report* (2008), which I will refer to throughout this paper simply as the "report," was initiated in June 2007 at the request of Ontario Premier Dalton McGuinty. The report emerged in response to a surge in gun violence in Toronto in 2005 that reached its peak in the shooting death of high school student Jordon Manners outside C.W. Jefferys Collegiate Institute in Toronto. Over a one-year period research was conducted in consultation with the communities most impacted by the violence, located in what the report refers to as "areas of concentrated disadvantage," to ascertain the "root" causes of youth violence. When asked what they thought were the "roots of violence," an overwhelming number of respondents replied that they felt that alienation from oppressive social conditions was a major issue in their communities. The authors of the report, in conversation with existing government bodies, read and represent the respondents' knowledge of a relationship between alienation and violence as proof of the need for a more coordinated and better-funded universal mental health system to help people living in disadvantaged communities cope with their disadvantage.

The "problem" of youth violence and its "solutions," as represented in the Executive Summary of the report, reveal a plan to garner public support for colonial reorganization and realign the interests of the most disadvantaged in Ontario with those of the Ontario government. This plan includes a proposal to increase the presence of social workers, psychiatrists, and counselors in "areas of concentrated disadvantage," which the report alludes to as primarily racialized communities. It also includes a recommendation for the collection of race-based statistics and diversity training for police as a way to address allegations of racism. Despite the fact that the premier of Ontario requested this report, the report's authors share their concern that the timing of the report might constrain the realization of its recommendations. They share their recognition that the report and its recommendations in the areas of "Children's Mental Health," "Anti-Racism" with a focus on the collection of race-based statistics and sensitivity training for police, and "Steps Towards Community Hubs" [1] emerge during a global recession, "at a point in time when the Province faces economic challenges" (McMurtry & Curling, 2008, p. 39).

The *Ontario Review of the Roots of Youth Violence Report* is authored by former Chief Justice and Attorney General Roy McMurtry and former Speaker of the Legislature Alvin Curling, both of whom were appointed by Liberal leader and Ontario Premier Dalton McGuinty. The authors' depiction of the causes of youth violence redirect attention away from the existence of a collective consciousness of alienation in "disadvantaged neighborhoods and individuals" by "disadvantaged neighborhoods and individuals," to the threat that these people and places pose to the province of Ontario because of their failure to acknowledge the prevalence of undiagnosed and treated mental illnesses. To rectify this, the report recommends that the Ontario government create a $200 million budget to increase the availability of psychiatric services for young children in disadvantaged schools and communities (McMurtry & Curling, 2008, p. 40). The report thus represents consciousness of the lived experience of oppression as an obstacle to overcoming the alienation of "disadvantaged neighborhoods and individuals." Its authors distance themselves and the Ontario government from the "problem" of youth violence through the espousal of a notion of violence that is abstracted from the complex reality of the violence of everyday life in a racist and ableist colonial society. Any specific reference to disability and race is omitted as part of a larger project of the cultural imposition of the colonial values of individualism.

Frantz Fanon's writings on the alienation of the colonized, [2] and more particularly the black man, provide an alternative way of encountering and responding to the current situation of youth violence in North America's most disadvantaged communities. Although Fanon shares a common interest in the disalienation of racialized and marginalized youths living in disadvantaged communities, his experiences as a black man and a psychiatrist living, working, writing, and thinking during the Algerian revolution for independence from France taught him that the existence of alienation is directly related to the presence of colonialism. Unlike the authors of the report, who understand alienation as a root cause of individual instances of violence that can be predicted and prevented, Fanon (1963/2004) understands alienation as the product of the violence of colonialism. For Fanon, violence is not something to be unquestionably avoided or contained. The performance of violence provides a unifying force for colonized people and is thus a necessary part of decolonization.

As Hussein Abdilahi Bulhan (1985) writes in *Frantz Fanon and the Psychology of Oppression*, Fanon saw the process of disalienation as central to decolonization. In colonization, "The colonized had been reduced to individuals without an anchor in history, alienated from themselves and others" (Abdilahi Bulhan, 1985, p. 139). In *Black Skin, White Masks*, Fanon asserts that the process of disalienation is conditioned by "an immediate recognition of the social and economic realities" (1952/2008, p. 11). He remarks that recognition of the social and cultural dimensions of alienation is obstructed within neoliberal societies where the colonialist bourgeoisie imposes on the colonized mind, "the notion of a society of individuals where each is locked in his subjectivity." According to Fanon, the colonial value of individualism and the notion of society it sustains can only successfully be destroyed in the struggle for liberation. As Fanon writes, "Involvement in the organization of the struggle will already introduce [the colonized] to a different vocabulary" (1963/2004, p. 11). With words like "brother," "sister," and "comrade," this "different vocabulary" embodies a communal spirit and a collective interest (Fanon, 1963/2004, p. 11). This language, developed in the struggle for independence from a colonial frame of reference, looses the chains of a singular subjectivity. Its appearance signals the emergence of a new situation, a realm of intersubjectivity, provoking a collective recognition of the escalating interpersonal violence in the most marginalized communities. This "different vocabulary" brings to awareness that in this life-or-death battle over meaning-making between the silent advantaged and the immense majority of Ontarians living in "areas of concentrated disadvantage," there is no time to compete for colonial status.

The way the report represents alienation as representative of the roots of violence exemplifies what disability studies scholar Rod Michalko refers to as the "nature-culture divide" (1999, p. 177). It naturalizes disadvantage and individualizes alienation, suggesting that even though alienation is a natural phenomenon for disadvantaged youth, this does not necessarily mean that all disadvantaged youth will become involved in violence. In the report, violence is inevitable for youths who fail to learn that their only hope for freedom lies in their ability to transcend what Fanon has referred to as the "corporeal schema" and accept in its place the "racial epidermal schema" as imposed by the representatives of colonial authority (Fanon, 1967, p. 112). This is distressing for the implications it has for oppressed peoples. According to Fanon, "The colonized ... have been prepared for violence from time immemorial" (1963/2004, p. 3). However, in representing disadvantaged youth as at a greater risk of involvement in violence because of their "experiences of oppression," and proposing that the only hope of *the province* escaping the irrationality of this violence is to implement a two-pronged approach, which (1) *coordinates* greater collaboration between community leaders, government agencies, and funders and (2) *fleshes out* a universal mental health system that targets disadvantaged children, the report justifies the continued domination of these peoples and suppression of their resistance.

The report suggests there are a number of different "roots," or ways of rationalizing, youth violence and these roots are often "intertwined" (McMurtry & Curling, 2008, p. 6). These include poverty, racism, community design, issues in the education system, family issues, health, lack of a youth voice, lack of economic opportunity for youth, and "issues" in the justice system. The Executive Summary acknowledges that there are multiple reasons given for becoming involved in violence. But, in keeping with its stated interest in coordination and collaboration, it orders these reasons and subordinates them to one dominant explanation for youth violence: the prevalence of alienation in specific communities, which it designates as "areas of concentrated disadvantage" (McMurtry & Curling, 2008, p. 3). Violence is then transformed from a lived reality to an isolatable problem that can be resolved given greater collaboration between the government and community leaders, the coordination of existing educational bodies and assimilationist policies, and the creation of a universal mental health system that targets children (McMurtry & Curling, 2008, p. 40).

The relevance of Fanon to disability studies can be found in the convergence of the categories of madness and race to stabilize unequal power relations in the province and reify the power of dominant groups.[3] The relationship between alienation conceived as mental illness and the performance of violence is captured in the stereotypical assumption that people with mental illness are inherently violent, and people who are violent are mentally ill. Fanon offers a way to rethink the relationship between this stereotypical representation of mental illness and the report's assertion that the root cause of violence can be located in the body of the alienated individual. For Fanon, the performance of violence is not a sign of a disordered individual. It is rather an embodied response to the violence of the racist ideologies of colonial governance.

WHEN SKIN MEETS MASK: RECOGNIZING WHITE PRIVILEGE

Before going any further, I feel it is important that I situate myself in this work. I write this from a position of power and privilege. The resources, time, and spaces I have access to as a graduate student in Equity Studies at the University of Toronto make my experiences of youth violence very different from the lived experiences of youth violence objectified in the report. Thus, one of the major difficulties I anticipated before embarking on my own analysis of the pedagogical and political implications of the report concerned how I would write my response in a way that could give life to a Fanonian reading of the situation, while at the same time resisting the temptation to wear Fanon's words like a mask, in the process denying my own position as a middle-class, white-identifiable woman who self-identifies as disabled. Because our experiences are shaped by our embodiments, for me to speak from the position of a universal "we" is to discount the significance of the always multiple and conflicting experiences of "the kinds of social and political relations that are established within bodies, minds, and senses" (Titchkosky & Aubrecht, 2009). It is to erase from view the complexities of the lived experience of race and disability, as well as their interrelations and departures. In this paper I am speaking from the perspective of someone whose body has been made to surface in the violence of psychiatric diagnoses and treatments. My particular understanding of disability is mediated by my embodied experience of a struggle to live with and in a racist and ableist society that privileges detached rationalism over emotion.

Identifiably white, I have benefited from white-skin privilege. Just as Fanon remarks in *Black Skin, White Masks* that the "Jewishness of the Jew, however, can go unnoticed," I move through the world with the ease that comes with knowing that for the most part I too "can pass undetected" (Fanon, 1952/2008, p. 95). The advantages this ability to pass has afforded me have also come with many costs, including an estranged relationship to myself, past, present, and future, and a constant anxiety that I am going to be "found out." My Czechoslovakian heritage on my father's side meant I would never be welcomed or at home in a white identity. This heritage, which found no voice in my primary education aside from the reference to the "influx of immigrants" that came to farm the lands or work in the coal mines in Cape Breton, as well as the name and the body it gave me, often made me an outsider in the rural, predominantly Scottish community in Nova Scotia in which I was raised. Even though my mother's father was Scottish, as a child I quickly learned that the parts of me which I was told I inherited from my father—dark hair, olive skin, and what I have been repeatedly reminded is a "strange" last name—opened me and my sisters to interrogation. I also learned that there was a multitude of cultural products and practices available that would help me mitigate the effects of my inheritance.

The community I was born and grew up in was Scottish insofar as the majority of people who lived there were descendents of people who had emigrated from Scotland. The name of the town—Antigonish—and the land on which our town was situated and on which the settlers grazed cattle, farmed, hunted, cut trees, built houses, streets, and shopping centres, were stolen from the Mi'kmaq people native to Nova Scotia. On the arrival of the settlers, the Mi'kmaq were violently displaced to reservations on the outskirts of settler communities, dispossessed of their land, their language and their culture (Reid, 1994). Even their children were stolen from them, removed from their families and sent to residential schools to be disciplined by forced labor and "civilized" by religious values that emphasized submission and obedience (MacDonald and MacDonald, 2007, pp. 34–45). Even though I may not have always felt at home in the community, I enjoyed the advantages living there afforded. In distancing myself from whiteness without taking critical account of the material advantages a white identity has afforded me, I reduced the complexity of my own ambivalent relations to my position. My thinking that my ethnicity distanced me from whiteness constituted a refusal to acknowledge my own implication in the reorganization of colonialism.

As I moved through my undergraduate and graduate studies, in paper after paper I struggled to make sense of the relationship between social justice and social difference. Paper after paper, I constructed around myself a space of supposed neutrality that I had a tendency of representing as a critical liminality, rarely pausing to consider what position I must be in such that I could even construct such a space. Over time this space hardened, crystallized, and became a mask that used my body as a mold. Safely concealed behind this mask, which restricted my reflections of the "we" to a more inclusive notion of "me," I voiced interpretations and made recommendations without having to take the time to think about how my own words and deeds were already embedded in the reorganization of colonialism. In this chapter, I turn to Fanon the teacher[4] to help me interrogate the cultural values that have structured my interpretations of the relationship between disadvantage, alienation, and oppression through a critical disability studies analysis of the Executive Summary of the Ontario *Roots of Youth Violence Report*.

THE DIFFERENCE THAT DISABILITY HISTORY CAN MAKE TO A FANONIAN ANALYSIS OF OPPRESSION

In "The Birth of Rehabilitation," Henry-Jacques Stiker (1999) traces the birth of a new awareness about disability, represented as rehabilitation, to World War I. After the war, many men and women were injured for life. They were not only amputees but also mutilated—the difference being that "Mutilation applied to all alteration of integrity, of integralness" (Stiker, 1999, p. 123). In response to the recognition of the damage and destruction that the war had caused there emerged the development of a notion of prosthesis, "the idea that you can *replace*" (Stiker, 1999, pp. 123–124) and the possibility that the integrity of the person and society that the war had destroyed could be replaced. Stiker asserts that at this critical juncture after the war, "A new will is born: to reintegrate" (1999, p. 124). For Stiker, the trouble with the appearance of disability as a "social fact" (1999, p. 121) made possible by the concept of rehabilitation is that "rehabilitation did not initially address the social and economic causes and conditions that gave rise to disability, no more than it questioned itself on the final outcomes of this [liberal] society" (1999, p. 174).

In the Executive Summary of the Ontario *Review of the Roots of Youth Violence Report* the government is represented as a kind of prosthesis for disadvantaged peoples. The reader, presumably not disadvantaged, is told that the only hope for disadvantaged people to live normal, productive lives in Ontario is for them to recognize themselves as ill and take the appropriate corrective measures. The language of mental health and illness is used to rationalize a natural relation between poverty, race, and disability. This language constructs individuals and communities who fail to transcend disadvantageous situations as a threat to the "social fabric of Ontario" (McMurtry & Curling, 2009). Here, one notices the presence of Western imperial culture in the demand that individuals remove themselves—their subjectivities—from the difficult situations in which they find themselves. Accepting the logic of this cultural imperative entails convincing ourselves and others that we can escape difficult situations, given the desire is present and the individual engages in the work required to make this desire a reality. This kind of thinking treats the appearance of difficulty as a sign of disadvantage and a symptom of moral and biological inferiority, thus legitimizing responses to those perceived of as disadvantaged, which would be considered unacceptable for less conspicuous bodies.

The report says that the truth about youth violence is that it is rooted in alienation, but what are we to make of this assertion given Fanon's contention in *Wretched of the Earth* that "In the colonial context there is no truthful behavior" (1963/2004, p. 14)? What are we to make of the report's call to recognize and accept the need for the creation of an "integrated governance structure" that will strengthen social bonds, thus restoring youths to their "normal" selves, reconnect them with their families and communities, and reintroduce them to their true potential? On first reading, the self-evident good of the report's appeal for integration as a necessary response to the violent appearance of alienation in today's youths is difficult to challenge. It is this sense of the supposed indisputability of the claim that tells us that it must be challenged. The text relies on readers already knowing what alienation is, even in the absence of a definition of alienation. This reliance on a psychologized Western understanding of alienation as a symptom of mental illness absences any consideration of whether what alienation means for one person, in one body and in one place in time, is irrevocably different from someone, somewhere else.

Given the fact that the report is written by members of the colonial government, the commonsense it evokes is that of the colonists, the dominant; the advantaged. The words of the people interviewed are recognized and represented from a colonist perspective for a colonial audience. The spirit they assume is European. Just as Fanon writes that "One must be accustomed to what is called the spirit of Martinique in order to grasp the meaning of what is said" (1967, p. 18), to understand what the authors of the report mean by "alienation," one must become accustomed to the spirit of Europe. A task made no less easy by the fact that the "European spirit has strange roots" (Fanon, 1963/2004, p. 313). As an imperial power, Europe has developed a habit of collecting peoples, cultures, and lands and discarding, resurrecting, and redistributing them at will. Its spirit is restless. If we are to understand what is at stake in the report, we need to develop a way of revealing the specters that haunt it.

How is it that the report and its recommendations can claim to be in the interest of all Ontarians? The ease with which this claim is made is related to the way the report represents the "problem" of youth violence as a symptom of a lack of integration. What kind of person would deliberately choose alienation? Who would ever say "no" to belonging and reject an invitation to being and feeling restored to being whole again? There need be no discussion on where or when or how this notion of being whole originated. Access to a shared understanding of the "integrated" or "normal" way of life that characterizes the ideal Ontarian is as there for the reader and as "naturally given" as the environment is for nondisabled peoples (Michalko, 2002, p. 128). Following this way of thinking, there is no sense unpacking the specific meaning of the word "alienation" in the context of the report or the colonial situation that produced it. It is not the appearance of alienation which is in question. What is in question in the report is how to get the disadvantaged to connect the appearance of alienation in themselves and their communities with objective knowledge about the possibility of their return to "normal" life. According to the report, the answer to this question can be found in the places where the people meet, like the local school. Gaining entry into these places and the conversations that happen there requires careful planning. Collaboration with the community leaders of these groups is the ideal, but in the absence of collaboration the government can always create new places, what the report refers to as "community hubs," already mapped and designed so as to allow for an easy transition into even greater colonial imposition and surveillance.

As good as integration may initially sound, we would do well to ask ourselves how it is that it resonates the way it does.

RESISTING THE COLONIAL WILL TO INTEGRATE

> *You do not disorganize a society, however primitive it may be, with such an agenda if you are not determined from the very start to smash every obstacle encountered. The colonized, who have made up their mind to make such an agenda into a driving force, have been prepared for violence from time immemorial. As soon as they are born it is obvious to them that their cramped world, riddled with taboos, can only be challenged by out-and-out violence. (Fanon, 1963/2004, p. 3)*

There is a real and pressing need to be attentive to the cultural will to integrate and rehabilitate the colonized subject redeployed in the report, to interrogate the "epistemological order" it reproduces and the historical situation it effaces (Stiker, 1999, p. 179). For, as Stiker warns, it belongs to a "certain kind of militant thought" and a way of thinking, "which directs the manner of addressing the question in the cultural zone of consideration" (1999, p. 179). This way of thinking, representative of what Fanon refers to as a "colonial mentality" founded on racist ideology (Fanon, 1963/2004, p. 108), erases histories of oppression and replaces them with oppressive histories thought better forgotten or left behind. It directs the gaze of colonized subjects away from the social structures and economic developments that have constructed them as disadvantaged, to the possibilities for advancement afforded by a place within.

Schooled in the values of this epistemological order, disadvantaged youths are taught that not only are their lives and their cultures less valuable than those of "normal" Ontarians, unmarked by difference, they are barely worth notice or mention—that is, except as proof of the progress of Western Eurocentric thinking, humanism, culture, and development. Racialized and disabled persons are taught that they should only be so grateful to be where they are today and that their even being there is proof of the justice and benevolence of colonial rule. Even if that place is located in a marginal space, on the peripheries of a core that systematically devalues their embodied knowledges and erases their histories, it is still far superior to where else they could be, and to where they once were. As Ellen Barton (2001, p. 169) writes:

> *Insofar as disability is thought of socially, culturally, or historically, it is usually represented in terms of improvement: After all, people with disabilities are no longer warehoused in large institutions, children with disabilities are being mainstreamed into schools, the Americans with Disabilities Act was passed in 1990, and Americans in general are thought to be growing ever more sensitive to the justice and importance of including citizens with disabilities in the multicultural melting pot.*

The "multicultural melting pot" Barton (2001, p. 169) describes is also represented in the report as the unspoken ideal. In this pot, all that matters and the only thing that counts is that you adhere to the cultural norms of the dominant group. Even making it into the pot is considered a privilege, for the only ones who make it are those whose predetermined attributes qualify them for the dominant's recipe for success. Because failure to conform could ruin the whole batch, anyone who looks, acts, thinks, or speaks differently is judged as having already gone bad. Differences are settled like land claims, with peace treaties drawn up by the dominant in the interest of the dominant. People born within the pot are taught to repress their differences or risk being expelled. It is thus that in so-called decolonized countries like Canada (decolonized in the sense that Fanon's Martinique was decolonized), "The colonist keeps the colonized in a state of rage, which he prevents from boiling over" (Fanon, 1963/2004, p. 17).

The textual representation of violence as a problem of individual alienation severs the connection between race and racism. The report treats violence as a sign of mental illness best resolved through the creation and circulation of more improved prognostic, preventative, and coping strategies specifically designed for managing the malaise of the "significantly disadvantaged." But Fanon says that there are other ways to read the appearance of alienation that recognize that the language of mental health and illness is the reigning civilizing language of contemporary colonialism. Rather than follow the authors of the report in locating alienation as the root cause of youth violence in Ontario, let us think with Fanon (1967) about what the appearance of alienation can tell us about racism and culture in contemporary Western "democracies" such as Canada and the United States:

> *The oppressor, through the inclusive and frightening character of his authority, manages to impose on the native new ways of seeing, and in particular a pejorative judgment with respect to his original forms of existing.*
>
> *This event, which is commonly designated as alienation, is naturally very important. It is found in the official texts under the name of assimilation.*
>
> *Now this alienation is never wholly successful. Whether or not it is because the oppressor quantitatively or qualitatively limits the evolution, unforeseen, disparate phenomena manifest themselves. (Fanon, 1967, p. 38)*

Where Fanon represents alienation as an "event" and the result of the imposition of a European demand to assimilate into colonial regimes, the report asks us to think of alienation as proof of the need for more quantitatively and qualitatively improved ways of managing ours and others' distance from white able-bodied colonial ideals. The language in the Executive Summary of the report decontextualizes and disembodies neighborhoods and individuals to the point where the only thing that seems to matter about alienation is that it can be used to identify potential threats to the health and well-being of the province of Ontario. It also gives the impression that race and disability only *really* appear as a result of racism or ableism, in the form of negative characterizations of inescapable attributes.

Represented as such, any mention of race or disability, let alone a relation between the two, is a risky business. Such an association could act as a stimulant for violence. The public acknowledgement of corporeal difference is thus represented as a potential "trigger" for youth involvement in violence (McMurtry & Curling, 2008, p. 6). The Executive Summary teaches its readers that any acknowledgement of the relationship between race and disability is better left to the experts, the doctors, lawyers, and psychiatrists, lest one inadvertently damage what are already understood as vulnerable self-understandings and notions of self-worth. In as much as racism and ableism make it difficult to stay in school or secure satisfying employment, embodied experiences of race and disability are represented in the report as always already potentially dangerous. The assumption is that since such experiences have the effect of recalling and invoking preexisting feelings of anguish or alienation they must therefore be effaced.

The text thus represents people who have been relegated to the periphery, in remote areas of concentrated disadvantage, as distanced from their true "subjective" selves. The emotions they have, or the apparent lack thereof, are attributed to their nature, and this nature is represented as a domain over which they have no authority or control. There is also the sense that they have frayed from the group and need to be restored to their proper place in the centre through a more integrated form of governance. No mention is made of the government's role in their marginalization, nor that of the City of Toronto, or England, the community design planners or the "funders" of the report and its recommendations who are never given a name (McMurtry & Curling, 2008, p. 6). All of these bodies are described in the text as benefactors, paving the way for a more optimistic future and a new safer Ontario. Even though the authors of the report assert that it has a "negative tone," they assert their belief that their "plan for the future is positive" (McMurtry & Curling, 2008, p. 1). But, who has to leave, be silenced, or left behind for this plan to work?

FRAMING THE PROBLEM AND FINDING SOLUTIONS: THE UNITED WAY MODEL

> *Before outlining our findings, we want to acknowledge the wise counsel and excellent advice we received from the two bodies our terms of reference identified as key partners: the City of Toronto and the United Way. (McMurtry & Curling, 2008, p. 2)*

In "Textual Practices of Erasure: Representations of Disability and the Founding of the United Way," Ellen Barton (2001) examines the appearance of disability in discourses of charity and how charitable organizations like the United Way have contributed to the social construction and textualization of disability. United Way is an organization that Barton tells us "began in 1949, in Detroit, Michigan, as an umbrella organization that collected funds from workplace campaigns and distributed them to member charities such as the United Cerebral Palsy association and the Epilepsy Foundation" (2001, pp. 170–171). In the United Way model there is a centralization of power and resources in one body that then redistributes funds to other affiliated bodies according to a predetermined order.

Just as the authors of the report share their optimism for a brighter future for Ontario, Barton writes that at the time of the emergence of the United Way model in the 1950s there was a general sense of optimism because of the perceived success of the American government and the victory of World War II (2001, pp. 170–171). She notes that in United Way campaigns, "The reader is constructed as being directly responsible for this happy ending and is urged to continue this pattern of gazing with pity and giving charity as an appropriate response" (Barton, 2001, p. 177). We need to consider the significance of the fact that the report is shaped by the United Way model. For, according to this model, the reader does not have to do anything or make any fundamental changes to his or her life to effect positive social change aside from welcoming and encouraging the "integrated" governance mentality the report espouses. This mentality encourages coordination and collaboration with like minds around the social dangers presumed to accompany a critical mass of people who are socially, economically and politically disadvantaged. It also leaves little time or space for questioning the economic and social conditions that produce the unhappy beginnings the government of Ontario wants to forget.

In the report, alienation, a sense of hopelessness, and the impulsivity of Ontario's most disadvantaged youth are represented as barriers to their maturation into productive and agentive adults. The recommendations it makes focus more on collecting, extending, and redistributing existing resources and services than developing and understanding the complex experience of social disadvantage brought on by racist, ableist, classist, sexist, or homophobic thinking. Unlike the United Way approach to disability, the report does not claim to cure Ontario's disadvantaged youths of their alienation and restore them to normalcy. On the contrary, the reader is to learn that the diversity of the province demands a different kind of strategy, one that "looks" to the future for ways to prevent mass social unrest.

A common "vision" (McMurtry & Curling, 2008, pp. 24–25) is required of those who enjoy the advantages of a safer Ontario. This vision foresees the demise of all that is enjoyed in a collective consciousness of oppression in Ontario's most disadvantaged. In sharing its greatest hope, the government's report also reveals its secret fear: unless the province acts immediately to thwart the growing masses of the alienated and oppressed on the outskirts of its major metropolitan centers, the advantages it enjoys are in serious jeopardy. How does it propose to do just that? Target the children, and do so under the pretense that government and corporate research shows that 80% of children in disadvantaged areas are not receiving the treatment they need (McMurtry & Curling, 2008, p. 13). Once the problem is diagnosed as alienation and treated as mental disorder, it becomes possible to justify the incursion of colonial officials in the schools, the community, the neighborhood, and the home. The strategy deployed: listen to what people say ails them, appropriate their language and use it to advance a colonial agenda. *Claim an interest in the hearts and souls and minds of the people, with the aim of systematically destroying the spirit of the resistance.*

THE COMPARTMENTALIZATION OF COMMUNITIES AND THE LIMITS OF A COLLABORATIVE APPROACH

> *"The first tactic of the colonial countries consists of basing themselves on official collaborators and feudal elements. These Algerians, who have been particularly singled out by a series of compromises, are regrouped and requested publically to condemn "the seditious movement that disturbs the peace of the community." (Fanon, 1967, p. 57)*

In the Introduction to the Executive Summary, the authors assert that they "joined a conversation rather than starting one." That is, they joined conversations already happening within and across communities, governments, and government-funded community agencies. As Fanon teaches us, dialogue on its own is not enough: " . . . once we have taken note of the situation, once we have understood it, we consider the job done. How can we possibly not hear that voice again tumbling down the steps of History: 'It's no longer a question of knowing the world, but of transforming it'?" (Fanon, 1952/2008, p. 1). Now that the colonial government has acknowledged the transformative potential of violence as a force of mobilization for the great masses of people living in Ontario in "significant disadvantage," how will we in the academy who identify as equity studies scholars, students and activists, respond? Will we accept its concessions and encourage others to follow suit? Given our privileged positions in the production of knowledge, it is imperative that we take responsibility for our role in the appearance of government documents like the Ontario *Review of the Roots of Youth Violence Report*. We need to question who is participating in this conversation, who has been objectified, who has been excluded, and how.

The agency represented in the text is not Ontario's youths or communities but a coordinated integrated governance structure through which youth groups and community groups can be brought into contact and conversation with existing action committees, government agencies, service providers, and funders. This contact is further mediated by the presence of gatekeepers and key holders such as building facilities managers, responsible for overseeing and relegating access to the resources in "community hubs" (McMurtry & Curling, 2008, pp. 25–26, 32, 34, 41) like schools, and the police, who patrol the neighborhoods bordering the "hubs." Only through an "integrated and collaborative approach" (McMurtry & Curling, 2008, p. 36) that welcomes the development of "neighborhood partnerships in the most disadvantaged areas," monitored and organized by government appointed staff, can Ontario build "strong communities" and "nurture healthy, well-educated and engaged youth" (McMurtry & Curling, 2008, p. 2). What are the consequences of this "collaborative approach" for the liberation movement?

We must consider the implications of the move to transform schools into "community hubs," and how this move could result in breaking up existing communities in concrete ways. This proposal, which recommends that school buildings can be leased out for community events and activities further compartmentalizes the school and the communities in which they are situated, preserving the use of school spaces for the highest bidder and enforcing the supervision of such spaces by "building facilities managers" (McMurtry & Curling, 2008, p. 43). The building facilities manager will be responsible for the maintenance and surveillance of spaces. Nothing can be moved out of order, everything will be behind lock and key and the facilities manager is the keyholder. This plan complements current trends in educational restructuring, which call for school amalgamation and privatization. In the construction of massive schools funded by corporate sponsors it is much more difficult for teachers to connect with the students and disconnect from colonial objectives. What is the purpose of the plan? Is it to create something new? Fanon reminds us, "There is no new entity born of colonialism" (1967, p. 102).

To further understand the meaning of creation in the colonial context, I turn to Jean-Paul Sartre, who Adele Jinadu describes as sharing Fanon's "conception of violence as a bond around which a group coalesces." (1986, p. 94). According to Sartre (1943, pp. 19–20):

> *One can conceive of a creation on condition that the created being recover itself, tear itself away from the creator in order to close in on itself immediately and assume its being; it is in this sense that a book exists as distinct from its author. But if the act of creation is to be continued indefinitely, if the created being is to be supported even in its inmost parts, if it does not have its own independence, if it is in itself only nothingness—then the creature is in no way distin-*

guished from its creator; it is absorbed in him; we are dealing with a false transcendence, and the creator can not have even an illusion of getting out of his subjectivity.

What is so dehumanizing about the proposed systematization of "integrated governance" is the way it modifies social relations through ideas which are steeped in the culture and traditions of the colonized; values such as the "professionalism" of the police (McMurtry & Curling, 2008, p. 15), so highly praised in the report. Even as the report speaks of the inhumanity of alienation, it locates this inhumanity in the bodies, minds, and spirits of oppressed peoples. The ideal of an integrated colonial order and a safer more cohesive province transcends the material needs of the most disadvantaged. For, as it says, there will always be disadvantaged and in this time of economic turmoil the very future of the province is at stake. Considering the fact that this report and the changes it proposes have emerged in response to a perception of violence, what of Fanon's assertion that the colonized can only regain humanity through violence? Does the report not herald the loss of humanity for even more people in even more remote places in the province?

Taking the appropriate bureaucratic channels to resist and redress the oppressive nature of many of these existing policies and policy recommendations will only modify or reform the current strategies and practices. It will not fundamentally change the system, its targets, or its objectives. There is not less colonial governance, but something else, a reorganized colonialism. The early childhood development programs for children from birth to age six and the implementation of extracurricular activities, which focus on sports and the arts from the time period 3 pm to 6 pm, organize the entire day and life of the student, which as the report states, "research confirms, that this period is a 'prime time for crime'" (McMurtry & Curling, 2008, pp. 20, 37). This is not to dispute the potential benefit these programs will have for some students but to bring to view the fact that such programs are most advantageous for those students who most closely resemble the government's projected image of the "normal" child and "average" student.

The report does not reflect a public acknowledgment by the Ontario government of the violence conditioned and produced by scientifically determined and medically sanctioned standards of normalcy. Any admission of violence performed in the cultural deraciantion of racialized communities in Ontario is dismissed as the unfortunate consequence of ineffective policies of the past. To make way for a more optimistic future, the report recommends the acceptance and adoption of more integrative ways of policing social relations to the normative standards that govern public understandings of youth violence and reorganize social space.

That countries such as Canada may have gained "formal" independence from imperial control does not necessarily mean that they have achieved total decolonization. Even though Fanon is speaking specifically about the situation in Algeria in the 1950s and 1960s, his writing on the creation of a national consciousness provides a counternarrative to the one offered by the government of Ontario. I am not suggesting that Fanon's specific understanding of the situation in Algeria should or even can be uprooted and transplanted across borders in other locales across the world. Nor am I asserting that decolonization could ever take the same form twice. What I am saying is that in reading *The Wretched of the Earth* one notices certain affinities between "the trials and tribulations" facing those committed to decolonization and the creation of a national consciousness in Algeria and the difficulties we face today as equity studies students, scholars, artists, and activists in the North American context. Even as we strive to reclaim space for our specific embodied differences, we ignore our shared histories and common experiences at our own peril.

If, as George Dei (2006, p. 2) suggests, colonialism "did not end with the return of sovereignty to colonized peoples or nation states," what are our possibilities for resistance here and now? How can we make concrete changes in the ways we view ourselves and conduct our lives that will make us people who question and people who read in others a perpetual questioning (Fanon, 1952/2008, p. 13)? To begin, we could reflect on the government of Ontario's interest in the school as a "community hub." The school, and more specifically the actual building of the school, is represented as a key site for instituting, implementing and enforcing the report's recommendations. This is also true of the university and college, in which proposed neighborhood assessment programs are to be formulated and assessed, providing a "resource" for government agencies and funders. Other key sites include the family and the community. In representing the school, the family and the community as strategic locations for implementing social change, the report signals the government's recognition of the disruptive power of these spaces and the activities that shape them. Rather than fight this power, the government of Ontario seeks to appropriate it, siphon off from it, and put it to use for its own objectives.

TACTICAL DIVERSIONS: THE REPORT CHANGES THE REFERENCE BUT KEEPS THE STRUCTURE INTACT

> *This hostile, oppressive and aggressive world, bulldozing the colonized masses, represents not only the hell they would like to escape as quickly as possible but a paradise within arm's reach guarded by ferocious watchdogs. (Fanon, 1963/2004, p. 16)*

Putting the solution to youth violence advanced by the report into practice entails teaching youths to negate the value of their lived experiences. It asks them to judge themselves, their families, homes, and communities against the colonial standards from an either-or perspective: they are either supportive of young people's development into good colonial subjects, thus providing a means of escape from violence, or they are "hostile" to the needs of young people and the "real" source of their disadvantage. Recall Fanon's words in *The Wretched of the Earth*, "The colonist's world is a hostile world, a world which excludes yet at the same time incites envy" (1963/2004, p. 16). How this approach produces a sense of responsibility in today's youths is highly questionable. Not only does it redirect the target of young people's feelings of anger, shame, or resentment from the structural violence of colonialism (Fanon, 1952/2008) to the youths themselves, their parents, families, communities, and schools, punishing them for their disadvantage and reproducing alienation.

It also redirects the actual bodies of youths out of the home, the community, the school. They are taught that the only "disadvantaged" who get to have a future in this scenario are those who accept that they have a problem and that the source of this problem is located in their neighborhoods and themselves. Implicit throughout the report is the suggestion that the best and most effective way for individuals to distance themselves from the immediacy of the risk of becoming involved in youth violence is to physically leave. This silent option, always present but never explicitly articulated, represents the most politically expedient response to the report's call for a more "overall and strategic" punishment that will facilitate community-police relations. As the report states:

> *Again, we do not take issue with where and how the police deploy their forces, but with the ways in which some of the officers use their powers. We do so in the context of deep appreciation for the hard and often-dangerous work police officers perform on our behalf, and respect for the professional way in which most of them carry out their responsibilities. (McMurtry & Curling, 2008, p. 15)*

The answer is not better, more improved but less "aggressive" colonial governance that will treat racialized youth with a greater degree of "civility" (McMurtry & Curling, 2008, p. 15). Nor is it instituting mental health intervention in the lives of preschool and younger school-aged children, to ensure they "get the help they need" before the "mental health condition" worsens and they become even more alienated, impulsive, with even lower self-esteem than they start with. The drive to mobilize people around a more integrated governance structure that mandates antiracism training for police, while at the same time applauding the police for their "high standards" and "professionalism," is reformatory, not revolutionary. It upholds the same epistemological order, safeguarding the advantages gained from colonial oppression of minoritized peoples. Rather than challenge modern capitalism, such a structure provides for the expansion of its domain, perpetuating capitalist interests in ever more remote spaces:

Instead we felt we first needed to understand the mindset of the youth who are at the core of the public's concern: the ones who walk our streets and enter our schools with guns and other weapons and seem to place no value on human life. Our analysis accordingly reasoned from the state of mind that puts no value on human life and leads to vicious assaults or killings, and to shootings in public places that also senselessly endanger far more people than the intended victim. We believe that it is only if we find and address the conditions that give rise to that state of mind that we will be able to stop the growing number of youth who think that way. (McMurtry & Curling, 2008, p. 5)

In this passage, oppression is represented as a "belief" instead of a lived reality, constructing a collective understanding of youth violence as something that exists outside of the historical circumstances of colonial oppression. Unlike Fanon, who proposes a critical pedagogy rooted in the recognition of the plight of the most disadvantaged, the report represents this group as the biggest threat to the well-being of the province of Ontario. Whenever the text makes explicit reference to the experience of oppression (McMurtry & Curling, 2008, p. 6), it is with respect to the need to teach disadvantaged youths to think of oppression as an experience that needs to be transcended so that Ontario can have a "safer future" (McMurtry & Curling, 2008, p. 1). Teaching people to treat oppression as a "state of mind" separates people from their embodied knowledges. The report leaves no room for interpreting the phenomenon of youth violence as a product of inequitable social structures and oppressive power relations. Experiences of oppression are stripped of their historical specificity, decontextualized and treated as a sign of the need for more interventionist and assimilationist policies, programs, and practices.

In *The Education of Black People: Ten Critiques 1906–1960*, W. E. B. Du Bois writes of the need to "carefully understand the age in which we live" (1973, p. 9). According to Fanon, "Revolution is mankind's way of life today. This is the age of revolution; the 'age of indifference' is gone forever" (1965, p. 1). It is vitally important that in today's age of colonial reorganization, marginalized peoples recognize that their self-understandings are shaped by a colonial agenda that erases historical specificity and suppresses corporeal difference. A pedagogy oriented to the liberation of the minds of marginalized peoples from the colonial mentality must therefore begin by troubling the suggestion that the answer to youth violence lies in greater access to psychiatric knowledge. Psychiatric knowledge is a tool the colonist employs as a way of re-turning the counterviolence of the colonized. Such knowledge is drawn on as a resource to deterritorialize, subjugate, and oppress. As an instrument of colonial domination and expansion, the discipline of psychiatry has been used to claim total control over the production of knowledge about of the psyche, suppressing the "psychic life of power" (Butler, 1997) of oppressed peoples.

CONCLUSION: THE COLONIAL ROOTS OF A RELATION BETWEEN DIFFERENCE AND DISADVANTAGE

> ... *decolonization is always a violent event.(Fanon, 1963/2004, p. 1)*

The seeming *naturalness* of the association between corporeal difference and disadvantage is cemented in the report's campaign to restructure policing, educational, and community infrastructures and establish a universal mental health system that targets disadvantaged children. The report reorganizes social relations to any conspicuous difference as a sign of imminent violence and a threat to provincial health and safety. In this plan to restructure the peripheries' relations to the core, the boundaries of places that once provided safe havens from the everyday violence of colonial domination, such as the home and the community centre, are becoming ever more eroded by governmental annexation and amalgamation. The community is further compartmentalized; the school is reduced to a designated community centre to be managed by a government appointed facilities manager who leases out the space to community groups and corporate interests; and pharmaceutical companies decide children's futures.

The reader is informed that in the new integrated governance system "disadvantaged" families will not have to worry about their children becoming involved in violence because the government is going to invest more to ensure that their children will not have a chance to feel and become alienated. They will be immersed in Western culture's values even before they are born: "supports to families should begin with prenatal care and should include outreach to early-years programs and the new all-day learning initiative for four and five year-olds" (McMurtry & Curling, 2008, p. 37). The unmarked reader, the good subject, the white able-bodied average Ontarian, learns through the report that if for whatever reason alienation still rears its ugly head, there is always the $200 million mental health system to make racialized and disabled youth learn to accept and cope with the reality of their misfortune of living life on the wrong side of the city. Barring that, the $850 million youth justice system will provide an absolute fail-safe, ensuring that the alienation of the disadvantaged and oppressed will not get in the way of a more prosperous future for the province of Ontario.

Only cursory attention will be paid to the fact that this alienation is a direct consequence of the impoverished and oppressive conditions of everyday life for racialized and disabled persons in a neoliberal society founded on the white able-bodied ideals of productivity and competition. Even though the report claims to find out where youth violence is "coming from—its roots" (McMurtry & Curling, 2008, p. 1), its commitment to "make Ontario safer in the long term" involves practices and procedures that may work to exasperate the ongoing pathologization, psychologization, and criminalization of today's racialized youths.

Despite the report's stated interest in "outcomes," there is little empirical evidence to support the report's claim that there even is an increase in youth crime. So the report calls for the construction of new measures, race-based statistics to legitimize its response to what it represents as an increase in youth violence, applauding the police and reinforcing the epistemic order. The report tells the reader there is no space, no time, to think about the violence perpetuated and sustained by the dominant. In fact, there is no dominant, only disadvantage. Following the report's blueprint for a "safer Ontario," there is no average or ideal when it comes to humanity, only "minimum acceptable levels of attainment" (McMurtry & Curling, 2008, p. 30). So goes the call. It echoes in the halls of parliament buildings, on national news reports, across the World Wide Web: the signs are everywhere; action must be taken before the "Great Fear" becomes a reality. What is the "Great Fear"? As Du Bois (1973, p. 8) writes:

> *Now the Great Fear has been variously named and designated—it has been called in the past, Mob-Rule, Sans-Cullotism, the Yellow Peril, the Negro Problem, and Social Equality. Whatever it is called, the foundation of the Great Fear is this: when a human being becomes suddenly conscious of the tremendous powers lying latent within him, when from the puzzled contemplation of a half-known self, he rises to the powerful assertion of a self, conscious of its might, then there is loosed upon the world possibilities of good or evil that make men pause. And when this happens in the case of a class or nation or race, the world fears or rejoices according to the way in which it has been trained to contemplate a change in the conditions of the class or race in question.*

How are we as teachers, researchers, and activists going to hear and respond to this call? Before we can answer this, we need to ask ourselves what we have already done and failed to do to resist the colonial imperative to think of corporeality as "useless-difference" (Michalko, 2002, p. 102)—difference that, as Michalko says, "does not and should not matter to the world", difference that matters only to the individual, and does so "in two important ways: it engenders 'suffering' in the other and has a psychological effect" (2002, p. 102). In the struggle to develop what Paulo Freire (1968) has described as the "pedagogy of the oppressed," we need new tactics; the originality and effectiveness of which can be measured only once these tactics have been situated in a history of struggle. As teachers, researchers, and activists, we cannot lay an unqualified claim to the embodied knowledges that characterize the diverse understandings of the world as voiced by our students, families, neighbors, and colleagues. Recognizing that colonialism conditions our experiences of ourselves is only the beginning. We need to continue to question the grounds of our commonalities and the meaning of our differences.

I conclude this chapter by returning to the words of the pedagogue whose ideas reshaped the way I thought about my own relation to the embodied knowledge that a disability studies perspective brought to my awareness—Frantz Fanon. The promise of social mobility and security through integration represented in the report is steeped in an implicit demand to associate corporeal difference with disadvantage.

Examining the Report from a disability studies perspective informed by the teachings of Fanon provides a way to re-read this relationship as a product of the colonial situation (Titchkosky & Aubrecht, 2009). As Fanon (1965, p. 1) writes:

> *Today the great systems have died or are living in a state of crisis. And it is no longer the age of little vanguards. The whole of humanity has erupted violently, tumultuously onto the stage of history, taking its own destiny into its hands. Capitalism is under siege, surrounded by a global tide of revolution. And this revolution, still without a centre, without a precise form, has its own laws, its own life and a depth of unity—accorded to it by the same masses who create it, who live it, who inspire each other from across boundaries, give each other spirit and encouragement, and learn from collective experiences.*

ACKNOWLEDGMENTS

I would like to thank George Dei of the Department of Sociology and Equity Studies in Education (SESE) at the Ontario Institute for Studies in Education (OISE) for the opportunity to think with Fanon the teacher and for much critical discussion and helpful comments. I am indebted to Rod Michalko at New College, University of Toronto, for reading the paper and providing valuable feedback, and Tanya Titchkosky, also of SESE at OISE, for her conversations and encouragement. Thanks most of all to my fellow students in the "Frantz Fanon and Education: Pedagogical Possibilities" class for creating new spaces for thinking about the social and political significance of our collective experiences of race and disability.

NOTES

1. For more on the "hub," please see Jijian Voronka, "Re/Moving Forward?: Spacing Mad Degeneracy at the Queen Street Site," *Resources for Feminist Research* 33, 1&2 (2008): 57. Voronka notes the emergence of the "hub" in plans to redesign and redevelop the Toronto Queen Street site, formerly the site of the first Provincial Lunatic Asylum in Ontario. The similarity between the redesign of psychiatric institutions and marginalized communities is troubling and in need of further research.

2. Frantz Fanon, A Dying Colonialism, trans. Haakon Chevalier (New York: Grove Press, 1965); Toward and African Revolution: Political Essays, trans. Haakon Chevalier (New York: Grove Press, 1967); Wretched; Black Skin, White Masks, trans. Richard Philcox, 1952 (New York: Grove Press, 2008).
3. For more on the relationship between racism and designations of mental illness, see Shaista Patel, "Encountering the Terrorism of 'Madness, Nation's Normal Race to Culture of Categories," Unpublished Manuscript (2009).
4. The role of Fanon the teacher has been discussed extensively in George Dei's course "Frantz Fanon: Advanced Topics in Social Research" in Sociology and Equity Studies in Education at the Ontario Institute for Studies in Education, University of Toronto, and Rod Michalko's course, "Equity and the Body" in the Equity Studies Program, New College, University of Toronto. Both courses were taught in 2008–2009.

REFERENCES

Abdilahi Bulhan, Hussein. (1985). *Frantz Fanon and the psychology of oppression.* New York: Springer.

Barton, Ellen. (2001). Textual practices of erasure: Representations of disability and the founding of the United Way. In James C. Wilson & Cynthia Lewiecki-Wilson (Eds.), *Embodied rhetorics: Disability in language and culture* (pp. 169–199). Carbondale: Southern Illinois University Press.

Butler, Judith. (1997). *The psychic life of power: Theories in subjection.* Stanford, CA: Stanford University Press.

Dei, George J. Sefa. (2006). Introduction: Mapping the terrain—towards a new politics of resistance. In George J. Sefa Dei & Arlo Kempf (Eds.), *Anti-colonialism and education: The politics of resistance* (pp. 1–23). Boston: Sense Publishers.

Du Bois, W.E.B. (1973). *The education of black people: Ten critiques 1906–1960.* Herbert Aptheker (Ed.). New York: Monthly Review Press.

Fanon, Frantz. (1965). *A dying colonialism.* Haakon Chevalier (Trans.). New York: Grove Press.

——— (1967). *Toward an African revolution: Political essays.* Haakon Chevalier (Trans.). New York: Grove Press.

——— (2004). *The wretched of the earth.* Richard Philcox (Trans.). New York: Grove Press. (Original work published 1963).

——— *Black skin, white masks.* (2008). Richard Philcox (Trans.). New York: Grove Press. (Original work published 1952).

Jinadu, Adele. (1986). *Fanon: In search of the African revolution.* London & New York: Taylor & Francis.

Freire, Paulo. (1968). *Pedagogy of the oppressed.* Myra Bergman Ramos (Trans.). New York: The Seabury Press.

MacDonald, Nancy, & Judy MacDonald. (2007). Reflections of a Mi'kmaq social worker on a quarter of a century work in First Nations child welfare. *First Peoples Child and Family Review* 3(1), 34–45.

McMurtry, Roy, & Alvin Curling. (2008). Executive summary. In *The Review of the Roots of Youth Violence Report*. Queen's Printer for Ontario. <http://www.rootsofyouthviolence.on.ca/english/reports/volume2.pdf> (30 November 2008).

Michalko, Rod. (1999). *The two in one: Walking with Smokie, walking with blindness.* Philadelphia: Temple University Press.

———— *The difference that disability makes.* (2002). Philadelphia: Temple University Press.

Patel, Shaista. (2009). Encountering the terrorism of "madness": Nation's normal race to culture of categories. Unpublished manuscript.

Reid, Jennifer. (1994). No man's land: British and *Mi'kmaq* in 18th and 19th century Acadia. *University of Ottawa (Canada), Dissertation Abstracts International,* 58–04A: 1–1352.

Sartre, Jean-Paul. (1943). *Being and nothingness: A phenomenological essay on ontology.* Hazel Barnes (Trans.). New York: Washington Square Press.

Stiker, Henry-Jacques. (1999). The birth of rehabilitation. In *A history of disability* (pp. 121–189). Ann Arbor: The University of Michigan Press.

Titchkosky Tanya, & Katie Aubrecht. (2009). The power of anguish: Re-mapping mental diversity with an anti-colonial compass. In Arlo Kempf (Ed.), *Breaching the colonial contract: Anti-colonialism in the US and Canada.* New York: Springer Press.

Voronka, Jijian. (2008). Re/Moving forward? Spacing mad degeneracy at the Queen Street site. *Resources for Feminist Research* 33 (1&2): 45–61.

CHAPTER FOUR

Resistance to Amputation
Discomforting Truth about Colonial Education in Ghana

PAUL ADJEI

The overarching theme of this chapter is to critically examine ways in which the writings of Frantz Fanon can inform, shape, and encourage resistance to colonial and racist relations in the education system in Ghana. I ask these six key questions to guide the investigation: How do Fanon's ideas resist colonial domination in knowledge production, validation, and dissemination? In what ways does Fanon's articulation of decolonization inform resistance to amputation? In what ways does Fanon's experience reveal the relevance of subjective voice, agency, and resistance power of the colonized subjects in antioppression work? In what ways do colonized bodies play a complicit role in their own colonization? Is there a role for spirituality in Fanon's thought about resisting amputation? What are the risks, perils, costs, and consequences of pursuing subversive politics and practices in the education system in Ghana?

I do not know the person who first came up with the statement: "truth hurts," but surely, there is something discomforting about truth; especially, if it challenges our deeply embedded emotional dimensions that frame and shape our daily habits, routines, and unconscious complicity with hegemony (see Boler and Zembylas, 2003). Truth sometimes tempers with things we hold dear, privilege, normalize, and even institutionalize. For instance, I was personally disturbed and disappointed when I realized that Christianity—a religion I hold dear and have devoted myself to since childhood—was complicit in the enslavement, genocide, and colonization of my people. It was a personal torture for me to deal with this truth. It took me months of denial before I accepted the truth. But I am also aware of 'Truth' as a site of contestation, as Foucault mentions, a discursive mechanism of power (Foucault, 1977), and the political implication and privilege of accepting Christianity as a truth.

Today, there is another disturbing truth I have to confront in this chapter. I am referring to the colonizing tendencies of the current education system in Ghana to amputate indigenous learners from the rich cultural knowledges and experiences they can bring into learning. In this chapter, I take education to imply the broadly conceived, varied options, strategies, and ways through which we all come to learn, know, and understand our world, make meaning, and act within this world (Adjei and Dei, 2008a). I argue that the colonial education system in Ghana through its terrible control of knowledge production, validation, and dissemination has managed to persuade and force local learners to reject their indigenous upbringing and sense of self. So, when Thesee (2006) argued that the colonial education system is a subtle and sophisticated garden in which the seeds of colonization and neocolonization are sown in the minds of girls and boys, she was invariably speaking about the conditions of schooling and education in Ghana. No wonder the local learners who are exposed to the education system in Ghana continue to find themselves consciously and unconsciously removed from their local culture and worldview into a new and different world that does not exist around them. Thus, the absence of inclusive school curricula in Ghana is responsible for reproducing an intelligentsia with little or no relevant skills and knowledge to address local needs (Adjei, 2007). Therefore, I strongly argue that for education to be meaningful to local learners in Ghana, the designed curricula must have local learners' history, cultures, values, and worldviews at the centre of learning.

AN ACADEMIC PLEA

Boler and Zembylas (2003) observe that pedagogy of discomfort does require not only the members of the dominant culture but also members of the marginalized culture to re-examine the hegemonic values inevitably internalized through violent education system. This observation is important because in colonial relations no one can claim to be immune from colonial influence. Colonial education is so insidious that even those who claim to have been decolonized occasionally gaze on things with colonized lenses. Therefore, it is highly improbable for educators oriented in Eurocentric values, culture, and knowledge systems to insist that those values, cultures, and knowledge systems do not affect the way they come to know, understand, process, interpret, and analyze reality. Smith (1999, p. 136) argues that to speak or write is thus always essentially dialogic because "texts never just get it right or wrong insofar as they are also a 'doing'—right or wrong, texts are always oriented social action, producing meaning" (Titchkosky, 2008, p. 21). Tanya Titchkosky further contends that the power dynamics invested in spoken, written, and imagined words can make visible that which appears invisible in certain spaces. For instance, the languages used to describe disability have become metaphors to express that which is inept, unwanted, detested, and disdained. This means that critical educators need to be mindful of our choice of words, because words can produce meanings beyond what they were intended for. Patricia Williams laments over the constant, unintended meanings others assign to her words in this way:

> *It seems I am running out of words these days. I feel as if I am on a linguistic treadmill that has gradually but unmistakably increased its speed, so that no word I use to positively describe myself or my scholarly projects lasts for more than five seconds. I can no longer justify my presence in academia, for example, with words that exist in the English language. The moment I find some symbol of my presence in the rarefied halls of elite institutions, it gets stolen, co-opted, filled with negative meaning. (Williams, 1995, p. 27)*

Therefore, I am issuing an academic plea for using the term "amputation" in this chapter. I am aware that the word "amputation" carries different meaning for different people. Therefore, for my readers for whom the word "amputation" may carry a personal and painful memory, I sincerely apologize. The concept "resistance to amputation" (Dei, 2008; Fanon, 1967) as used in this chapter implies a desire to subvert colonial domination and racist thinking in the current education system in Ghana. It is an effort to subvert the dominant strategies, policies, and politics in the education system that continues to contextualize standards and excellence to the needs and conditions of the West while stubbornly delegitimizing indigenous ways of knowing and living.

THE JOURNEY TOWARDS REMEMBRANCE: FANON AND MY MEMORY

Commenting on Homi Bhabha's position that the education system needs to remember Frantz Fanon, Sekyi-Otu (1996, p. 11) asks: what will the remembrance look like if it is solicited by a somewhat different situation in the world, a somewhat different geopolitical affiliation? In other words, the act of remembering Frantz Fanon is informed by different historical and geopolitical situations. Personally, I remember Frantz Fanon from a location of pain, anger, bruise, and a spirit injury. The pain and the spirit injury were inflicted on me by the colonial education system in Ghana. As argued elsewhere (Adjei, 2007), although I was born and raised in an era where Ghana was supposed to be an independent country, yet I went through an education system that trained me to be more a European/American/Canadian than a Ghanaian. For instance, I grew up with the understanding that my ancestors still guard over me, and as custodians of the land they expect me to follow certain traditions, customs, and moral values that serve the general interest of the community. So, long before the environmentalists in the West started their campaign against global warming, I knew through oral teachings not to farm at river banks or in virgin forests because those are sacred habitats of deities and my ancestors. Yet, as soon as I went to a colonial classroom, I was told that this knowledge—the knowledge of my mother, grandmother, and the entire ancestry—is primitive, myth, and superstition; for that matter, they have no place in a Cartesian classroom. Like Jacob' ladder pointing to Heaven (Genesis 28) where those highest up the rungs are best placed to tell everyone else what paradise is or could be, Cartesian science and behaviourist knowledge systems have become the tacit norm by which all other knowledge is judged and assigned legitimacy in schools in Ghana.

Not surprisingly, the history lessons I received in the colonial school barely mentioned the achievements and contributions of my Ghanaian ancestors to world civilization (see Adjei, 2007). Where references were made to them, they were done in demeaning and derogatory ways that made me ashamed to relate to them. Thus, the school system succeeded in initiating me into the world of Julius Caesar, Plato, Shakespeare, Aristotle, Socrates, Chaucer, and other Western civilizations; meanwhile, my own world of myths, fables, superstitions, proverbs, storytelling, and riddles were dismissed as unreal, primitive, and illegitimate. Today, my anger and frustration is not placed in the Western knowledge system I was exposed to during schooling days in Ghana, but the indigenous Ghanaian upbringing that my teachers failed to include in the curricular. For instance, I still do not understand why my geography teacher taught me all about Niagara Falls of Canada, yet he did not see the need to teach me about Boti Falls located in my community.

Understandingly, this education system has paved the way for me. I am, today, pursuing doctoral education in Canada and even teaching a course at the university. Yet, these opportunities have come at a great cost, the cost of losing my local upbringing and everything I have held dear. Today, I have become a stranger to my own birthplace because the colonial education system has succeeded in alienating me from my local knowledge, culture, values, and worldviews. I feel lost, I feel pain, and I feel injured. I am also asking—just like Avatara (Avey) Johnson, the protagonist of Paule Marshall's novel *Praisesong for the Widow*—asked herself when she realized that their material success as a black couple (Avey and Jay) in the United States has come at the expense of their black identity, culture, and values:

Would it have been possible to have done both? That is, to have wrestled, as they have done over all those years, the means needed to rescue them from Halsey Street and to see the children through, while preserving, safeguarding, treasuring those things that had come down to them in a particular way. The most vivid, the most valuable part of themselves! (Marshall, 1983)

Today, I ask a similar question knowing that the answer is not within grasp. Yet, like Avey Johnson, I can also recover myself, relearn my past culture, values, worldview, and identity if I can find a way of resisting the colonial amputation in schools in Ghana. I can re-affirm and celebrate my ancestry. bell hooks assured me that the journey home—to that place of mind and heart, where we recover ourselves in love—is constantly within reach if only I can dare to awake from the sleep-walk, I will see the path clearly ahead of me (1992, p. 20). Today, I have dared to follow the clear path leading home. Home is the place that rejects the dominant ideology that a black person can only succeed in a white supremacist world if she or he rejects blackness (see hooks, 1992). Home is the place that resists the amputation, pathologization, inferiorization, and criminalization of blackness. Yes, home is the place where blackness is loved and celebrated. Home is the place where there is on-going effort to reclaim that which is distorted, falsified, forgotten, ruptured, stole, and lost. I have also resolved, like Fanon (1967, p. 115), that "since others hesitate to recognize me, there remained only one solution: to make myself known." And the only way I can make myself known is by going to that place called home. This is how I remember Frantz Fanon.

WHAT IS FRANTZ FANON DOING IN A NICE PLACE CALLED EDUCATION?

Frantz Fanon, who died at the young age of 39 (June 20, 1925–December 6, 1964), produced an impressive body of works: *Black Skin, White Masks; A Dying Colonialism;* and *Toward the African Revolution.* But, perhaps, *The Wretched of the Earth* is considered his most famous work partly because of the fierce preface penned by Jean-Paul Sartre and also the fact that this particular book was written when Fanon was dying of leukemia in the United States. Unfortunately, Fanon did not live to see the outcome of his revolutionary manifesto. He died not long after the book came out. The very fact that all the copies of *The Wretched of the Earth* were seized from all bookshops in France immediately after Fanon died is an indication that there is more to this book than probably Fanon himself anticipated. In fact, many revolutionary groups attributed their source of motivation to *The Wretched of the Earth:* First, Huey Newton and Bobby Seale, the founders of the Black Panther

Party, for self-defence as an alternative to the nonviolent civil rights movement in the United States in the 1960s, are believed to have been influenced by *The Wretched of the Earth* (Adell, 1996, pp. 50–51(also see Major, 1971, pp. 138–139). Second, sometime in 1973, in the notorious H-Block cell of Belfast prison, a young apprentice coach builder and a member of the Irish Republican Army, Bobby Sands, first read the book *The Wretched of the Earth*. Later when Richard English was recounting the history of the Irish Republican Army (IRA), he concluded that the passion that set the IRA on fire was found in passages in the first chapter of *The Wretched of the Earth* (English, 2003, pp. 197–199). Third, the Shiite revival of the 1960s and 1970s, which developed into the Iranian revolution led by the Ayatollah Khomeini, was based on a revision of Shiite doctrine influenced by Marxism and ideologies in *The Wretched of the Earth* (Bhabha, 2004). Thus, if many violent revolutionary leaders have once claimed and are still claiming the works of Frantz Fanon as their model for resistance, then, what is the work of Fanon doing in a nice place called "education?"

Understandingly, this is a legitimate question. However, Frantz Fanon did not prescribe violence; he simply diagnosed violence (Austin, 2006). Thus, to describe Fanon as an apostle or glorifier of violence is to ignore the relevant message he has for humanity. Writing about Frantz Fanon's influence in the world, Emmanuel Hansen notes:

> *It is clear ... that simplistic interpretation of Fanon as 'apostle of violence,' 'glorifier of violence,' 'apologist for violence,' 'prisoner of hate' should be rejected. Fanon was a great humanist. It was in the name of man that he rose up against oppression; it was in the name of man that he fought against degradation and it was in the name of man that he affirmed the dignity of man. If Fanon was a prisoner, he was a prisoner of a cause, the cause of the people, and the cause of freedom. (1974, pp. 45–46)*

In my own judgement, Frantz Fanon's ideas are relevant for looking at the contemporary education system. Fanon devoted his time, life, and energy to the fight against injustice, inequity, unfairness, and oppression. Fanon displayed by his life examples that apathy and rhetoric without political commitment and actions has no place in decent society. These virtues of Frantz Fanon are worth emulating in the current education system; especially, in the era where people still have lingering doubts about social justification of antioppression work in education. What is the purpose and usefulness of education if it cannot motivate learners to show interest and commitment to issues of social justice, fairness, and equity? In this era of global economic restructuring and transnational corporations, at least we need learners who have the conscience to speak against human poverty, environmental abuse, and denial of human rights. Frantz Fanon's commitment to justice, fairness, equity, and respect for humanity are exemplary qualities that can guide today's education system. Homi K. Bhabha (1986, p. xxii) noted a long time ago that the time for the education system to return to the work of Frantz Fanon is now: "Remembering him is never an act of introspection or retrospection, but rather a putting together of the dismembered past to make sense of the trauma of the present." Fanon's commitment to end injustice is needed in the era of schooling, where apathy is rampant. I am convinced that Frantz Fanon's ideas can help learners depart from the current hegemonic conditioning of "me" that constantly interferes with one's ability to speak up against injustices and oppression that affect others. Thus, if, today, we are rethinking Frantz Fanon in the nice place called "education" it is because he has earned his place in history and in education, and the least we can do in this historical moment is to simply celebrate his works and let his ideas guide us.

RESISTANCE TO "AMPUTATION": RESISTANCE TO COLONIAL RELATIONS IN EDUCATION

In his famous book *The Souls of Black Folk,* W. E. B Du Bois (1903, p. 1) poses an important question: "How does it feel to be a problem?" Naturally, everybody has one or more problems (from financial needs to emotional stress); thus, there is nothing unusual about Du Bois's question. However, Du Bois's question is not about having "a problem"; it is about being "the problem." Du Bois (1903, p. 1) contends that being a black person in Euro-American/Canadian society is "the problem" and being "the problem" is a strange experience. Du Bois's assertion is based on the reality that blackness is viewed in Euro-American/Canadian society as an existential threat to the security and safety of whiteness (see Fanon, 1967; Butler, 1993). Not surprisingly, persons of color are constantly judged in Euro-American/Canadian society not based on the content of their character but by the color of their skin. Blackness has become an epidermal schema that attracts hatred, despising, detestation, and punishment, not by a group of lunatics or self-insufficient individuals but by a system of domination that assigns privilege and power to whiteness.

It is within this context that the veteran of the Pacific War told Frantz Fanon's brother to accept his blackness just as he has accepted that his two legs are forever lost to the Pacific War: "Resign yourself to your color the way I got used to my stump; we're both victims" (Fanon, 1967, p. 140). In a sense, the crippled veteran of the Pacific War is encouraging Fanon's brother to accept his burden as a black person in a white supremacist world just as he has accepted his burden as a disabled person in a world that treats disability as a burden.

In (Adjei, 2008), I recounted my conversation with a white administrative staff in my own institution of learning, the University of Toronto, when I went to his department to look for a summer job. The white administrative staffer asked me what I was doing at the University of Toronto. I told him that I was studying for my Ph.D. degree in education. He looked at me for some time and then said to me: "You can lie to me, I don't care" (see Adjei, 2008). Even when another administrative staffer who knows me from my department told him that I was telling the truth, he still disbelieved me. Why did this white male assume that I cannot be what I claim to be? Surely, he does not know me and has not engaged in any intellectual discussion with me to determine my intellectual capability, yet he is willing to draw the conclusion that I cannot be a Ph.D. candidate. I argue that the white male, although meeting me for the first time, knew me through the imagination of whiteness. This imagination of whiteness was created through a colonial education system that scripted black bodies as the quintessence of evil, less educated, lazy, dishonest, and inferior (see Memmi, 1965; Fanon, 1963). Therefore, in the imagination of this white administrative staffer, not only must I be black as scripted in the colonial education system, but also be black in relation to whiteness (see Fanon, 1967, p. 161). Thus, if he, a white male, does not possess a Ph.D. degree, then he finds it hard to believe that a black male like me should be pursuing one. In the perspective of this white administrative staffer, blacks are not supposed to possess any "ontological resistance" (Fanon, 1967, p. 110) but, rather, should appear exactly as they have been woven out of a thousand detailed, anecdotal stories: lazy, uneducated, dishonest, criminal, violent, immoral, and unintelligent. Therefore, it defiles the law of reason, according to the expectation of my "white friend," that a black male like me should be highly educated. Fanon (1967) offers a description of how the black male is constituted through fear and through naming and seeing in the white world:

> *In the white world the man of color encounters difficulties in the development of his bodily schema. Consciousness of the body is solely a negating activity. It is a third-person consciousness. The body is surrounded by an atmosphere of certain uncertainty.... The elements that I used had been provided for me not by 'residual' sensations and perceptions ... but by the other, the white man, who had woven me out of a thousand details, anecdotes, stories. I thought that what I had in hand was to construct a physiological self, to balance space, to localize sensations, and here I was called on for more. "Look, a Negro!" ..."Mama, see the Negro! I'm frightened!" Frightened! Frightened! Now they were beginning to be afraid of me. (Fanon, 1967, pp. 111–112)*

In Fanon's articulation of the racial interpellation, the black male is already pathologized, criminalized, and degenerated even before he enters the white world. It is like going to a place for the first time, but you realize that residents of that place have preexisting knowledge of you. For racialized bodies, this preexisting knowledge is not comforting because it is negative. Judith Butler asks:

If racism pervades white perception, structuring what can and cannot appear within the horizon of white perception, then to what extent does it interpret in advance "visual evidence"? And how, then, does such "evidence" have to be read, and read publicly, against the racist disposition of the visible which will prepare and achieve its own inverted perception under the rubric of "what is seen? (1993, p. 16)

What can be taken from Judith Butler's assertion is that in the natural world, everybody is innocent until proven guilty, but in the white world, a person of color is guilty until she or he proves his or her innocence. One can therefore conclude that the white administrative staff's accusation that "I cannot be what I claim to be" is not neutral to the question of race. If anything, it is itself a racist formation. Within the white world, a person of color is unmercifully imprisoned in what Fanon (1967, p. 111) calls "the historico-racial schema" to the extent that the only ontologically endowed means to liberate oneself is to literally amputate or excise the self from blackness, or better still go through a hemorrhage that will splatter the black blood in the whole body (Fanon, 1967, p. 112). So, when the veteran of the Pacific War told Frantz Fanon's brother to accept his blackness just as he has accepted his disability, he was invariably reminding Fanon's brother that they both occupy spaces that unmercifully shape, control, and define how they should be treated in the white supremacist world.

In response to the charge of the veteran of the Pacific War, Frantz Fanon, a black male from Martinique, argues: "Nevertheless, with all my strength I refuse to accept that amputation" (Fanon, 1967, p. 140). By refusing "amputation," Frantz Fanon is denouncing the manner in which the identity of blackness has been scripted, read, and imposed on bodies of color within the imagination of whiteness. He is also resisting the colonizing knowledge system that constantly pathologizes and criminalizes blackness and misrepresents it as an agent of malevolent powers there to cause harm to the white world. Like Frantz Fanon, I have also resolved to resist the colonial and racist narration within the current education system that charges me to amputate myself from blackness. In pursuing this task, I draw on anticolonial and antiracism education to guide my understanding and interpretation of Frantz Fanon.

As critical thoughts, both anticolonial and antiracism prisms are perfect for this task because they both challenge the Western paradigms that guide today's educational systems and social diversity by agitating for more inclusive and better responses to varied local concerns about colonial education (Dei, 2002a). Anticolonial and antiracism education contend that only when the subjective accounts of the marginalized communities are accorded a discursive integrity can imperialist projects destabilized. Elsewhere, Dei (2002b) has observed that the anticolonial education is an epistemology of the colonized anchored in the indigenous sense of collective and common colonial consciousness. Although anticolonial thought works with the notion of colonial, it nevertheless defines colonial in terms of imposed relations and power inequalities engendered by history, tradition, language, worldview, culture, and contact and not necessarily foreign or alien (Dei and Asgharzadeh, 2001). This means that "the colonial relations" as used in this chapter are not limited to the asymmetrical power relations between the West and "others," but also include relations of power within indigenous communities that continue to reproduce violence against women, people with disabilities, people with different sexual orientations, and ethnicity.

The discursive frameworks interrogate institutionalized power, privilege, and the accompanying rationale for dominant reproduction of what is considered 'legitimate' knowledge, culture, and language (Dei, 2002a). They acknowledge the role of schools in producing and reproducing inequalities that are based on race, sexuality, class, gender, ethnicity, disability, and religious beliefs. The frameworks allow us to understand how these (colonial remnants) are being reproduced and challenged in schools and education in Ghana. Within this context, I utilize anticolonial and antiracism frameworks to critically examine the readings of Frantz Fanon. At this juncture, I want to examine in depth the six key questions I posed at the beginning of the chapter to show the relevance of Fanon's ideas to education.

HOW DO FANON'S IDEAS RESIST COLONIAL DOMINATION IN KNOWLEDGE PRODUCTION, VALIDATION, AND DISSEMINATION?

In the foreword note to Dei and Kempf (2006), Molefi Asante, a foremost scholar of Afrocentric education, contends that "if colonialism's influence had been merely the control of land that would have required only one form of resistance, but when information is also colonized, it is essential that resistance must interrogate issues related to education, information, and intellectual transformation" (Asante, 2006, p. ix). Molefi Asante's comments vindicate the existing argument that resistance to colonialism requires more than reclaiming the land and resources stolen through colonialism. Colonialism, through its terrible control of knowledge production, validation, and dissemination, continues to persuade and force local learners to reject their indigenous upbringing and sense of self. According to Smith (1999), the major agent of imposing positional superiority over knowledge, language, and culture of the colonized is through colonial education. Smith (1999) further contends that colonial education that came either in the form of missionary/religious schools or public/secular schools has managed to create new breeds of indigenous elites who align themselves with the culture, values, and worldviews of the colonizer. In a similar way, an educationist, Dore (1976) has long argued that the effect of schooling, the way it alters a person's capacity to behave and to do things depends not only on what is learned, but also on how and why it is learned and the environment within which it is learned. The observation of Dore is extremely important because it shows the relevance of knowledge production, validation, and dissemination in maintaining or resisting colonial domination in Ghana. There is currently a dichotomy between knowledge individuals are exposed to during their upbringing in Ghana and the knowledge they get exposed to when they enter formal schooling (see Dei, 2004; Adjei, 2007). The effect is that schooling in Ghana continues to reproduce students who are conscious of Western cultures, values, and knowledges, yet very ignorant of their own indigenous cultures, values, and worldviews. Probably, the excerpt from the *Song of Lawino* eloquently speaks to the negative implications of colonial schooling in Ghana:

> My Husband
> Has read at Makerere University.
> He has read deeply and widely,
> But if you ask Him a question
> He says
> You are insulting him;
> He opens up with a quarrel
> He begins to look down upon you
> Saying
> You ask questions
> That are a waste of time!
> He says
> My questions are silly questions,
> Typical questions from village girls.
> Questions of uneducated people,
> Useless questions from untutored minds.
> My husband says I have a tiny little brain
> And it is not trained,
> I cannot see things intelligently,
> I cannot see things sharply.
> He says
> Even if he tried
> To answer my questions
> I would not understand
> What he was saying
> Because the language he speaks
> Is different from mine

> So that even if he
> Spoke to me in Acoli (*local language*)
> I would still need an interpreter.
> My husband says
> Some of the answers
> Cannot be given in Acoli
> Which is a primitive language
> And is not rich enough
> To express his deep wisdom.
> He says the Acoli language
> Has very few words
> It is not like the white man's language
> Which is rich and very beautiful
>
> A language fitted for discussing deep thoughts. (P'Bitek, 1986, pp. 87–88)

Although this song was written in reference to the Luo culture of Northern Uganda, it no doubt depicts the reality of the education system in Ghana. There are many characters like Ocol in Ghana who pride themselves in learning from the best universities, yet their acquired knowledges have no relevance to the local environment. They boast of being familiar with the ancient world of Julius Caesar, Plato, Shakespeare, Aristotle, Socrates, and other founding fathers of Western intellectual traditions, yet they have no knowledge of the philosophy of their own ancestors. They can fluently write and speak in the English language, yet they cannot write or read the alphabets of their own local languages. Like Ocol, many Ghanaian educators have read extensively and deeply to challenge any European or American in the knowledge and history of the West, yet to their own Ghanaian history and knowledge, they are at a great lost. It is this situation that probably informed the humorous quip of the former President of Ghana, J. J. Rawlings: "Ghanaians were free some times in the past that is why Europeans needed chains to enslave us. But, today there is no need for chains because, we have our minds trapped and we are struggling to break free. This is the struggle to deal with entrapment/enslavement of the human mind." (Cited in Adjei and Dei, 2008, p. 142)

This clearly indicates that the only means ontologically endowed to address the problem of colonialism in Ghana is to resist the current approach to knowledge production, validation, and dissemination in schools in Ghana.

The understanding that Frantz Fanon has of colonial relations makes his ideas relevant to the Ghanaian context.

Frantz Fanon argues that structures of colonialism were designed to amputate the colonized subjects from their history, culture, values, and worldview till they believe that the colonizer is their saviour and only source of hope:

> When we consider the efforts made to carry out the cultural estrangement so characteristic of the colonial epoch, we realize that nothing has been left to chance and that the total result looked for by colonial domination was indeed to convince the natives that colonialism came to lighten their darkness. The effect consciously sought by colonialism was to drive into the natives' heads the idea that if the settlers were to leave; they would at once fall back into barbarism, degradation, and bestiality. (1963, pp. 210–211)

What this implies about knowledge production, validation, and dissemination in Ghana is that the continuous centering of Euro-American/Canadian knowledge in the school curriculum in Ghana compromises any effort to resist colonial domination in Ghana. The influx of Western-centered books in the libraries and schools in Ghana continues to reproduce hyperopic intellectuals; although they can see and effectively discuss issues affecting the West, they have no knowledge of issues affecting their own communities. As Frantz Fanon rightly observes:

> The native intellectual has thrown himself greedily upon Western culture. Like adopted children who only stop investigating the new family framework at the moment when a minimum nucleus of security crystallizes in their psyche, the native intellectual will try to make European culture his own. He will not be content to get to know Rabelais and Diderot, Shakespeare and Edgar Allan Poe; he will bind them to his intelligence as closely as possible. (1963, p. 219)

Frantz Fanon's observation is a wakeup call to Ghanaian educators that the continuous imposition of Western curriculum on local learners presents a dangerous and worrisome challenge to the task of resisting colonial domination in Ghana. The recentering of indigenous knowledge, culture, values, and worldview in the school curriculum in Ghana remains the single most important move to resist colonial domination in Ghana. George Dei (2004) argues that the epistemic knowledge of a learner is instrumental in how the learner defines the 'self' and its connectedness to others and the community at large. In a sense, George Dei is claiming that since indigeneity and identity are powerfully linked, we cannot dismiss the power of indigenous and local cultural knowing to resist colonial domination. Frantz Fanon, therefore, submits that resistance to colonial domination should begin by acknowledging the relevance of local knowledge and culture in the struggle:

> We would also uncover the same transformation, the same progress and the same eagerness if we enquired into the fields of dance, song, rituals, and traditional ceremonies. Well before the political or armed struggle, a careful observer could sense and feel in these arts the pulse of a fresh stimulus and the coming combat. Unusual forms of expression, original themes no longer invested with the power of invocation but the power to rally and mobilize with the approaching conflict in mind. Everything conspires to stimulate the colonized's sensibility, and to rule

> *out and reject attitudes of inertia or defeat. By imparting new meaning and dynamism to artisanship, dance, music, literature, and the oral epic, the colonized subject restructures his own perception. The world no longer seems doomed. Conditions are ripe for the inevitable confrontation. (Fanon, 2004, p. 176)*

Thus, Molefi Asante's point that resistance must interrogate issues related to education, information, and intellectual transformation is relevant to Fanon's argument. The first Prime Minister of Ghana, Kwame Nkrumah, concluded that only when Ghanaians learn to question the colonial and colonized thinking that our knowledge and value systems are inferior to European and American knowledge systems can the stirrings of revolt begin and the whole structure of colonial rule will come under attack (1963). Therefore, one should read the re-centering of indigenous knowledges in the school curriculum in Ghana as an act of stirring academic revolt in Ghana.

IN WHAT WAYS DOES FANON'S ARTICULATION OF DECOLONIZATION INFORM RESISTANCE TO AMPUTATION?

Frantz Fanon saw decolonization as a tool of resistance to colonial domination. Fanon (1963) enthused that decolonization can only be understood as a historical process that ultimately culminates in changing the social order. It is an initial violent encounter of two forces (colonial domination and resistance power of the colonized subjects) opposed to each other by their very nature:

> *Decolonization is the veritable creation of new men. But this creation owes nothing of its legitimacy to any supernatural power; the "thing" which has been colonized becomes a man during the same process by which it frees itself. In decolonization, there is therefore the need of a complete calling into question of the colonial situation. If we wish to describe it precisely, we might find it in the well-known words: "The last shall be first and the first last." Decolonization is the putting into practice of this sentence.... The naked truth of decolonization evokes for us the searing bullets and bloodstained knives, which emanate from it. For if the last shall be first, this will only come to pass after a murderous and decisive struggle between the two protagonists. (1963, pp. 36–37)*

Frantz Fanon noted that while violence is wrong and causes physical, emotional, psychological, and spiritual damage to its victims; it also teaches the oppressed groups to resist. Thus, for the oppressed groups, violence is a necessary choice not just to redeem their freedom from the oppressive regimes but also to cure the internalization of their own inferiority created through colonialism. One can therefore assume from Fanon's articulation of decolonization that violence is a cleansing force that frees the oppressed from despair and inaction. In this case, the violence of the marginalized is not intrinsic but instrumental because its goal is to remove the chains of oppression. Understandingly, every oppressive relation needs to be halted at every cost; nevertheless, since violence dehumanizes both the perpetrator and its victim (see Memmi, 1965; Fanon, 1963), at what point does violence start healing? Gail Presbey (1996) contends that for the victims of violence, it is hard to say that there is healing taking place. There can never be retribution enough to help victims of violence to forget their pain and suffering let alone obtain healing. Indeed, Frantz Fanon's own works catalogue the damage violence creates to the physical and mental well-being of the oppressed (Fanon, 1963, 1967). Presbey (1996) argues that rather than healing, violence stubbornly positions individuals against reform, change, and even healing (p. 287). Although Frantz Fanon spoke within a particular historical context and the conditions pertaining in his time could have influenced his diagnosis of violence, yet there are still unanswered questions to Fanon's solutions to oppressive relations.

Frantz Fanon rightly saw colonialism as fundamentally a violent situation because colonialism generates two competing interests: the interest of the colonizers and the interest of the colonized subjects. From the standpoint of colonizers, their place in the colony and everything they have acquired at the colony are just and fair (see Gordon, 1996). Thus, to replace them or seek to reclaim their possessions is unfair and unjust. On the other hand, the colonized subjects are aware that their place in society is unjust. Thus, any effort to restore them to their rightful place in society is a just cause. Here is the irony: the oppressors face the threat of violence; the oppressed are living violence. The former are not willing to change position without a fight, and the latter are willing to fight till changes come. Even if the oppressed are to succeed in removing the oppressors violently, the latter will also seek other opportunities to restore themselves back to power because to the delusional minds of the oppressors, they are also innocent victims. Let us even, for purpose of argument, ignore the shrilling cries of victimization of the oppressors and focus on the oppressed. If violent decolonization is to restore the balance of power by installing the oppressed to their rightful position, who supervises such transition? At what point do we agree that the balance of power has been duly restored? Who ensures that the oppressed do not end up becoming the oppressors? What happens, if in the process of violent decolonization, the oppressed do become the oppressors? The contemporary examples of vicious cycles of violence in the Middle East—between Israel, on the one hand, and Hamas/Hezbollah, on the other; the United States/Canada/Britain, on the one hand, and Jihad fundamentalists, on the other—clearly raise new questions on whether violent decolonization can indeed offer true healing or permanent relief to either the oppressors or the oppressed.

Having said that, I still think Frantz Fanon talked about decolonization from a particular historical context. The history of colonialism in Algeria was enmeshed in violence. Therefore, Frantz Fanon saw violence as the only option available for the Algerians if they were to resist colonial amputation. The inconsistency in the argument of those who accuse Fanon of being the apostle of violence is that the same individuals ignore the historical conditions within which Frantz Fanon wrote *The Wretched of the Earth*. If the French were dominating Algerians with brute force, then how can anybody condemn the resistance groups of Algeria for using violence to resist the French domination? How can something be right when committed by the French army but wrong when committed by the resistance groups in Algeria?

Pedagogically, Frantz Fanon's concept of decolonization offers us a principle that can guide the struggle for decolonization: If Western hegemony is constructed and maintained through a colonial education system, then it requires an anticolonial education system to counter the Western hegemony. This means that decolonization is a subversive act because it calls into question the whole colonial situation and its aftermath. Dei and Asgharzadeh (2001) argue that colonialism and colonization accedes to a false status through the authority of the Western canon. Therefore, decolonization is breaking away from the human condition as defined and shaped by Western culture, values, and knowledge system. It is one's willingness to confront all forms of political, ideological, and socioeconomic injustice. It is an approach that engages without reverting to the colonizing forms of social relations. As already mentioned, decolonization can only be understood as historical process that ultimately culminates in changing social order (Fanon, 1963). Dei and Asgharzadeh (2001) point out that the concern raised by Frantz Fanon is legitimate because it makes a connection between what is and what ought to be. Thus, decolonization is an on-going dialectic between a hegemonic centrist system and peripheral subversion; between European Imperial discourse and their anticolonial dismantling (Dei and Asgharzadeh, 2001). It is a process that seeks to interrupt and rupture the "the political economy of knowledge production" (Dei, 2002a, p. 129) that accords certain privileges and legitimacy to Eurocentric systems of thought while invalidating indigenous knowledges. Also, decolonization is an effort to reclaim indigenous cultures, languages, values, and worldviews and reposition them into the education system in Ghana. Therefore, the journey towards decolonization will be impeded when local learners lose their ontological, epistemological, and axiological resistance, because resistance knowledge offers learners the necessary groundings to challenge the dominant knowledge and to reclaim that which is forgotten, stolen, and lost. Thus, decolonization should be seen as an effort to empower the colonized subjects to reclaim everything they have lost through colonial domination.

In view of that Fanon (1963) recommends that decolonization should produce literature of combat against colonialism. He also calls for the modification of oral traditions such as storytelling, epics, and songs to celebrate the names of indigenous heroes and ancestors who hitherto are depicted in derogatory manner in the colonial classroom (ibid.). More than three decades ago, Fonlon (1978) made similar appeals to African schools, colleges, and universities to contribute towards a genuine, multifaceted, liberation of the continent and its people by including indigenous knowledge in the educational policies (Copans, 1990, 1993; Zeleza and Olukoshi, 2004). The school curriculum in Ghana needs to recognize, legitimize, and validate a central space for indigenous storytelling, proverbs, fables, Adinkra symbols, riddles, local languages, myths, and superstitions. Through the strategy of incorporating indigenous knowledge, culture, values, and worldview into the school curricula, the schooling system in Ghana can create an environment for decolonization.

IN WHAT WAYS DOES FANON'S EXPERIENCE REVEAL THE RELEVANCE OF SUBJECTIVE VOICE, AGENCY, AND RESISTANCE POWER OF THE COLONIZED SUBJECTS IN ANTIOPPRESSION WORK?

How did Fanon come to know about his world? To what extent did his experiential knowledge inform his writings? Writing under the theme "The Fact of Blackness" in *Black Skin, White Masks,* Fanon (1967) points to the knowledge that comes with showing up in the white world as a black person. Although Frantz Fanon had an academic understanding of racism long before he went to Algeria, the racist discrimination he was exposed to in Algeria taught him that he was not adequately prepared to experience racism in the flesh (see Azar, 2000). Frantz Fanon's experience is an insightful lesson because it warns us against any superficial interpretation of oppression; especially, if a particular oppression (racism) is deeply ingrained in socially constructed ideologies and practices. Frantz Fanon's experience in Algeria raises important questions for those of us in the academy: when we claim to know, is the knowing based on personal experience? Or is the badge of knowledge simply part of the trappings the academy bestows on its members just to set them apart from the subjects they study? While academic knowledge is an essential component of understanding social issues, Fanon's experience in Algeria points to the limits of intellectual analysis when it is based only on academic knowledge without personal experience. Dei and Asgharzadeh (2001) argue that there are oceans of difference and privilege that divide and separate those who have the gift of a voice from those who do not have such a gift, who in fact cannot dream of having a voice. Thus, antioppression works cannot ignore the resistance voices and subjective politics of the marginalized groups. Although the very complex nature of social identity can make one an oppressed person in one area of social identity (race, gender, class, sexuality, disability, religion) and an oppressor in another area of social identity, yet we cannot flatten out oppression as if it impacts different bodies in the same way. Fanon's experience shows that body matters in antioppression work; therefore, the resenting voices of the marginalized groups affected by a particular oppression cannot be ignored when that issue is tabled for discussion. As Prah (1997) rightly admonishes us, we have to guide against this insulting idea that somehow we know and understand other people's problems better than they do. Fanon's life experience teaches us that knowing an issue by merely reading or researching it, cannot be the same as experiencing the issue. Gayatri Chakravorty Spivak (1988) asks: Can the subalterns speak? The exact response should have been the subalterns speak—although not through the complex intellectual jargons we throw around just to claim discursive integrity on issues that do not directly affect us—but rather they speak through the physical, psychological, emotional, spiritual, economical, social, and cultural scars and chains they bear from oppression. These scars and chains are the irrefutable evidence that they have a deep and complex understanding of their issues. Therefore, part of our responsibility as antioppression workers is to ensure that we do not only hear the subaltern speak but also help others hear the subaltern voices.

IN WHAT WAYS DO COLONIZED BODIES PLAY A COMPLICIT ROLE IN THEIR OWN COLONIZATION?

bell hooks (1994) rightly notes that part of doing critical work is to start with oneself. While we are eager to challenge oppression in society, we need to bear in mind that such action does not inoculate us from criticism. Fanon (1967b, p. 3) asks "Have I not, because of what I have done or failed to do contribute to an impoverishment of human reality? . . . Have I at all times demanded and brought out the man that is in me?" These questions raised by Frantz Fanon call for self-implication, self-critical, and self-reflexivity as we engage in antioppression work. How are we complicit in Western hegemony? How do we deal with the questions of complicity, accountability, and responsibility? The black theologian James Cone says that our survival and liberation depend upon our recognition of the truth when it is spoken and lived:

> *If we cannot recognize the truth, then it cannot liberate us from untruth. To know the truth is to prepare for it; for it is not mainly reflection and theory. Truth is divine action entering our lives and creating the human action of liberation. (Cited in hooks, 2003, p. 160)*

As a child going to Sunday school every Sunday, I heard a particular story of the Bible that stayed with me. It is a passage in the book of Luke 24:13–31. In this passage, we are told of an incident that happened on the road to Emmaus after Jesus Christ resurrected from death. According to the story, Jesus joined his two disciples who were travelling to the village called Emmaus, about seven miles from Jerusalem. The story goes on to describe almost ridiculous interactions during which Jesus drops all kinds of hints about who he is, yet his stolid disciples—perhaps still heavy with the tragedy of losing Jesus—miss every reference that might have helped them to recognize Him. In order to continue their discussion, these two disciples invited Jesus to stay and eat with them. It is only when they were sitting around the table waiting for Jesus to break and bless the bread that their eyes finally opened and recognized him. For me, the road to Emmaus is a real road in every way. The two travelers in the story were walking with troubled minds, so engrossed that for a long time they could not see the gift that their ordinary journey was offering them. Similarly, our struggles as antioppression workers will be meaningless if we fail to recognize the truth being presented to us. Sometimes, this truth lies within us; it speaks out to us in our daily interactions with others. Thus, as we are eager to seek justice and fairness, we need to ask ourselves: how fairly do we treat others? In her letter to Professor Cornel West, bell hooks writes:

> *We bear witness not just with our intellectual work but with ourselves, our lives. Surely the crisis of these times demands that we give our all. Remember the song which asked "Is your altar of sacrifice late?" To me, this "all" includes our habits of being, the way we live. It is both political practice and spiritual sacrament of a life of resistance. How can we speak of change, of hope, and love if we court death? All of the work we do, no matter how brilliant or revolutionary in thought or action loses power and meaning if we lack integrity of being. (2003, p. 166)*

For me, the pedagogical lesson from the story in Luke 24, the questions posed by Fanon, the observation of James Cone, and the correspondence between Cornel West and bell hooks is that our commitment to fight against oppression will be hypocritical, if we only recognize oppression when we see others doing it and not when it exists within us.

Within the current antiracism and anticolonial education, marginalized groups have to constantly remind the privileged and dominant members engaged in critical work that oppression, colonialism, and racism also exist in them (Dei, 2008). Oftentimes, some of the dominant members take such comments as an indictment on the good works they are doing. Of course, we are fully aware, as bell hooks (2003) also reminds us, that if we fail to acknowledge the value and significance of individual dominant groups in antioppression work, we do not only diminish the work they have done and do to transform their thinking and behaviour, but also we prevent other dominant people from learning by their example. For instance, any racialized person who has suffered racism knows that racial exploitation will never end until racist whites change. hooks (2003, p. 57) insists that "anyone who denies that this change can happen; that one can move from being racist to being actively antiracist is acting in collusion with the existing forces of racial domination." Thus, asking individuals to own up to their complicit role in colonialism and racism does not imply that those individuals are disqualified from doing anticolonial and antiracism work, but rather serves to remind all of us that doing antiracism and anticolonial work does not "inoculate" anyone from criticisms.

IS THERE A ROLE FOR SPIRITUALITY IN FANON'S THOUGHT ABOUT RESISTING AMPUTATION?

In his recent book *Racist Beware: Uncovering Racist Politics in the Contemporary Society,* George Dei poses this question: "What is the place of spirituality and spiritual knowing in antiracist teaching and political practice" (2008, p. 68)? Perhaps, embedded in this question are these multiple questions: What motivates us to do antioppression work? What compels us to challenge injustices and oppression even when they do not affect us? What sustains us to continue the struggle against oppression even when the odds are against us? Answers to these questions will show that spirituality plays a central role in antioppression work. Dei (2002b) defines spirituality as:

> *The building and rebuilding of human spirit to embrace gentleness, humility, and compassion in learning about others and ourselves. It is about a powerful force beyond the immediate and more physically observable culture, one that directs social action beyond the perspective of human control in terms of that which can be counted, measured, evaluated, and physically grasped. (p. 38)*

Spirituality, at the most basic level, refers to the understanding of the self as encompassing body, mind, and the spirit. It also includes the sense of interconnection that moves beyond the knowable and the visible material world. This sense of interconnectedness has been described variously as divinity, the sacred, spirit, or simply the universe. But spirituality can be as much about the practice of compassion, love, ethics, and truth defined in nonreligious terms as it can be related to the mystical reinterpretations of existing religious traditions (Fernandes, 2003, p. 10).

Leela Fernandes observes that "in a world marked by violent ethnic, racial, and religious conflict and deepening social and economic inequality, any possibility of social transformation also requires a spiritual revolution, one which transforms conventional understandings of power, identity, and justice" (2003, p. 11). My argument is that if resistance to amputation is to be fully transformative, then, it must link the spiritual with the material realm. History has shown that even the progressive social movements that rest on the assumption that spirituality has no role in resistance work often end up reproducing another form of social oppression while addressing one form of oppression (see Fernandes, 2003). For instance, the well-intentioned attempts of Western feminists to speak on behalf of global women's oppression have often implicated them in colonial and racialized discourses that have stereotyped Third World countries as backward and oppressive (Fernandes, 2003, p. 12). The truth is that without compassion and love, resistance groups will be overwhelmed by anger and hatred toward the person who has harmed them. The world is filled with cruel and wicked people that sometimes the only reasonable thing to do with such individuals is to shoot and kill them. But Thich Nhat Hanh reminds us that "meeting hatred with hatred, meeting violence with vengeance and retaliation can never lead to the end of hatred and violence. Love is the only force that can protect us and others from harm" (2008, p. 192). Spiritual revitalization helps us to regain our sense of humanity. It helps us to look deep into the oppressor and realise that she or he too is a victim of ideas, misinformation, and conditions in his or her own life, culture, and society. According to Albert Memmi, "oppression is the greatest calamity of humanity. It diverts and pollutes the best energies of oppressed and oppressor alike. For if colonization destroys the colonized; it also rots the colonizer" (1965, p. xvii; also see Fanon, 1963, 1967). Thus, resistance work should not be about committing harm to the oppressor but, rather, should be about rescuing him or her from the oppressive structures that continue to violate and dehumanize him or her. We can only reach this decision when we allow spirituality to guide our resistance work.

Again, spirituality allows us to link our struggles to the collective struggles of others. For many conservatives and liberal educators, the historic victory of Barack Obama as the first black president of the United States, the success story of Oprah Winfrey as the most successful TV host in the United States, and the achievements of Condoleezza Rice, Colin Powell, and others are indications that racism is something of a distant past (see Elder, 2008). Spirituality allows us to see the picture beyond the specific successes of individuals. It helps us to understand that we cannot sing "we have overcome," when other people are still experiencing racism, classism, sexism, homophobia, Islamophobia, antisemitism, and disability. Spirituality abhors and resists any forms of oppression that affect individuals, especially the weak in society. Hindman (2002) challenges educators to work towards the spiritual development of students and inspire them to dedicate their lives to the struggle against social injustices, inequity, and unfairness that affect every member of society. Within this understanding and conceptualization spirituality becomes a relevant framework for antioppression work.

Spirituality was pivotal in the activist life of Frantz Fanon. He devoted his entire life to the fight for justice, fairness, and equity. As a professional and practising psychiatrist, Fanon was well positioned to benefit tremendously from the oppressive regimes in France and Algeria, yet he rejected all these colonial benefits just for the suffering life of an activist. In his personal letter to a friend, Roger Tayed, just before he died, Frantz Fanon observed: "We are nothing on earth if we are not, first of all, slaves of a cause, the cause of the people, the cause of justice, and the cause of liberty" (Geismar, 1971, p. 185). Yes, even in his last days before his death at the early age of 39, Fanon was only thinking about the cause of the people, the cause of justice, and the cause of liberty. Even when suffering with leukemia, Frantz Fanon did not take his eyes off the goal of ending colonial and racist oppression in Algeria; he constantly went to Ghardimao, a small town at the Algeria-Tunisian border, to deliver lectures to ALN (Armée de Libération Nationale) officers. Surely, it takes a person well grounded in spiritual knowing to care more about others than himself.

WHAT ARE THE RISKS, PERILS, COSTS, AND CONSEQUENCES OF PURSUING SUCH SUBVERSIVE POLITICS AND PRACTICES IN THE EDUCATION SYSTEM?

bell hooks (1994, p. 74) reminds us that those who go through oppression find it difficult to name their pain and even theorize from that location. Patricia Williams (1991) poignantly observes that even those who are aware are made to feel the pain of homophobia, class exploitation, Islamophobia, sexism, disability, and racism:

> *There are moments in my life when I feel as though a part of me is missing. There are days when I feel so invisible that I can't remember what day of the week it is, when I feel so manipulated that I can't remember my own name, when I feel so lost and angry that I can't speak a civil word to the people who love me best. There are times when I catch sight of my reflection in store windows and I am surprised to see a whole person looking back ... I have to close my eyes at such times and remember myself; draw an internal pattern that is smooth and whole. (p. 228)*

The task of changing the academy is difficult and it is only when one begins to take a whack at shaking the structure that one sees how the opposition is well consolidated (Spivak, 1990). The words of these critical educators clearly indicate that there is high risk and cost to resistance work. Thus, resisters of oppression need to weigh in the cost and ask themselves if they are willing and prepared to pay the cost. Probably the most important question is not about who can do antioppression work, but who is willing to face the consequences?

CONCLUSION

In *Black Skin, White Masks,* Frantz Fanon recounted what his philosophy professor, a native of the Antilles, told him:

> 'Whenever you hear anyone abuse the Jews, pay attention, because he is talking about you.' And I found that he was universally right—by which I meant that I was answerable in my body and in my heart for what was done to my brother. Later I realized that he meant, quite simply, an antiSemite is inevitably antiNegro. (Fanon, 1967, p. 122)

Leon Bass, a 19-year-old African American and a sergeant of the 183rd Combat Engineer Battalion, was part of the team that entered Buchenwald, a Nazi concentration camp in Germany, to liberate the Jews in April 1945. Later, Leon Bass recounted what he saw at the camp in his interview with Pam Sporn: "There I saw the walking dead.... It made me see clearly what can happen when racism is left unchallenged. It removed my blinders.... I now understand that the pain of racism is not relegated just to me and mine ... your pain is my pain, and my pain is your pain" (Sporn, 1999, n.p.). I believe the words of Sergeant Leon Bass and the advice of Fanon's professor can guide us in our work as educational activists. We should pay attention whenever we hear anyone abusing racialized people, women, gays and lesbians, persons with disabilities, Aboriginal people, poor people, Jews, Muslims, and other members of marginalized groups because that person is also talking about us. Frantz Fanon offers us pedagogical knowledge that can be applied to everything we do as educators and activists. The Akans of Ghana have warned that "only the fool goes to sleep when his or her neighbour's house in on fire." Our struggle as activists will be incomplete if we cannot link our struggles with other struggles. The power of intersectional marginalities calls for inclusive politics and practices. As antioppression workers, we cannot afford to operate within our own silos and fail to make linkages with others in the pursuit of social justice because oppressions are multifaceted and complex (Dei, 2008). Thus, our ability to intersect all forms of oppression puts us on the road to securing justice for all (Dei, 2008, p. 6). This is why the ideas expressed in the essay cannot be seen as isolated to Ghana alone.

I believe "resistance to amputation" cannot be complete if we do not link the struggles of indigenous Ghanaian students to the struggles of Aboriginal and Indigenous students to have a voice in schooling and education in Euro-American/Canadian society. Many indigenous scholars (see Dei, 2008; Graveline, 1998; Iseke-Barnes, 2004; Smith, 1999; and Lester-Irabinna, 1997) have expressed concerns about high increase of students' disengagement and drop-outs in schools in Euro-American/Canadian society. These educators have suggested the need to broaden the teaching and pedagogic practices to accommodate alternate forms of learning. I am sure the views expressed in the essay and the writings of Frantz Fanon can serve as important references to any conversation about restructuring education in Euro-American/Canadian society. The works of Fanon offer a very important understanding of colonial relations and useful ways to address them in society. Yes, Fanon may be dead and gone, but his ideas are still relevant today. Society only ignores Fanon at its own risk.

REFERENCES

Adell, S. 1996. *African American Culture.* Detroit, MI: Gale Research.

Adjei, P. B. 2007. Decolonising Knowledge production: The Pedagogic Relevance of Gandhian Satyagraha to Schooling and Education in Ghana. *Canadian Journal of Education* 30 (4):1046–1067.

Adjei, P. B. 2008. Unmapping the Tapestry of *Crash.* In *Crash Politics and Antiracism: Interrogations of Liberal Race Discourse,* edited by P. Howard and G. Dei. New York: Peter Lang.

Adjei, P. B., & Dei, G. S. 2008. Decolonizing Schooling and Education in Ghana. In *Education and Social Development: Global Issues and Analyses,* edited by A. A. Abdi & S. Guo. Rotterdam: Sense Publishers.

Asante, M. 2006. Foreword. In *Anticolonialism and Education: The Politics of Resistance,* edited by G. J. S. Dei & A. Kempf, Rotterdam/Taipei: Sense Publishers.

Austin, D. 2006. Frantz Fanon's diagnosis: Fanon Did Not Prescribe Violence; He Diagnosed It. *Toronto Star,* October 23.

Azar, M. 2008. *In the Name of Algeria: Frantz Fanon and the Algerian Revolution* 2000 [cited December 20 2008]. Available from http://www.eurozine.com/pdf/2000-12-06-azar-en.pdf.

Bhabha, H. K. 2004. Foreword: Framing Fanon. In *The Wretched of the Earth,* by F. Fanon. New York: Grove Press.

Bhabha, H. K. 1986. Foreword: Remembering Fanon: Self, Psyche, and the Colonial Condition. Introduction to Franz Fanon's *Black Skin, White Masks,* Liberation Classics. (m. b. Charles Lam Markmann of Peau noire, Trans.). London and Sydney: Pluto.

Boler, M. & Zembylas, M. 2003. Discomforting Truths: The Emotional Terrain of Understanding Difference. In *Pedagogies of Difference: Rethinking Education for Social Change,* edited by P. P. Trifonas. New York, London: Routledge Falmer.

Butler, J. 1993. Endangered/Endangering: Schematic Racism and White Paranoia. In *Reading Rodney King: Reading Urban Uprising*, edited by R. Good-Williams. New York: Routledge.

Copans, J. 1990. *La Longue Marche de la Moderniite Africaine: Savoirs, Intellectuals, Democratie.* Paris: Karthala.

Copans, J. 1993. Intellectuels Visibles, Intellectuels Invisibles. *Politique Africaine, 51*(October), 7–25.

Dei, G. J. S. 2002b. Spirituality in African Education: Issues, Contentions and Contestations from a Ghanaian Case Study. *International Journal of Children Spirituality,* 7(1), 37–56.

Dei, G. J. S. 2002a. Rethinking the Role of Indigenous Knowledges in the Academy. *International Journal of Inclusive Education,* 4(2), 111–132.

Dei, G. J. S. & Asgharzadeh, A. 2001. The Power of Social Theory: The Anticolonial Discursive Framework. *Journal of Educational Thought,* 35(3), 297–323.

Dei, G. J. S. & Kempf, A. (Ed.). (2006). *Anti-colonialism and Education: The Politics of Resistance.* Rotterdam/Taipei: Sense Publishers.

Dei, G. J. S. 1996. *Theory and Practice: Anti-racism Education:* Halifax: Fernwood Publishing.

Dei, G. J. S. 2004. *Schooling and Education in Africa: The Case of Ghana.* Trenton, NJ: Africa World Press.

Dei, G. J. S. 2008. Lecture Notes: Frantz Fanon and Pedagogical Challenges. Unpublished manuscript, Toronto.

Dei, G. J. S. 2008. *Racist Beware: Uncovering Racist Politics in the Postmodern Society.* Rotterdam/New York/Taipei: Sense Publishers.

Dore, R. 1976. *The Diploma Disease: Education, Qualification and Development.* London: George Allen and Unwin.

Du Bois, W. E. B. 1903. *The Souls of Black Folk.* Chicago: A.C. McClurg & Co.

Elder, L. 2008. *Stupid Black Men: How to Play the Race Card.* New York: St. Martin's Press.

English, R. 2003. *Armed Struggle: The History of the IRA.* New York: Oxford University Press.

Fanon, F. 2004. *The Wretched of the Earth.* New York: Grove Press.

Fanon, F. 1967. *Black Skin, White Masks.* New York: Grove Press.

Fanon, F. 1963. *The Wretched of the Earth.* New York: Grove Press.

Fanon, F. 1967b. *Toward African Revolution.* New York: Grove Press.

Fernandes, L. 2003. *Transforming Feminist Practice: Non-Violence, Social Justice, and the Possibilities of a Spiritualized Feminism.* San Francisco: Aunt Lute Books.

Foucault, M. 1977. Truth and Power. In *Power/Knowledge: Selected Interviews and Other Writings 1972–1977,* Colin Gordon, ed. New York: Pantheon Books. 109–133.

Fonlon, B. 1978. *The Genuine Intellectual.* Yaoundé: Buma Kor.

Geismar, P. 1971. *Fanon: A Biography.* New York: Dial Press.

Gordon, L.R. 1996. The Black and the Body Politic: Fanon's Existential Phenomenological Critique of Psychoanalysis. In *Fanon: A Critical Reader,* edited by L.R. Gordon, T.D. Sharpley-Whiting, and R.T. White. Oxford: Blackwell Critical Readers.

Graveline, F J. 1998. *Circle Works: Transforming Eurocentric Consciousness.* Halifax: Fernwood Publishing.

Hanh, T. N. 2008. *Peaceful Action, Open Heart: Lessons from the Lotus Sutra.* Berkeley, California: Parallax Press.

Hansen, E. 1974. Frantz Fanon: Portrait of a Revolutionary Intellectual. *Transition* (46), 25–36.
Hindman, D. M. 2002. From Splintered Lives to Whole Persons: Facilitating Spiritual Development in College Students. *Religious Education* 97 (2):165–182.
hooks, b. 1992. *Black Looks: Race and Representation.* Boston: South End Press.
hooks, b. 1994. *Teaching to Transgress.* New York: Routledge.
hooks, b. 2003. *Teaching Community: A Pedagogy of Hope.* Routledge: New York.
Iseke-Barnes, J. M. 2004. Politics and Power of Languages: Indigenous Resistance to Colonizing Experience of Language Dominance. *Journal of Thought* 39 (1):45–81.
Lester-Irabinna, R. 1997. Internationalisation of an Indigenous Anti-Colonial Cultural Critique of Research Methodologies: A Guide to Indigenist Research Methodology and Its Principles. *Journal for Native American Studies* 4 (2):109–125.
Major, R. 1971. *A Panther Is a Black Cat.* New York: William Morrow.
Marshall, P. 1983. *Praisesong for the Widow.* New York: Penguin Books.
Memmi, A. 1965. *The Colonizer and the Colonized.* Introduction by Jean-Paul Sartre. Boston: Beacon Press.
Nkrumah, K. 1963. *Africa Must Unite.* London: Heinemann.
P'Bitek, O. 1986. *Song of Lawino:* Nairobi: East African Educational Publishers.
Prah, K. 1997. Accusing the Victims—Review of *In My Father's House* by Kwame Anthony Appiah. *Codesria Bulletin, 1,* 14–22.
Presbey, G. M. 1996. Fanon on the Role of Violence in Liberation: A Comparison with Gandhi and Mandela. In *Fanon: A Critical Reader,* edited by L.R. Gordon, T.D. Sharpley-Whiting, and R.T. White. Oxford: Blackwell Critical Readers' Series.
Sekyi-Otu, A. 1996. *Fanon's Dialectic of Experience.* Cambridge, MA: Harvard University Press.
Smith, D. 1999. *Writing the Social: Critique, Theory, and Investigations.* Toronto: University of Toronto Press.
Smith, L. T. 1999. *Decolonizing Methodologies: Research and Indigenous Peoples.* London: Zed Books Ltd.
Spivak, G. C. 1988. Can the Subaltern Speak? In *Marxism and the Interpretation of Culture,* edited by C. Nelson and L. Grossberg. Chicago, Urbana: University of Illinois Press. 271–313.
Spivak, G. 1990. Criticism, Feminism, and the Institutions. Interview with Elizabeth Grosz. In *The Post-Colonial Critic: Interviews, Strategies, Dialogues,* edited by S. Harasym. New York: Routledge.
Sporn, P. 1999. *Blacks and Jews: Are They Really Sworn Enemies?* Documentary.
Thesee, G. 2006. A Tool of Massive Erosion: Scientific Knowledge in the Neo-Colonial Enterprise. In *Anti-Colonialism and Education: The Politics of Resistance,* edited by G. J. S. Dei, & A. Kempf. Rotterdam/Taipei: Sense Publishers.
Titchkosky, T. 2008. *Reading and Writing Disability Differently: The Textured Life of Embodiment.* Toronto, Buffalo, London: University of Toronto Press.
Williams, P. J. 1991. *The Alchemy of Race and Rights.* Cambridge, MA: Harvard University Press.
Zeleza P. T. and Olukoshi, A. 2004. *African Universities in the Twenty-First Century.* Dakar: CODESRIA books.

CHAPTER FIVE

The Fact of Blackness[1]
A Critical Review of Bermuda's Colonial Education System

DONNA OUTERBRIDGE

The writing of this chapter comes with much struggle and anxiety. I write from a precarious space that renders me both fragile and fragmented: a place where I must look back and remember, critique, and analyze a system that has shaped me into a particular subject while robbing me of my identity, culture, and language. I speak with a foreign tongue; the colonizer's language I was taught would grant me acceptance and entry into the white world. Similar to Fanon, I now question, struggle, and contest the Eurocentric knowledge that privileges one group of people while rendering the "other" inferior. With a new awakened consciousness and desire to be a woman who always questions; it is incumbent on me to answer the challenge that Fanon has presented to either " . . . discover my mission, fulfill it, or betray it." I choose to fulfill it (Fanon 1963, p.206).

In this chapter, I discuss the relevancy of using Fanon's notion of blackness, and how it speaks to the schooling and education system in Bermuda. How can a reconceptualization of humanism[2] as engaged by Fanon and as it related to blackness be envisioned in order to eradicate structures that promote a lack of self-esteem and disrupt the sense of belonging and identity? I argue that although the Bermudian education system has undergone many reforms, at least compared to the period of its first inception; these reforms have ignored the fundamental crisis of schooling and education in Bermuda by failing to address how the school curriculum[3] continued to socialize learners into the Eurocentric educational system that does not reflect their identity or lived experiences. In order to contextualize this discussion,

I present the significance of utilizing anticolonial, indigenous knowledge epistemology, and antiracist discursive framework and provide a historical synopsis of marginalization in Bermuda's education system followed with three themes: (1) blackness/inferior complex in Bermuda, (2) politics of identity—dialectic of experience, (3) and loving blackness as a tool of decolonization—towards Fanon's new humanism. I will conclude by reemphasizing Fanon's relevancy to the process of decolonization, and subsequent move towards a new humanism; as I imagine loving blackness. By loving our blackness we will begin to decolonize our minds thus enabling us to start the process of reclaiming, healing and gaining our total liberation, and our sense of self. Hence, loving our blackness is the first step of decolonization by examining the way in which colonization has instilled and reinforced internalized racial hatred via white supremacist thinking reflective in Bermuda's colonial education. I, therefore, affirm that loving our blackness is our ontological resistance.

With respect to the epistemological implications of colonial education complexities, it is important to highlight my rationale for choosing to utilize an anticolonial discursive framework and indigenous knowledge epistemology and antiracist framework in my analysis. These respective discursive frameworks allow me to speak from an autobiographical voice while simultaneously utilizing artifacts, reports, newspapers, magazines, and books to engage in this discussion. Accordingly, an anticolonial discursive framework challenges the dominant paradigm and provides a critical lens for looking at the denial and erasure of black Bermudian identity. It also allows for a critical reading of colonial power relations that has been oppressive to specific groups of people.

With respect to Bermuda's education, an anticolonial framework acknowledges the role of the school in producing and privileging different knowledge forms by developing an awareness of the urgency for creating an educational system that is liberatory, empowering, reciprocal, and transformative. Moreover, the anticolonial perspective is grounded in indigenous ways of knowing and understanding of a spiritual sense of self and each other, an important component that is missing from the Bermudian education system. It further provides possible solutions for a holistic way of living and learning that is nonlinear and offers a form of cultural resistance (Wane, 2005, p. 29). In addition, anticolonialism departs from the notion of postcolonialism; this factor is of particular importance especially while Bermuda is still under colonial rule; albeit self-governed. Anticolonialism challenges the idea that the colonial encounter has ended by looking at what colonialism has done to us, (Bermudians) controlling our minds and education. Accordingly, an anticolonial discursive framework makes the invisible control visible.

In conjunction with anticolonial and indigenous knowledge epistemology, I employ an antiracist discursive framework to assist me in understanding how race, class, and gender influence teaching, learning, and educational administration, and how that understanding can help me to critically look at issues such as, students' engagement and disengagement from school (see Dei, 1996, p. 29, and 1997, p. 85); how identities are constructed by knowledge producers such as the education system, and how this construction has real consequences with respect to self-worth, life chances, and economic mobility. Moreover, I will look at how misrepresentation of Bermudian history can/does raise questions of identity and representation relevant to understanding how people make sense of the knowledge imparted to them in the school system. By utilizing an antiracist discursive framework issues of power relations are identified and challenged by looking at existing values, structures, and behaviours that continue to reproduce colonial violence within the education system. In this regard, antiracist discursive framework resists imposing and dominating knowledge by challenging colonial and imperial relationships that have been instrumental in rendering young black Bermudian youth as deficits. By placing black youth at the centre of analysis and focusing on their lived experiences, Bermudian educators can assist them in moving towards loving their blackness.

Before I begin this discussion, I believe it is important to locate myself and how I am positioned within this discussion. I locate myself in the Bermudian context. I also write from the standpoint of having the opportunity to distance myself both physically and mentally as I now reside in Toronto. This distancing has afforded me the space to look more critically at Bermuda in general and the education system in particular.

PERSONAL LOCATION

As I forge forward in this discussion I am aware of the complexity of interrogating Bermuda's educational system, especially, when going against a colonial system that has and continues to subjugate Bermudians through a racialized linear interpretation and representation of who Bermudians are. I have chosen my interest/learning objective in this paper due to three important factors: discovery of self, my commitment to my teenage son, and the scarcity of research conducted on this specific area in Bermuda. As a black Bermudian/Canadian woman I have come to realize the importance of revisiting my colonial past, I must look back and remember, critique, and analyze a system that has shaped me into a particular subject while robbing me of my identity, culture, and language. I have come to understand the importance of finding my own voice and the necessity of returning, of knowing my history, and anchoring myself to advance beyond my distorted colonial perception of self. As a mother, I have a responsibility to my son to impart the importance of knowing his Bermudian history that will help ground him in his identity, culture, and language, thereby providing him with a strong sense of belonging.

Similar to Hanohano (1999), my "purpose is not to replace the present educational system, but to introduce another perspective on how we may better relate to each other as human beings, to our Mother Earth, and to other creatures of this planet" (Hanohano, 1999, p. 2). The days of accepting the colonial educational system unquestionably need to cease. I would be remiss and equally complicit to discount what historical accounts have revealed without imparting this knowledge to my son and my Bermudian community. In my quest to decolonize my state of being, I have taken on the task of retracing histories in order to better understand myself and others. Dei stresses the importance of this undertaking when he stated that "identity is powerful in helping us understand not only ourselves, but our place in society and how we connect with each other as a way to understand our collective destinies" (Gismondi, 1999).

HISTORICAL OVERVIEW OF BERMUDA'S EDUCATION SYSTEM

Bermuda is Britain's oldest self-governing colony. Not only is Bermuda unique in its size of 21 square miles, the population composite of the island's 65,000 is unlike any other British colonial territory (present and past) except South Africa, with the majority of people being predominately black with a strikingly powerful white minority. Bermuda's recorded history is one of discovery, with no historical account of indigenous people prior to discovery. We had "no culture, no civilization, no long 'historical past' so it seemed the crossing of seas had erased traces of our identity (Fanon, 1967, p. 34). The fact that Bermuda is still colonized and is relatively small makes the effects of colonization more devastating, thus having a greater impact on the social, political, and geographical landscape. These factors undoubtedly have impinged upon the education system, albeit Bermuda has shifted from relying heavily on Britain for its educational reform to encompass a more American influence, nonetheless it is still Eurocentric in its ideology.

I often remind myself that I ought to think about the way in which Bermudians come to understand their experience with the fear of the unknown. A number of us took comfort in knowing that we are still connected to Britain, it provides a safety net, a superficial sense of belonging and acceptance of all that was/is espoused by Britain. For instance, I felt privilege to be afforded a colonial education, similar to Wane (2006), "I was only partially aware that there was much missing about my culture and my knowledge. As a researcher and scholar, I have come to know in greater depth the scope and meaning behind these absences" (pp. 88–89).

In 1663, the Bermuda Company [4] had three schoolhouses built for the primary purpose of training Indians from the mainland, New England, and Bermudians. Succeeding the Bermuda Company era there was a disinterest in education because Bermuda's leaders at the time were uneducated men who turned teaching over to the clergy. On 1 June 1725 Bishop George Berkeley solicited England for funding to set up a college, known as St. Paul College that would educate Americans and Indians to the Master of Arts level. "The college would not only educate the Indian, "savage Americans," but supply them with clothing, lodging, diet at the rate of 10 pound, per annum for each"; however, blacks and Indian enslaved were not included in this educational plan (Packwood, 1975, p. 99).

By 1825, the Church of England adopted a "regular system" that was religion based to direct blacks in their school. Near the end of the 18th century, Rev. Joshua Marsden, a Methodist began to educate poor and enslaved people. By 1832 the Methodist ministers had nine functioning Sunday schools staffed by 50 white and 16 black teachers. Attending were 283 enslaved children and 96 white children who were taught reading, writing, and the scriptures (Zuill, 1999, pp. 222–223). In the same year, a classical academy was opened, teaching Greek, Latin Classics, mathematics, and geography. The school comprised of 25 pupils, none of whom were blacks (Packwood, 1975, p. 99). The aforementioned synopsis clearly indicates that the way blacks were taught had not changed from 1663 to 1832. Blacks were still only taught to read, write and understand the Bible; academic learning was reserved only for white students.

In 1837, Chief Justice John Christie Esten proposed a radical educational plan, advocating that it was a moral obligation of white people to train children of the former enslaved. He argued that the lives of the sons and daughters of whites have been enriched by the fruit of enslaved labours; thus, educating them would be the least Europeans could do in return (Zuill, 1999, p. 224). Esten's radical reform and comment was nothing more than token reparation for exploiting enslaved labour.

In the years that followed Bermuda saw a succession of schools implemented. In 1839 the government granted the permission to educate blacks in the public school (ibid). By the end of the 19th century, Sandys Grammar School, Bermuda High School for Girls, Mount St. Agnes, Whitney Institute, and St. George's Grammar School opened as white schools funded by the neighbourhood. In the mid-1930s, there were only two secondary schools for black children, Berkeley Institute and Sandys Secondary School. By 1949 free primary education was introduced. In 1956 the Technical Institute was built as the first post-war school to be declared biracial by the government (Zuill, 1999, p. 227). In 1965, St. George Secondary School opened along with other secondary schools for the sole purpose of concentrating on vocational training and was not expected to produce college-entrance graduates. The government decided that Berkeley Institute, Saltus

Grammar School, and Warwick Academy would be responsible for preparing students for college entrance.

Despite Bermuda's historical records that have consistently indicated the marginalization of blacks, black educators still espouse white ideology that continues to place Bermudian society in a colonial cage. According to Fanon (1967), "the native intellectual has thrown himself greedily upon Western culture. Like adopted children who only stop investigating the new family framework at the moment when a minimum nucleus of security crystallizes in their psyche, the native intellectual will try to make European culture his own" (p. 218). Moreover, blacks have forgotten consciously or unconsciously that, "the colonizer never intended . . . to remake the colonized in his own image! He cannot allow such equation—it would destroy the principle of his privileges" (Memmi, 1965, p. 69). The current education system is designed to keep a certain level of unsuccessfulness because it's in the best interest of the dominant group to maintain the education and bureaucratic system in order to maintain individuals within a certain racialized, gendered, and classed position. Therefore, I contend that Bermudian educators cannot continue to ignore the impact of colonial education on Bermudian youths. Bermudians know, whether admittedly or not that the colonial invasion, lies, and subsequent manipulations have been the impetus behind black Bermudian youth's lack of self-esteem, disruption of sense of belonging, culture, and fragmented identity that was based upon colonialist imposition. As a result, Bermuda's education system has inadvertently constructed blackness in a violent and psychologically traumatizing way that has caused rejection and internalized hatred of blackness by failing to teach black existence via Bermudian culture and history. This failure has resulted in what Fanon (1967) called a "dependency complex" a reluctance to disentangle from the colonial web.

When blacks reaffirm their self-definition, whites are no longer able to maintain their hegemonic normalizing status. For instance, colonialism makes people what they are not by hiding the truth in order to sustain itself. Fanon spoke to colonialism untruths calling it "the lies of the colonial situation" (Fanon, 1965, p. 128). He further points out that in the colonial situation, " . . . colonialism is predicated only on force and fraud. Colonialism 'succeeds' thus to the extent its social relations of power remain invisible, so long as their presumed naturalism goes unchallenged" (Goldberg, 1996, p. 183). Accordingly, anticolonial, Indigenous knowledge epistemology and antiracist discursive frameworks provide a diverse spectrum of discourse that offer an alternative for one to remap their historical identity and account for lived experiences and reality. It also provides a means to contest, talk back and sometimes evade the risk of violence inherent in the process of reaffirming blackness.

The first step towards education liberation is to acknowledge that colonial education is fashioned in a way to make blacks believe that we are included, that we are one of them, British, on equal footing. As a result, we bought into the conspiracy of "school fascinating the soul" (wa Thiong'o, 1986, p. 9). This psychological imprisonment has produced two different outcomes: the continuous struggle of blacks to find themselves, their voice, and their place in a white-dominated world and their forced assimilation. Colonial education has served to rob us of our history by creating a pseudo representation of who we really are. Thus, blacks' worth and contribution to the world has been negated and falsified. Evidence of this negation and falsification can be seen in the textbooks. As wa Thiong'o (1986) so aptly states, "Language and literature [has taken] us further and further from ourselves, to other selves, from our world to other worlds" (p. 12). This psychosocial and political battle has been ongoing despite black people's resistance to forced assimilation into the dominant European world that still rejects us no matter how refined we have become. We are still considered unequal to our European oppressor (Eshleman & Smith, 199, p. 77).

The rejection Eshleman and Smith (1993) spoke of was conveyed in "Report of Royal Commission into the 1977 Disturbances—Bermuda," stating that "Black people were expected to know their place and be thankful for favours" (1977, p. 1). The report further stated that " . . . frustration of those who, having gained education and experience, were still not rewarded caused intolerance and rebellious attitudes" (1977, p. 3). Time has come to question the fate imposed upon us by the colonizer. The "most important area of domination was the mental universe of the colonised, the control, through culture, of how people perceived themselves and their relationship to the world" (wa Thiong'o, 1986, p. 16). By acknowledging our history through written and taught curriculum, we will begin to stake our rightful belonging in the world and, only then, will the process of mental freedom and liberation begin.

According to Wane (2006), this journey of returning to the past is necessary because it is through such a journey that we can understand the present in order to prepare for the future (p. 87). In other words, understanding our past is a necessary component of decolonizing the mind. Wane (2006) further encourages us to heighten our awareness by being cognizant of the "historical objectification that emerged as a central tool of social control, . . . hierarchies of difference [that] were the basis of colonial relations of ruling, . . . and of the violent consequences and psychic imposition of colonial education" (p. 88). Wane's (2006) concern is based on the understanding that the colonial education did not only facilitate the normalization of Western education but also actively left deep spiritual and mental scars, causing mental and physical enslavement (p. 88). If Wane's (2006) comment is anything to go by, then the education system in Bermuda cannot and should not be allowed to reproduce psychologically and spiritually injured learners. It is on these premises that I implore for a new education system in Bermuda that is based on Frantz Fanon's notion of the new humanism. According to Fanon (1963), "humanity is waiting for something from us other than such an imitation ... if we want humanity to advance a step further, if we want to bring it up to a different level than that which Europe has shown it, then we must invent and we must make discoveries" (p. 315). In other words, let us not reinvent Europe.

BLACKNESS/INFERIOR COMPLEX IN BERMUDA

In this section, I will discuss blackness and inferior complex as espoused by Fanon and how it applies to Bermuda's education system. Under "the fact of blackness" in *Black Skin, White Masks*, Frantz Fanon argues: "For several years certain laboratories have been trying to produce a serum for 'denegrification'; with all the earnestness in the world, laboratories have sterilized their test tubes, checked their scales, and embarked on researches that might make it possible for the miserable Negro to whiten himself and thus to throw off the burden of that corporal malediction" (1967, p. 111). A review of Fanon's statement indicates that perhaps, Fanon was speaking directly about Bermudian education. An education system, that borrows continuously from Eurocentric ways of knowing, moreover, a system whose definition of reform is renaming and reshuffling of old white ideology. Woodson's (1933) statement echoes my concerns that we need to hold Blacks responsible for following white ideology but we cannot hold them accountable for "the origination of this nonsense ..." (p. 60). Blacks have been so busy doing what they were told, that we have "borrowed the ideas of [our] traducers instead of delving into things and working out some thoughts of his own" (p. 61). The over-reliance on Eurocentric way of knowing taken up by Fanon (1967) and Woodson (1933) has been to Bermudian's detriment and subsequent "denegrification."

Writing under the theme "On National Culture," Frantz Fanon rightly observed in the *Wretched of the Earth* that: "Colonialism is not satisfied merely with holding a people in its grip and emptying the native's brain of all form and content. By a kind of perverted logic, it turns to the past of the oppressed people, and distorts, disfigures, and destroys it" (Fanon, 1963, p. 210). No place is Fanon's words more appropriate than the case of Bermuda. To date there have not been any historical accounts (either written or oral) that suggest the land was inhabited before the arrival of Europeans. What is intriguing and quite disturbing is the fact that early accounts, at least from the perspectives of the Europeans, suggested they discovered wild hogs, edible fruits and food on the Island (Smith, 1976). In their opinion, the items might have been left there by either the Portuguese or the Spanish in the previous century. There are several questions to be asked on this account: Could it be that the land was originally inhabited by indigenous people and the early Portuguese or Spanish sailors who first arrived on the Island killed all of them? Or could it be that the indigenous people were killed by those who came later and their presence was deliberately erased from the history books? The answers to these questions are almost impossible to find. Thus, the contemporary historical account of Bermuda has to rely on the one presented by the early Europeans.

There is no doubt that the education system in Bermuda was designed with the sole goal of whitening the black Bermudian. Consequently, there is a high level of inferiority complex residing within some black Bermudians. Black Bermudian educators consciously or unconsciously have been socialized into the white supremacists ideology that continues to perpetuate the colonial project with little or no room left for the critical interrogation of the erasure of Bermudian's culture, language, and history within the curricular. Fanon (1967) speaks more to the depth of this erasure and colonization in his words:

> *Every colonized people . . . every people in whose soul an inferiority complex has been created by the death and burial of its local cultural originality- finds itself face to face with the language of the civilizing nation; that is, with the culture of the mother country. The colonized is elevated above the jungle status in proportion to his adoption of the mother country's cultural standards. He becomes whiter as he renounces his blackness, his jungle. (p. 18)*

A large part of the population of Bermuda has not questioned their history or their limited control for fear of the unknown. A number of us took comfort in knowing that we are still connected to Britain, it provides a safety net, a superficial sense of belonging and acceptance of all that was/is espoused by Britain, particularly the education system. The only Bermuda history I recalled taught was how Bermuda was discovered in 1503 by a Spanish captain Juan de Bermudez. Dr. Lou Matthews, a former teacher of two local Bermuda high schools and one of the researchers of the Hopkins Report (*Review of Public Education in Bermuda*), inadvertently touches on the issue of history when he expressed his sense of disquietedness of the colonial education system in Bermuda stating that "our national mindset has been to borrow 'things' from other places, which in and of itself isn't bad, it just doesn't automatically lead to excellent and innovative practice. . . . one of the problems was that over the years Bermuda has taken on methods from abroad but not incorporated them with the strength of Bermudian culture" (O'Kelly-Lynch, 2007). I agree with Matthews's (2007) concern in part, however, my concern is that Bermuda has continuously borrowed from Eurocentric educational systems that have disenfranchised black Bermudian people from their culture, language, and history.

Purpel (1989) rightly points out that "the crisis in education is a moral and spiritual crisis . . . the social and other ills that beset our cities and communities call for a new paradigm" (Hanohano, 1999, p. 207). Education is commonly viewed as a preparation for life, it allegedly teaches students survival knowledge that will sustain them in society, yet the same education is instrumental in their disconnectedness. Makris (2003) extends Purpel's (1989) claim to include the intellectuals who are in the position to effect change within the educational system. Makris (2003) emphasizes that the commonly accepted belief of postcolonial studies is the British educational system is a double-edged sword. It provides a level of "respect and admiration for British values and culture that were essential for the smooth maintenance of a vast overseas empire" while simultaneously providing "Britain's colonies with small group of native intellectuals with the knowledge and confidence to challenge British colonial policies" that will eventually assist in the de-colonization of their countries (Makris, 2003, p. 1). The question I must ask here is: Why are Bermudian educators, and more specifically the Ministry of Education, reluctant to take responsibility for their complicity in not delivering an educational system that is transformative, liberating, reciprocal and representative of Bermudian identity and culture? I postulate that the reason for their complicity is a denial of their blackness.

The fact of blackness as it is played out in Bermuda has similar psychological effects to Fanon's account of Algeria's colonization, both were insidious, albeit French colonialism was about assimilation of "Natives," and British colonialism sought to imbue "Natives" with British values, hence, mimicry. Both produced and fostered an inferior complex. This inferior complex has had a direct effect on Bermuda's education system as educators continue to reproduce domestication of education that perpetuates hegemonic practices of the colonizer. Matthews highlights the problem claiming that Bermuda requires "a paradigm shift in teaching ... in short, changes in the culture of teaching have not kept apace of modern day expectations for teaching and learning" (O'Kelly-Lynch, 2007). I agree with Matthews that a shift in teaching is required however, the latest teaching methods he was alluding to are unclear. But, as a consideration for Bermuda's teaching methods, educators can glean from the black-focused school proposal. Although Dei's (2005) proposed solutions are focused on Canada, Bermuda can also benefit. He stated that:

> *black-focused school is organized around communal principles and non-hierarchical structures. In making the totality of black-lived experience relevant to all parts of the curriculum, the school would foster the social, physical, spiritual, and academic development of students. In breaking down the separation between the formal school and the wider community, incorporating the family/home and the workplace, the school offers new and creative ways of thinking about knowledge, and then engaging students to use this knowledge to make positive social changes.(Dei [quoted and responding to Cahis], 2005; and see also Dei, 1997, p. 144)*

Dei also addressed the previously raised issue of the discovery story, asserting that "the school wouldn't talk about history in terms of enslavement or who discovered A or B ... it would teach about history in terms of its totality and not sweep things under the carpet." (Robinson, 2007, and see also Dei, 2005, p. 7). Bermudian educators could benefit from Dei's alternative way of teaching history—a history that is not linear, riddled with misrepresentations, and violence and erasure of identity.

POLITICS OF IDENTITY: DIALECTIC OF EXPERIENCE

Fanon (1967) noted that "ontology—once it is finally admitted as leaving existence by the wayside—does not permit us to understand the being of the black man. For not only must the black man be black; he must be black in relation to the white man. ... The black man has no ontological resistance in the eyes of the white man" (p. 110). The production of this identity in which the black man (and by extension black woman) becomes situated occurs through the media, colonial discourse, constant surveillance, and their subsequent punishment. For example, in Bermuda's *Show off* Magazine, R. Andre Bassett talked about being a black male living in the 21st century, and how he was acutely aware of being "ignored, labelled and set upon on a daily basis." He proclaimed that it was:

> not so much for any activity that [he is] involved in, but for the mere sake of being born a Black male. Rapist, drug-dealer, womanizer, thief and dead-beat dad are just some of the tags [he is] stuck with. ... As long as [he had] skin color that is a few shades darker than that of the average Caucasian, in the eyes of many White people [he has] no chance of nor [is he] capable of being a positive and productive citizen of this country. (Bassett, 2007)

According, to Bassett (2007), and I concur, society has labeled most young black men as dangerous in need of constant surveillance, discipline, and punishment. Bassett continues by saying that despite all the negative labels:

> so many other optimistic Black males, who have received advice and guidance, do not live "down" to those names. Instead, conscious decisions are made daily to lead as constructive a life as possible. And these are the great majority of Black males. No, not everyone is a rocket scientist or Nobel Peace prize recipient but there are so many young and not-so-young Black tradesmen, businessmen and educators who make a positive difference every day. (Bassett, 2007)

Bassett emphasizes that there is an invisible factor at play, the media (electronic, print, Internet) that does not report on the good black men do. Instead, they focus on the minority of those black males who make decisions that lead to criminal behaviour. For example, Bassett exclaims "Just look at the headlines of the daily and bi-weekly tabloids. Those headlines lead to constant discussion among Whites and some Blacks that further cements in their minds that Black males are worthless human beings" (Bassett, 2007).

In addition to Bassett's (2007) comments, Bermuda's *Royal Gazette* newspaper dated 7 February 2007 stated that "two-thirds of young men and more than half of young women had inadequate literacy skills to excel in life, according to a survey of Bermudians aged 16 to 25" (Strangeways, 2007a). These statistics revealed that the "Island lacked the skills to fully function in a knowledge-based society" and that students were likely to struggle when learning new tasks" (Strangeways, 2007a). Chief Statistician Valerie Robinson James stated that despite the findings of the statistics, "the results did not mean young Bermudians were illiterate or not productive in society" (Strangeways, 2007a). Even though statistical results are open to interpretation, the role of the "objective" social sciences is in creating statistics as truth. Statistics have a "perceived" legitimacy not only because they come from authorities but also because they reinforce statements that certain youth are problems specifically black male youth.

Young black Bermudian males are being depicted as casualties of failing institutions: the family, the education system, the economy, the political, security, and religious systems that are fundamental to their development. In May 2007, a *Review of Public Education in Bermuda: Summary of Findings and Recommendations* was conducted. The Report was a collaborative effort of four foreign and two local researchers wherein it was stated: that the Ministry lacked strategy, vision, and skills, exercised a lot of control but little leadership, it was secretive and operated through direction, it stifled initiatives suggested by schools and its own education officers. Last but not least, the Ministry urgently needs a radical overhaul together with the appointment of exceptional leadership, and first rate management in order to improve public education (Hopkins et al., 2007, p. 3). The report's proposed changes consisted of a closer curriculum link between schools or groups of schools, which would allow for an easier transition into the local college.

With respect to the standards of achievement, the report confirmed the public's perception that standards in Bermuda's schools are very low. Other underlined observations indicated that students in a great majority of preschools and primary schools achieved at least satisfactory standards. Students who started out slow and made insufficient progress generally attained inadequate standards by the end of middle school, which contributed to low graduation rates. By the end of schooling these low standards compared unfavourably to private schools in Bermuda and public education in England and the United States (Hopkins et al., 2007, p. 2). At this juncture, it is imperative to ask ourselves how much control we have over shaping our own identities and our education system. Are we more certain about our identities now than in the past or are we still lost? Is it possible to consider a reimagining of a new humanism that incorporates our history infused with new vision, empowerment, and rebuilding of sense of self? This new humanism, new beginning, is continuous, ever evolving, it includes an understanding of people who are different; it is free from labels, and most of all offers hope, and a loving of blackness.

LOVING BLACKNESS AS A TOOL OF DECOLONIZATION: TOWARDS FANON'S NEW HUMANISM

We have to change our own mind.. We've got to change our own minds about each other. We have to see each other with new eyes. We have to come together with warmth.
—Malcolm X

In order to begin the process of decolonization and move forward towards a new humanism and loving blackness, we need to decolonize our minds thus enabling us to start the process of reclaiming, healing and gaining our total liberation, our sense of self. Loving our blackness in its complexities, tensions, and ambiguities is the first step of decolonization by examining the way in which colonization has instilled and reinforced internalized racial hatred via white supremacist thinking that is saturated within Bermuda's education system. Loving our blackness is our ontological resistance, our terms of engagement; therefore, "[l]et us waste no time in sterile litanies and nauseating mimicry" (Fanon, 1963, p. 311). Let us not reinvent Europe. "European spirit has strange roots" (Fanon, 1963, p. 313). In other words, we cannot leave the restoration of our humanity to Europe. According to Freire (1970), "this struggle is possible only because dehumanization, although a concrete historical fact, is *not* a given destiny but the result of an unjust order that engenders violence in the oppressor, which in turn dehumanizes the oppressed" (Freire, 1970, p. 44). Freire (1970) supports and shares Fanon's (1963) caution to us, stating that in our struggle to dispel the notion of not being fully human and regaining our humanity we should not become the oppressor but rather the restorers of humanity of both, the oppressor and oppressed. This task of the restorer is the great humanistic and historical task of the oppressed to liberate themselves and their oppressor as well (Freire, 1970, p. 44). Decolonization is invariably the search for new humanism. Decolonizing the mind is synonymous with loving blackness, a political process, a struggle to redefine ourselves; it is a form of resistance to white domination. In our search for a new humanism we need to reclaim and rewrite our history, failing to do so we relinquish our autonomy. As hooks (1992) eloquently points out, "we are always in the process of both remembering the past even as we create new ways to imagine and make the future" (p. 5). wa Thiong'o (1986) adds to hooks's (1992) statement by emphasizing the importance of creating new ways to imagine by adding that "to control a people's culture is to control their tools of self-definition in relationship to others" (p. 16).

Accordingly, it is essential for black Bermudians to take control of their self-definition and move towards a new humanism. The fact that Bermuda has a predominantly black population does not exclude Bermudian educators from looking at how black students are marginalized and, how "learning, for a colonial child, became a cerebral activity and not an emotionally felt experience" (wa Thiong'o, 1986, p. 17). Therefore, it is imperative that Bermudian educators create a context within the education system where students can love blackness as a worthy standpoint for bonding. As a means of loving our blackness, hooks (2000) proposes that we " . . . bring love ethic to every dimension of our lives . . ." (p. 87). She further believes and agrees with Fanon (1963) that we need to do things differently. I believe that hooks's (2000) concept of love ethic is a viable solution and a positive move towards a new humanism.

The love ethics can transform our lives by offering blacks a different set of values to incorporate into our lives. Although hooks (2000) looks at love ethics in terms of family and friends her concept can be extended to Bermuda's education system and serve as an expanded articulation of Fanon's (1967) statement of "understanding and love amongst coloured brothers" (p. 7). Bermudian educators can incorporate love ethics into their course curriculum and liberatory pedagogy. hooks (2000) further states that by embracing a love ethic we can incorporate all the dimensions of love— "care, commitment, trust, responsibility, respect, and knowledge of love—in our everyday lives" (hooks, 2000, p. 94). She also points out that "there is a gap between the values citizens claim to hold and their willingness to do the work of connecting thought and action, theory and practice to realize these values and thus create a more just society" (hooks, 2000, p. 90). Valenzuela (1999) adds to hooks's (2000) love ethics as a possible manifestation of Fanon's (1963) proposed new humanism with her concept of "politics of caring." She argues that students reflect their noncaring attitude towards school and learning similarly to the non-caring attitude teachers' exhibit towards them. Despite their noncaring attitude, teachers still expect student to care about schooling and participate in a unilateral exchange of knowledge that is devoid of caring and minus a reciprocal relationship between teacher and student (Valenzuela, 1999, p. 63).

Freire (1970) also addresses the issue of unilateral exchange in *Pedagogy of the Oppressed* when he stressed the importance of dialogue between teacher and student, where both the student and the teacher can learn simultaneously from each other (p. 80). Freire (1970) further states that only through communication can human life hold any meaning, for instance, the "teacher's thinking is authenticated only by the authenticity of the student's thinking;" one cannot exist without the other (Freire, 1970, p. 77). The teacher and the student teach and learn simultaneously, both learn, question, reflect, and participate in meaning making. In this regard, education becomes an experience capable of naming or using a vocabulary that dismantles perceived notions and steers students towards more innovative thinking. Quick judgement immediately closes the door of possibility for a more relational and compassionate pedagogy previously articulated in hooks's (2000) love ethics and Valenzuela's (1999) politics of caring. Wane (2006), Dei (2005), hooks (2000), Valenzuela (1999), wa Thiong'o (1986), and Fanon (1967 and 1963), all agree the significance of individual histories students and teachers bring to their classroom encounters can influence the chances for successful relationship building. Teachers need to be more concerned with the overall well-being of their students and should endeavour to provide an environment that will allow them to flourish both personally and academically.

Loving our blackness is our political resistance, our decolonization and a beginning of our new humanism that will enable us to look critically at Bermuda's education system. In the words of Fanon (1967), "I, the [woman] of color, want only this: That the tool never possess the man or woman. That the enslavement of man by man cease forever. . . . That it be possible for me to discover and to love man, wherever he may be" (Fanon, 1967, p. 231).

NOTES

1. In the Bermudian context, it is a redefining and reclaiming of one's racial identity as a reality to oppositional force.
2. Fanon's notion of humanism I believe is an "understanding and love among mankind ... (.7)..." coupled with "black man ['s] [ability] to free himself from arsenal of complexes that has been developed by the colonial environment" (30). And "...Always [be] a man who questions!" (232).
3. Curriculum in this context is being defined as pedagogy, rules, social organization and notion of culture. Curriculum as site of change needs to use critical lens to empower the learner to move beyond Eurocentric way of knowing.
4. Virginia Company, and then the Bermuda Company, ran the islands like a fiefdom. This wearied the settlers so much they sued to have the company's charter rescinded, and in 1684 Bermuda became a British crown colony.

REFERENCES

Bassett, R. A. 2007. August. The shade of race. In the *Showoff*. [Retrieved from local magazine published in Bermuda.]

Burchall, L. 2007. February 2. Education system is creating a mass of economic misfits. *Bermuda Sun*. [Retrieved from local newspaper published in Bermuda.]

Cahis, C. 2005. March 1. *Race or Class*: Addressing "black-focused" school in Toronto. Retrieved 29 February 2008, from http://www.marxist.ca/index2.php?option=com_content&do_pdf=1&id=94.

Dei, G. 1996. *AntiRacism Education Theory and Practice*. Halifax: Fernwood.

Dei, G. J. S., J. Mazzuca, E. McIsaac, and J. Zine. 1997. *Reconstructing "Dropout": A Critical Ethnography of the Dynamics of Black Students' Disengagement from School*. Toronto: University of Toronto Press Incorporated.

Dei, G. 2005. Critical Issues in Anti-racist Research Methodologies: An Introduction. In G. J. S. Dei and G. S. Johal (eds.), *Critical Issues in Anti-Racist Research Methodologies* (p. 7). New York: Peter Lang.

Dei, G. J. S., and A. Kempf (eds,) 2006. *Anti-colonialism and Education: The Politics of Resistance*. Rotterdam: Sense Publishers.

Eshleman, C., and A. Smith, (2006). *Notebook of a Return to the Native Land*. Los Angeles: University of California Press.

Fanon, F. 1963. *The Wretched of the Earth*. Grove Press. New York.

Fanon, F. 1965. *A Dying Colonialism*. Grove Press. New York.

Fanon, F. 1967. *Black Skin, White Masks*. Grove Press. New York.

Freire, P. 1970. *Pedagogy of the Oppressed*. New York: The Continuum International Publishing Group Inc.

Gismondi, M. 1999. *Aurora Online with Geroge Sefa Dei*. Retrieved 29 April 2003 from http://aurora.icaap.org/index.php/aurora/article/view/22/33.

Goldberg, D. T. 1996. In/Visibility and Super/Vision: Fanon on Race, Veils, and Discourses of Resistance. In Lewis R. Gordon, T. Denean Sharpley-Whiting and Renee T. White, (eds.), *Fanon: A Critical Reader*. Oxford: Blackwell Critical Reader Series. pp. 179–202.

Hanohano, P. 1999. The Spiritual Imperative of Native Epistemology: Restoring Harmony and Balance to Education. *Canadian Journal of Native Education*, 23 (2), 206–217.

hooks, b. 1992. *Black Looks: Race and Representations*. Boston: South End Press.

hooks, b. 2000. *All about Love: New visions*. New York: William Morrow and Company, Inc.

Hopkins, D., Matthews, P., Matthews, L., Woods-Smith, R., Olajide, F., & Smith, P. 2007. *Review of Public Education in Bermuda: Summary of Findings and Recommendations*. London: Institute of Education, University of London.

Makris, P. 2003. Beyond the Classic: Legacies of Colonial Education In C. L. R. James and Derek Walcott. *Revista/Review Interamericana*, 31 (1–4), 1–17.

Memmi, A. 1965. *The Colonizer and the Colonized*. Boston: Beacon Press.

O'Kelly-Lynch, R. 2007, May 8. Public education has turned into a political football, says expert. *Royal Gazette*, pp. 1–3.

Packwood Outerbridge, C. 1975. *Chained on the Rock*. New York: Eliseo Torres & Sons.

Purpel, D. E. 1989. The Morale and Spiritual Crisis in Education: A Curriculum for Justice and Compassion in Education. Grandy, MA: Bergin & Garvey.

Smith, J. E. 1976. *Slavery in Bermuda*. New York. Vantage Press.

Strangeways, S. 2007. May 4. Premier Brown reveals the education review's ten recommendations for a "rapid raising of standards": Education 's failing grade. *Royal Gazette*, p. 1.

Valenzuela, A. 1999. Subtractive Schooling U.S.-Mexican Youth and the Politics of Caring. Albany: State University of New York Press.

Wane, N. 2005. African Indigenous Knowledge: Claiming, Writing, Storing, and Sharing The Discourse. *Journal of Thought*. San Francisco: Summer 2005; 40, 2; ProQuest Education Journals pp. 27

Wane, N. 2006. Is Decolonization Possible? In *Anti-Colonialism and Education: the Politics of Resistance*, edited by G. J. S. Dei and A. Kempf (eds,) 2006. *Anticolonialism and Education: The Politics of Resistance*. Rotterdam: Sense Publishers.

wa Thiong'o, N. 1986. Decolonising the Mind. The Politics of Language in African Literature. Nairobi: Heinemann Kenya.

Woodson, C. G. 1992. *The Mis-Education of the Negro*. Hampton, VA: United Bothers & Sisters Graphic & Printing.

Zuill, W. S. 1999. *The Story of Bermuda and Her People*. Oxford: Macmillan Publishers Limited.

CHAPTER SIX

Reading Fanon in "Homosexual Territory"
Towards the Queering of a Queer Pedagogy

RORY CRATH

A rainbow flag, the now ubiquitous symbol of LGBTQ[1] pride and community activism, stretches along the entire length of the main classroom wall of Toronto's Triangle School, "Canada's only high school program for LGBTQ youth" (Triangle Mission Statement, 2007). The size of the flag, together with its place of prominence in the classroom, speaks to the way in which this space can and should be read as part of a wider, nonlocally specific globalised movement: an imagined panhistorical, pancultural collectivity of allies and identifying members, who struggle to disrupt heteronormativity by declaring presence and creating spaces free from heterosexist, transphobic, and homophobic violence.

    I would like to take a step into the Triangle Program to query to what extent this institutional/pedagogical space, one that presumes a level of freedom and transgression, and is viewed currently by a number of Ontario Secondary School Boards as source of inspiration for "good practice," may function at times as a mechanism for reproducing discourses and practices that pathologise or normalize different subjectivities and different lives. In other words, I wish to question the way in which difference, and specifically racialised differences, is not only imagined and practiced discursively and materially within the space of the Triangle School Program, but how these spatialised politics might function to enable or dis-enable the movement of racialised/nonracialised youth (and teachers) in relationship to themselves and others, and in what directions. I will argue that these questions have direct relevance for the ways in which schools are able to open up space for students, teachers, caregivers and community members that are free from racist, classist, homophobic, and transphobic violence. To assist me in this work, I will engage in a selective reading of Frantz Fanon's writings, with an eye to the critical explorations emanating from "Queers of Colour." Specifically, Fanon's insights into the unconscious mechanisms of racism and colonialism and his deliberations over the decolonization process (as a site of violence and transformation) I would suggest, are not only essential to this project but any project that seeks to initiate fundamental change within schooling and educational environments.

Before proceeding, and to mimic the process of "coming out" (a phrase often deployed in Western sexualities discourse), I would like to make clear my use of specific terminology, my intentions in writing this paper, and, importantly, what this paper will not be about. I would also like to make clear my own personal investments and subjective positioning, which orients me in certain directions and not in others.

A NOTE ON TERMINOLOGY

In this chapter, I will be positioning the word queer (as a site of desire and as a form of activist intervention) beside and against the more liberally inclined acronym LGBTQ, a categorical device used to signal the inclusion of a range of sexual desires and gender expressions that make reference to the specific subjectivity of individuals ("I am gay," "I am a lesbian" "I am transgender"). In other words, the individual initials within LGBTQ suggest identity categories that are stable, fixed and stand in direct relationship to a set of Eurocentric hierarchically organized binary categories that organize human subjectivity (homosexual/heterosexual; female/male). To be "gay" or any other identity category, "purports to fully describe those it seeks to represent" (Butler, 1993, p. 3)—a mind-set, a sensibility, and a "matching between chromosomal sex, gender and sexual desire" (Jagose, 1996, p. 3). In and of themselves, identity categories suggest nothing of the politics that will be embraced or of the level of critique that will be levied against normative organizational systems of sex and gender. The term "queer," as I use it here in a reclaimed sense,[2] resists the apolitical stance of this model of stable categorizations, not only in terms of how desire and gender are organized, but also in the way queerness acts as a site of contingency, metaphor, and critique in its relationship to heterosexuality and gender conformity. "Queer" can thus be thought of as a radical theoretical device to critique the normalizing technologies of the state and other social institutions that are mobilized to name and regulate sexual and gendered subjects. As Eng argues, in relationship to the historic origins of the term:

> Given its commitment to interrogating the social processes that not only produced and recognized but also normalized and sustained identity, the political promise of the term resided specifically in its broad critique of multiple social antagonisms, including race, gender, class, nationality, and religion, in addition to sexuality. (Eng et al., 2005, p. 1)

In this chapter, I will employ the two categories strategically to signal the type of politics in operation at that particular and respective site.

MY INTENTIONS

I see this chapter as having two overlapping aspirations: the first is to think about the ways in which the writings of Frantz Fanon might inspire a rethinking of how issues and experiences of sexuality and gender variance are understood and practiced within the classroom space—a decolonization to use Fanon's terminology—that would involve (1) the exposure and dismantling of colonialist mechanisms that operationalise universalizing Western sexual, gendered, and cultural norms and (2) dares to think at the limits of what these engagements might be like once the work of disengagement has begun. To this first end, the Triangle Program will be employed as a test site for these theoretical explorations. The second aspiration is to contribute to both a growing body of literature—what Eng, Halberstam, and Munoz (2005) refer to as "a renewed queer studies"—and a growing body of queer activism in Toronto and elsewhere, seeking to re-queer queer space by interrogating the ways in which queer or LGBTQ practices might be contingently engaged or complicit with "dominant formations" of whiteness and normative sexuality and gender (Puar, 2005). In this sense, given that the Triangle Program exists on the cutting edge of pedagogical practice, such attempts at re-queering (or "decolonizing") can only help us as educators move in directions that open up, rather than foreclose (or at worse, disavow), possibilities for radical educational change. I am hoping that my appreciation for what the school has accomplished to date and my gratitude to the teachers at the school who provided written material and generously answered my questions will be read as self evident. Finally, I urge that this chapter not be read as a definitive critique but as a catalyst for dialogue about inclusive and expansive pedagogy.

I also feel it is important to recognize what I would argue are the limitations of this chapter. First, the scope is narrowly focused on my reading of the Triangle Program's institutional surfaces: how the program frames itself publicly and discursively (through its mission statement and Web site); how the space of the classroom is visually organized and oriented; and the pedagogical orientation of curriculum, as gleaned from a brief interview with one of Triangle's teachers, written correspondence from another teacher, and reading from print material offered. Second, and as a qualifier to the first limitation, I have not devoted sufficient time to allow for the institutional voice of the program to display itself in its fullness (and, I imagine, complexity). I have not sat in on classes, I did not engage in a series of formal interviews with the teachers, nor have I had access to the full curriculum offered in the program. My reading must, therefore, be viewed as impressionistic and exploratory, but also, hopefully, not wholly un-insightful. Finally, and perhaps most important, by adhering exclusively to a reading of institutional surfaces, what I am not offering is a window into the myriad of ways in which the students themselves (and teachers) make accommodations to, resist, and, perhaps, resignify, the discursive and material frames that they inhabit at the Triangle Program. In other words, by occluding youth voices and experiences, and by not offering a comprehensive review of curriculum, I run the serious risk of representing or reposting a story of dominance and normalization, where that story may well be shot through with significant holes or might even be eclipsed in moments of transgression or reclamation.

Finally, I wish to position myself within the writing. My investment in this project stems from a multiplicity of places: my ongoing commitment to queer, antipoverty, antiwar/imperialist activism initiated at local levels; almost two decades of experience working with street-involved, queer, and trans-identifying youth and inner-city racialised youth in Toronto and Los Angeles during which I have been challenged to rethink my understanding of the effects of, and resistances to, the mix of racialization, poverty, and heterosexist normativity; along with my own subjectivity as a queer man with mixed racial heritage (European, Aboriginal), although both are most often/sometimes invisible because of my markings of whiteness and presentation of my gendered self. Because I identify with queer spaces as a type of home (although tangentially, at times, and with a sense of discomfort, anger, alienation, and irony at others), I see this chapter as being part of the necessary "homework" (Visweswaran, 1997, cited in Kunstman, 2008) that comes with the territory of expanding understandings of belonging and citizenship (Kunstman, 2008). Moreover, although I am not a teacher at the high school level, I have taught and continue to teach at the postsecondary level in Social Work, and am, thus, forever curious about how to co-create pedagogical environments in which fields of normativity are displaced and replaced in creative ways. I am also fully aware that to experience and learn from critique is hard and often painful. And it can be pleasurable too! Finally, I am unequivocally supportive of the Toronto District School Board's initiatives in creating alternative educational spaces for students who have experiences with colonialism (Toronto's First Nation's School); racism/colonialism (the soon-to-be-initiated black-centric school) and heterosexism/homophobia/transphobia (the Triangle Program) in the "mainstream" school system and wider spheres, and who have the ability/desire to be schooled in less violent spaces.

READING FANON IN "HOMOSEXUAL TERRITORY"

Readers familiar with footnote 44[3] in *Black Skin, White Masks*, together with scholarly works criticizing Fanon for his failure to engage with issues of sexuality (Mercer, 1996; Pellegrini, 1997) might find a paper that draws inspiration from Frantz Fanon's insights as a vehicle for re-queering LGBTQ space, surprising, if not a bit queer. I would argue, however, that Fanon's attempts to write at the junction of psychoanalytic theory and anticolonial/imperial politics (Fuss, 1994) resulted in a number of critical contributions that are directly relevant to my current attempts at diagnosing the following problematics: in what ways are the generative properties of whiteness and normativised Eurocentric understandings of sexuality and gender actively at work in the space of Triangle; and, if present, what effects might these "colonizing" mechanisms have on both formations of subjectivity and identification of differently racialised students enrolled in the program? Moreover, I would argue that Fanon's prescriptive thoughts on the decolonization process in spaces that have experienced the violence of colonialist neuroticism and crisis might prove useful in allowing us to re-image a queer pedagogy that is attentive to the realities and potentials of difference. What follows in this section is an examination of Fanon's productive reading of the construction and operation of "psychical alterity" as a "formulation" of colonialist economics and politics (Fuss, 1994). This will be followed by a brief sketching of Fanon's "prescription" for the decolonization process. I will then take up these reflections to enable a reading of the programming of Triangle. Finally, I will reintroduce Fanon towards the conclusion of the paper, or, in what might more precisely be called the reconstructive section, of my reflections.

In her reading of Fanon's treatment of the embodiment of difference, Teresa de Lauretis notes that there is a difference between the concept of "identity" and that of "identification." For de Lauretis, identity signals an assimilation of an individual into a socially regulated, normativised subject position marked by class, gender, nationhood, etc. (e.g., "I am Aboriginal"; "I am Canadian"). Identification, on the other hand—and this is what Fanon was concerned with—suggests a journey that is shaped by both concerns about being (the quest of ontology—"who am I?") and knowledge about who one is (epistemological concerns—"what am I and in relation to whom?" (de Lauretis, 2002, p. 54). Although these are properly questions of psychoanalysis, Fanon is intent on grounding them in the materiality of a space that lies at the juncture between the particularities of an individual's own psychical and embodied formation and the socio cultural and historical properties that are inherited by, and ground, the individual. As de Lauretis suggests, "Fanon's sociogeny identifies the place of culture in the individual psyche more precisely, by articulating constructions of subject, difference, and otherness that are specific to a given social and cultural formation" (p. 55).

If colonialism operates within the logic of hierarchicalized difference (and specifically the positioning of subjects as inferiour/superior, subject/other),[4] we might ask two interrelated questions: first, according to this logic, or what Fanon insightfully calls the "psychopathology of colonialism," what are the effects of the construction of racialised alterity (materially, psychically, in terms of power); and, second, how it is that individuals take up their positions of difference (the process of "identification") within the spaces of colonialism?

PROCESSES OF IDENTIFICATION WITHIN THE COLONIAL ENCOUNTER

Although the postcolonial writer Homi Bhabha (1986) argues that this space of inferring "inferior positionalities" occurs at the level of cognition, other writers such as Hall (1996), de Lauretis (2002), and Martin Alcoff (2001) suggest that this drive to otherness is also, and, perhaps most important, spatially located in the body. For these authors, difference is always an embodied experience. Fanon refers to this spatial process as "epidermalization," in which race, as a discursive, cultural, and economic practice (and, most emphatically, not one grounded in genetics or the physiognomy of the subject) is inscribed onto the skin of the subject deemed black (to paraphrase Hall, 1996, p. 16), a process that confers what Fanon calls an "alternative 'corporeal schema' (Hall, 1996, p. 16): "Below the corporeal schema I had sketched a historico-racial schema…woven…out of a thousand details, anecdotes, stories" (Fanon, quoted in Hall, 1996, p. 16).

"Corporeal schema" for Fanon (borrowing from and reworking Freud) is a mental projection of the body's limits (internal/external) onto the surface of the body that proceeds "in a slow composition of my self as a body in the middle of a spatial and temporal world […] a definitive structuring of the self and the world—definitive because it creates a real dialectic between my body and the world" (Fanon, quoted in de Lauretis, 2002, p. 56). Fanon understands that the phenomenological body (the phenomenal, corporeal schema) is a universalist promise of Humanism—that the body's ability to move, to extend expansively outwards, permits or is implicated in the project of self-realization. And yet, within the logic of colonialism, the difference that is ascribed to raced bodies renders these bodies out of place and immobile in spaces inscribed by universality and privilege of movement (Ahmed, 2007). As Fanon suggests, "I thought that what I had in hand was to construct a physiological self, to balance space, to localize sensations, and here I was called on for more" (p. 111). This "more," de Lauretis interprets, is the effect of the materiality and discursivity of racism; the mapping of an "epidermal," an alternative "corporeal schema"; a deluge of images about blackness that are fixed by the white gaze "onto the skin of the racialised black body in the sense in which a chemical solution is fixed by a dye" (Fanon, quoted in de Lauretis, 2002, p. 57). What transpires is a cognitive/physical inchoateness of perception about, and experience of, one's own body in the presence of whiteness. The phenomenal body schema is called into question, "burdened and thrown into disarray" (Fanon, quoted in de Lauretis, 2002, p. 57) by the presence of the projected epidermal schema. As de Lauretis argues:

> *In the black subject's lived experience, then, the displacement of the corporeal schema by the racial epidermal schema causes the body-ego to be continually fractured, time and again denied and re-asserted, in a traumatic, ongoing process of dislocation. (de Lauretis, 2002, p. 58)*

What results from this experience of "disjoining or disidentification" from one's own body self is a racialised self that not only splits discursively (consisting of both an imagined "constructed racist blackness" and an imagined stereotypical whiteness—the white as superior, heroic to which one is meant to aspire) but also splits as a lived, embodied experiencing self as well. For Fanon, then, splitting for the racialised person takes place at both a psychical and an embodied level—two bodily schemas and two embodied personas of racialised stereotyping of white and black (de Lauretis, 2002).

To summarize, the process of colonized identification—the process of epidermalization and the effect of inhabiting two conflicting corporeal schemas—constructs the racialised body both materially and discursively, and as Martin Alcoff and de Lauretis identify, is reinstated or reconstituted at the level of the body. Thus, the body is both discursively imagined and provides a material ground upon which racism is manifested and importantly, resisted. Racism is experienced as real and reproducible through daily interactions. And racism can be countered by accessing a knowing that arises in moments of interaction (de Lauretis, 2002).

De Lauretis argues that it is the imperative of being "excess of body," of being irreducible to the materiality of one's own body, that has resonance also in the lives of people rendered other to heteronormative economies of sex and gender (58). Queer bodies, trans bodies are understood as perverse, excessive, deviant, defective, in the projected gaze of heteronormativity. Indeed, it is the very act of fixation of subjectivity and identification to a projected physiognomy that ensures the reproduction of gender and sexual object choice normativity. Of course, de Lauretis is careful not to conflate the experiences that result from the psycho-pathological impulses of each respective economy (racism and heteronormativity). Her reading here allows us to see how Fanon's insights into the effects of "epidermalization" for the black body, and the resulting dislocation of the subject's bodily ego, may be productively utilized in thinking about queer bodies and trans bodies which are deemed out of place in the spaces of heteronormativity.

THE EFFECTS OF THE CONSTRUCTION OF RACIALISED ALTERITY

On one level, then, Fanon argues that within the psychopathological economy of colonialism, racial othering is a process of subjection projected onto the black (racialised) body, "for not only must the black man be black; he must also be black in relation to the white man" (Fanon, 1967, p. 110, quoted in Fuss, 1994). It is the black, racialised body under the colonialist system of representation that is rendered racialised other, the recipient of a phobic projection by the colonialist subject of all that is despised, disavowed ("licentiousness, orgiastic desire repressed within the white soul" (Fanon, 1967, p. 61; Fuss, 1994). According to this logic of the psychical schema of the colonizer, the black body, perceived "on the level of the body image," is deemed the "not self" of the white; it is the racialised body that is intended to bare the weight of colonialist fear, self-loathing, and repressed fantasy. As Fanon argues, "the real other for the white man is and will continue to be the black man" (1967, p. 161).

Fuss suggests that an alternative reading of Fanon's thoughts on the process of racialised alterity reveals a more insidious, and perhaps more psychically tortuous process at work within the colonial schema of power and violence. Indeed, a second reading questions whether racialised others can even be thought to constitute subjects in the first instance, a positioning that is guaranteed in the first reading—a fractured, insufficient subject, but a subject that is nevertheless understood to be capable of aspiring to sameness. Fanon reveals that blacks are excluded from even occupying the category of Other within a dynamic of intersubjective interaction,[5] an exclusion that eclipses or curtails the possibility of black self-realization/actualization. Indeed, this exclusion of blackness from securing the position of the Other, along with the simultaneous appropriation of the category by white subjects, gives breath to the colonialist illusion that the positionality of whiteness guarantees "an unfettered access to subjectivity" (Fuss, 1994, p. 21). To quote Fuss:

> *Colonialism works in part by policing the boundaries of cultural intelligibility, legislating and regulating which identities attain full cultural signification and which do not. For the black man, the implications of his exclusion from the cultural field of symbolization are immediate and devastating. If psychoanalysis is right to claim that "I is an Other" [Lacan, 23], then otherness constitutes the very entry into subjectivity; subjectivity names the detour through the Other that provides access to a fictive sense of self. (Fuss, 1994, p. 22)*

In this particular reading of Fanon, the implications of the implementation of this type of (inter)psychical violence are threefold. First, racial difference implies blocked movement, a freezing of the black body into a "static ontological space of the timeless 'primitive,'" what Fanon calls a "crushing objecthood" (quoted in Fuss, 1994, p. 24). Second, denial of alterity through the policing of representation and material access to citizenship, as well as the white gating of subjectivity, culminates in whites' ability to claim universality, while effectively foreclosing the ability of racialised others to lay claims to universalities' promises. As Fuss so eloquently argues, "While the racialised other is always raced in relation to whiteness, whiteness can abdicate its dependent relationship to blackness for its constitution because it has effectively evacuated itself from the logic of negation by declaring itself its own Other" (Fuss, 1994, p. 25). In the racist colonialist discourse, whereas whiteness can occupy the position of exalted subject (Thobani, 2007), black continually functions as the negative term to reaffirm/reify whiteness's superiority. "The Negro is comparison" [Fanon, 1967, p. 211] (Fuss, 1994, p. 25). Third, the narcissism that is inherent in the gating of subjectivity for whiteness demands that the colonizer be able to see himself (and, importantly, what he is not) in the face of other subjects and in the face of racialised others. Denied access to being a subject for itself, the racialised Other is intended to occupy the impossible ontological place of abjected/fetishised other and, simultaneously, the place of "similitude" (an other that mirrors back the characteristics of whiteness). In other words, the imperative set by whiteness for the racialised other is to "be like me, act like me AND be the other that has already been previously fantasized, imagined, abjected by me" (Fuss, 1994, p. 27).

If, as Fanon suggests, universality is conferred and disavowed at the level of the representational and the ontological under the guise of colonialism, colonialism's power to reproduce itself also resides at the level of the epistemological.[6] Reading Fanon against perhaps his best intentions, Fuss discovers in Fanon's denial in Footnote 44, that "homosexuality doesn't exist in the Antilles ..." a possible interrogation of the epistemological proclivities of the West to universalize and globalize its own understandings of sexual desires and acts.

As Fuss notes, it is imperative to:

focus attention on the ethnocentrism of the epistemological categories themselves —European identity categories that seem to me wholly inadequate to describe the many different consolidations, permutations, and transformations of what the West has come to understand, itself in myriad and contradictory fashion, under the sign "sexuality." (1994, p. 37)

Throughout this section, I have been attempting to demonstrate how Fanon's writing (albeit interpreted in specific ways) draws our attention to the ways in which mechanisms of colonialism operate materially, inter- and intrapsychically, and epistemologically to create the conditions for the "orientation of the world around whiteness" (Ahmed, 2007, p. 155) as well as a heterosexual orientation that, in part, sustains it.

PROCESSES OF DECOLONIZATION

Fanon's thinking on the convergence of the problematics of the materialist and discursive manifestations of colonialism and subject-intersubjective formations and embodiments opens up a more productive and, one could argue, critical space in which to think through processes of decolonization. For Fanon, "the struggle for national liberation [the struggle for decolonization and the dawning of a "new history of humanity"] does not exist in spanning the gap in one stride: the drama has to be played out in all its difficulty every day.... Day after day goes by" (Fanon, quoted in Bhabha, 1996, p. 188). Homi Bhabha argues that there is an inherent tension within the decolonization process itself that is necessary for fulfilling its transformational aspirations—a tension between the necessary explosion of violence/insurgency force (a violence that results in "a bi-polar antagonism") and what Fanon refers to as "the knowledge of the practice of action":

> *The people will thus come to understand that national independence sheds light upon many facts that are sometimes divergent and antagonistic. Such a taking stock of the situation at this precise moment of the struggle is decisive, for it allows the people to pass from total, undiscriminating nationalism to social and economic awareness ... (Fanon, quoted in Bhabha, 1996, p. 189)*

The agency of decolonization thus takes on three forms: first, as an epistemological and materialist rupture to the logic and practice of colonialism (the initial expression of determinant "violence" resulting in antagonistic positionings); second, as an emergent and concentrated taking stock of the effects of colonialism in creating heterogeneous and differential conditions for living and the disjunctures that occur in the production of differently racialised subjectivities (a pedagogical process of an "enlightening" of both "white" and "black" subjects of the encounter); and third, the "resolution" to persist in the crafting of a decolonized space that resists the temptation to reinscribe an ontological consciousness of self sameness (the practice of Humanist thinking) or a radical alterity between Self or Other. Specifically for Fanon, the process of resolution is dynamic, contradictory at times, and emergent—a process of negotiating and interpreting ethical and political truths from fragments left behind by history and gathered together in the moment of transformation—in the moment of becoming new. As Fanon so passionately declares "So comrades, let us not pay tribute to Europe by creating states, institutions, and societies that draw their inspiration from it. Humanity expects other things from us rather than this grotesque and generally obscene emulation" (Fanon, 2004, p. 239).

In the following section, I take up these selective thoughts of Fanon—his reflections on processes of colonization, subjectification, and decolonization (as violence, as education, as reformulation)—as a means of critically examining the workings of the Triangle Program. In other words, I will argue that it is through Fanon's insights that we can re-imagine Triangle's space and practices, not in their current states of embodying and exercising the effects of colonization, but as sites of pedagogical emergence and possibility.

THE TRIANGLE PROGRAM: MISSION IMPOSSIBLE

An incidence of homophobic violence in which a Toronto District School Board (TDSB) teacher was beaten to death by a group of students because of his presumed sexuality, together with a growing awareness that acts of homophobia and heterosexism targeting "gay and lesbian students" were rampant in school corridors and classrooms, culminated in the development by the TDSB of a program entitled the Human Sexuality Program in1986 (Schneider, 1998, p. 146) The program's mandate was to provide counseling and other supportive services to youth affected and targeted by this violence and to provide training opportunities, together with curriculum materials, to challenge or guide teachers and administrators on "gay and lesbian issues" (Schneider, 1998, p. 146). The Triangle Program grew out of the work of the Human Sexuality Program, as a "logical step" in providing support to students whose ability to pursue their studies was threatened by their experiences of homophobia (either within the school, or in the family environment). Since its inauguration in 1995, the Triangle Program has witnessed a remarkable spurt of growth in terms of both scope and student enrollment. Operating independently as one of three programs housed within OASIS Alternative Secondary School (TDSB), and in tandem with the Human Sexuality Program and a community based Advisory Board, the Triangle Program currently has three full-time teachers and a part-time social worker, all of whom are white (although this was identified as being "a problem"), "out and Queer identifying" (Anthony Grandy 2009). Over 300 students have benefited from the program since its inception. Forty-one students are currently enrolled at the school, and they are able to select from a wide range of high school curriculum courses (grades 9 through 12). In the mornings, students work independently on a "generic" curriculum designed by OASIS. In the afternoon, students come together as a "community" (a word now emphasized by teachers in the program (Grandy, 2009)) to study units of "English, Science, Social Studies, and Personal Life management," which are "focused through a LGBTQ lens." As the newly revised Mission Statement states, this program provides students with an "opportunity to learn about LGBTQ literature, history, and lives" (Triangle, 2008).

I would like to pause for a moment to examine the introductory paragraph of the revised Mission Statement that was developed by teachers at the school in January 2008. The first few lines read as follows:

> *The Triangle Program is Canada's only high school program for LGBTQ youth. It is a safer space, free from homophobia, transphobia and heterosexism where LGBTQ youth can be themselves, be respected, and valued for who they are. It is a program where all will be respected and treated equally regardless of gender, race, ethnicity, religion, class, ability, gender identity or sexual orientation. Racist, sexist, homophobic and other oppressive behaviour, language and/or symbols are not tolerated.*

The language employed is consistent with that used in other TDSB printed material, reflecting the general tone and tenure of rights-based language employed through liberal discourses. What I wish to argue is that, despite conscious and best intentions by the authors, the way in which language is mobilized in this document effectively normativises whiteness through a discourse of normative sexuality. The unit of focus is the individual and specifically an individual whose defining marker of identity is oriented around sexuality and gender. Here, the phrase "youth can be themselves, be respected and valued for who they are" is set within the context of the signifier LGBTQ. Freedom to "be," to "self-realize" then, is clearly predicated on the ability to be free from "homophobia, transphobia and heterosexism" and on the ability to embrace gender/sexuality as a stable identity. Oppression based on experiences of gendered and sexual transgressions of normative sexuality/gender is thus viewed as axiomatic and articulated as a singular unifying principle. Occluded from view are the ways in which experiences of racialization and classism simultaneously function to eclipse or curtail this movement towards freedom for racialised students.[7] We can recall Fanon's claim that the prerogative of whiteness is its ability to think of itself in terms of its freedom to take up the subjectivity of humanist promise—to self-realize. And it is this very claim to subjective space, without recognition of the racist exclusionary politics at work within that space, that problematically fixes blackness/racialised Otherness within an ontological no-place. Moreover, the promise of "respect and equality of treatment regardless of gender, race ..." further entrenches the liberal promise of belonging within a common polity oriented around sexuality/gender without requiring an interrogation of the mechanisms allowing whites to imagine that identification can take place outside of the interstices of racialised, classed dynamics and interactions. In other words, as Fanon suggests, racialised bodies are beckoned to be part of a process that has been lactified (as signified by the word "regardless"), without acknowledging the effects that this pacification might have on not only racialised students' ability to claim equality of respect and treatment, but also on white students' (and teachers') ability to assume "the naturalness" of rightness of place because of their inclusion within the operating logic of rights language.

In addition, I would suggest that we need to pay attention to a reading of Fanon that challenges a Eurocentric predilection to assume the universality of an economy of desire centred in categories of identity and aligned to binary classificatory systems organized in relationship to heterosexuality and maleness. By emphasizing the ontological truth claims inherent in expressions of sexual desire and gender experience (as evidenced in the language of "being themselves, being respected for who they are"), what is being enacted through the Mission Statement is a sexual epistemology that effects erasure of other systems of organizing/regulating sexuality and gender, both historically, and in other sociocultural locations, and reenacts modernism's desire to essentialize difference. Moreover, it is this understanding of essentialism that animates programs like Triangle's politics of liberation and secures an (unspoken) alignment with a larger, Western-based globalised movement that is attempting to colonize the conditions of gender and sexual expression (Oswin, 2008). As Joseph Masad argues, "In espousing this liberation project, however, [organizations like the U.S.-based Human Rights Organization] Gay International is destroying social and sexual configurations of desire in the interest of reproducing a world in its own image, one wherein its sexual categories and desires are safe from being questioned" (Masad, 189, cited in Kouri-Towe, 2008). I would argue that the Mission Statement opens up the possibility for quite similar acts of epistemological and ontological erasure to be enacted on a local level—on students belonging to cultures that embrace other formations of subjectivities, other means of regulating and organizing desire and gender. To be specific here, I am arguing not for a static, reified understanding of "cultural difference," what Yukio Hanawa calls a "pure local episteme" (Hanawa, 1996, p. vii, cited in Oswin, 2006), but, rather, for a mobile and more fluid understanding of desire and gender identification that reflects diasporic movement, cultural hybridity, and the economics/violences of globalization and how these differences get mapped onto identification and feelings of belonging. Thus, in the space of the Mission Statement, rather than being mobilized as an opportunity to disrupt and redefine the limits of Western discourse, difference is instead foreclosed as a site of possibility, resulting perhaps in the pathologising and then reorientation of students around the privileged operating signs of whiteness and heterosexuality.

Finally, I would like to comment on the section within the revised Mission

Statement labeled "what we value." The first bulleted point reads as follows: "A safer, social justice, community-focused, and equity-based high school program for students who have left school, or are thinking of leaving school, because of the homophobia, the transphobia, and the heterosexism that exists in the school system" (2008). Although I applaud the inclusion of a key word such as social justice (although it remains undefined in the text), I wonder to what extent an exclusive focus on the school system (family was also included in the older statement) and on the system of heteronormativity/gender conformity as the interconnected sites responsible for making students feel "unsafe" ignores the effects of wider systems of globalization, and discourses of race, citizenship and belonging on the racialised and nonracialised students of Triangle. What is assumed by Triangle's Mission Statement, I would suggest, is an "assimilated immigration" (Desai, 2002, p. 968) (and in Fanon's term, a "lactified" presence) and a "homonormative settlement" (Desai, 2002, p. 968) that renders impossible subjectivities that fail to attain a sufficient level of (racialised) accommodation and that reifies the superiority of whiteness.

SPATIALIZING UNIVERSALITY

Part of Fanon's insight was his ability to think about the effects of colonialism on the space of the body and the body politic, and specifically, about the ways in which differently racialised bodies are positioned or oriented towards the directives of whiteness (or the "lactifying gaze"). Moreover, Fanon argued that Humanism's promise of an unfettered phenomenological body (the movement of the body in space necessary for the realization of the body-self) is eclipsed within the logic of colonialism; the difference that is ascribed to raced bodies renders these bodies out of place and immobile in spaces inscribed by universality and privilege of movement (Ahmed, 2007). Following Fanon's line of thought, I suggest that within the physical space of the Triangle Program are different "orienting devices" (Ahmed, 2007) that align individuals within a Western sexual economy that maps desire onto object choice and self-identity. This incitement to "homonormativity" (and by implication, as has been suggested, an incitement to the normativity of whiteness) involves the spatial positioning of cultural artifacts that might well serve as constant visual reminders to the correct positioning of desire and to the place of othered experiences within the spatial organization of this desire.

I began this chapter by describing the overarching presence of the rainbow flag within the main classroom space of the "school community." To return to this flag for a moment, I suggest that its presence functions as the central orienting devise for students, teachers, and visitors, demarcating their entrance into a space with an affirming LGBTQ sensibility. This is positive space, LGBTQ space. Not only should one expect a certain sensibility to be played out in words, actions, and behaviours within that space, but an expectation resides with the presence of the flag that one's own course of behaviour also needs to be aligned with this sensibility. What is realised then, with the situating of the rainbow flag on a prominent wall, visible to all who have the ability to see, is the simultaneous orientation of bodies towards a coded set of expectations intended for the specificity of this place and time, and towards a universalist, globalised understanding of sexualized and gendered identities. The effect of this codification of sexuality (and gender) within the framework of a Western, modernist understanding of esssentialised sexual/gendered identification is to negate the possibility that other expressions/systems of organizing sexual desire might coexist within this space. Moreover, by positing the rainbow flag as the overarching symbol of the Triangle School (in the classroom and on its Web site), by positioning liberationist sexual/gender identity politics as centric to this space to the exclusion of all other politics, there transpires a privileging of certain subjectivities that can "naturally" experience the logic of its centrifugal pull. To be able to parse off the intersectionality of one's racialised, classed experiences and to pronounce a singularly focused politics is, as Fanon reminds us, the privilege of whiteness; it is its delusion and its pathologising force. Just as the normativising force of homonormativity and gender conformity tend to the lactification of desire, whiteness, through the symbolic presence of the flag, offers both to racialised and "racially mixed" bodies the fantasy of being able to position themselves/ourselves around and within the space of whiteness. And yet, as Fanon so perceptively notes, not only is the ability to move in white spaces contingent on an anything but stable or fixed assessment of proper class disposition and genealogical background, but the very fantasy of being white is a "melancholic impulse" (the pathologised import of colonialised experience) that seeks to murder all or part of what "it" has inherited, as well as a demobilizing identification with the orientation that repudiates it. (Ahmed, 2007, p. 146).

Two other visual representations, one situated within the main space, the other positioned above student work stations within the resource/computer room, adjacent to the central classroom space, are noteworthy for the way in which they reaffirm normative orientations. The first piece, located within the resource room, is a visual time line of "140 years of our Modern Queer History" that moves along the top third of the wall, just above where the computer work stations are located. A few posters from different HIV/AIDS service organizations (one from an agency servicing an ethnoracialised community) are posted just below the time line. The timeline provides a visual complement to the three-week curriculum unit of the same name.[8] The timeline is remarkable, I would argue, because of its complete censuring of a non-European, non-white, and trans contribution to the history that is being represented. First, what is effected is a colonialist erasure of not only what existed in Canada before European presence (two-spirit teachings and practices amongst First Nations) but also the violence that was enacted on these practices in the name of a colonialist system of heteronormativity to which this particular articulation of sexuality history is aligned. Moreover, nowhere on this historical trajectory are we reminded of the ways in which systems of racialization affect sexual and gendered expression (for example, Fanon's articulation in Footnote 44 suggesting that sex work by racialised men (and women) is effectively produced within a racist economy of Eurocentric/Capitalist desire). Nor are we granted access to the many ways in which racialised Canadian artists, academics, and activists have resisted and rearticulated the fetishised black (Asian and Orientalist) body of which Fanon speaks so passionately. A space is devoted to acclaiming the presence and importance of the AIDS Committee of Toronto (the largest resource-rich HIV/AIDS service agency in the city, founded by gay white men) and the Metropolitan Community Church of Toronto (a Christian-based "LGBT" affirming church) in articulating health rights and religious freedoms for LGBTQ identifying Christians. The work of other faith-based groups working to make a space for queer desire and gender expression within their respective traditions together with the fearless contributions that ethnoracialised HIV/AIDS service agencies have made in shifting and creating policies and practices, are simply absent from this timeline and supporting curriculum that celebrates Eurocentric stories of liberation, persistence, and white, biological males' exalted position within queer space.

The second piece,[9] which occupies a substantial section of the back wall, is visible as one leaves the classroom. A series of beautifully painted, stylized portraits of young people, representing a spectrum of races, ethnicities, and genders, and etched in the six different colours of the rainbow flag are situated throughout the visual field of the piece and are intermingled with popularized LGBTQ symbolism (triangles, rainbows, interlocking same gender signs) etched in pink. Meant to be read as an expression of the "diversity" within the wider LGBTQ "community," this portrait betrays the way in which a specific articulation of sexuality (and, marginally, gender) becomes a unifying marker of difference, but that this difference is to be read in terms of a universalized and hegemonic understanding of sexuality (and gender). In other words, here in this piece, racialised and gendered formations are constituted by, and thus unified through, a prescribed formation of sexuality, instead of other alternative symbols of experience that might possibly tie the youth together in the visual space (for example, signs of the disruption of war, activism against globalization, the effects of capitalism, imperialist expansionism, and environmental degradation on global patterns of migration, etc.). Embedded within these ubiquitous symbols of liberal sexual politics and representations of freedom/justice is a transparent white subject, the unacknowledged presence of which signals the ability to occlude from view all experience that is presumed to fall outside of the experiences and entitlements of whiteness. And yet, as Fanon reminds us, the psychical and material inequalities that exist within civil society, as well as, the important contributions that racialised groups are making to disrupt this inequality, are directly implicated in the story of whiteness.

What I have attempted to argue is that the prominent forms of representation visible within the space of the "Triangle Program Community" offer a promise of liberation and freedom that is oriented around a specific politics of prescription that threatens to become/becomes that which it disavows initially—a "straightening," colonizing effect that precludes a host of sexual, gendered, and racialised others/Others depending on whether or not (and how) their personal histories permit them to gain entrance to this point of orientation(Ahmed, 2007, p. 175).

QUEERING CURRICULUM: "WRITING OUR WAY OUT OF THE MARGINS"

I wish to conclude this section with a reading of the "Writing Our Way Out of the Margins Unit," a centrepiece "for community development" and a point of departure for the afternoon "Community Curriculum" (White, 2009). A central premise of the unit is that regardless of where one positions one's own sexual/gender identity within the "LGBTQ continuum" (White, 2009), "coming out" (in terms of that identity) is an inevitable (and desirable) process that happens in some fashion in the classroom, in this particular unit and over the "course of a lifetime." As White suggests, "we make decisions each time we meet new people on whether this is something we can safely do [to come out or not]." Over the course of a three-week period, the students are exposed to a range of "coming out" tales, from children's books (*Asha's Mums*; *The Sissy Duckling*; *King and King*; *Uncle-What-Is-It Is Coming to Visit*), to comic books (*Rusty Is a Homosexual*) and music, to Hollywood films (*Torch Song Trilogy*). Students are then invited to offer their own "reader response" to the tales that have just been told. A four-day writing workshop facilitated by Dinah Smith, founder of "A is for Orange" (a writing group for queer Caribbean writers), together with peer feedback, result in the production of a student's "own coming out story," which the students then present to each other over the course of two days in a "Storytelling Circle." (Although the students have the option of creating a fictionalized account, most choose to represent themselves in a "realist" mode [Grandy, 2009].) Teachers also tell their "coming out" stories in the Circle, both for the purposes of modeling how to tell and in terms of being able to impart life wisdom to the students.

What I find interesting about this curriculum is that there appears to be a tension between the various mechanisms seemingly being operationalised within the school that orient students to the exaltedness of whiteness and homonormativity, the inclusion of reference material within this unit that mirrors this orientation and the inclusion of Smith as the central workshop facilitator of students "coming-out stories." This tension highlights both the problematic of normativising trends and the possibility of rupture, and as such, is worthy of further exploration.

In the fall 2008 issue of *Shameless Magazine*, Dinah Smith wrote a piece entitled "And in This Corner: Writing through Trauma," in which she explains her relationship to the writing process:

> *Writing became a way for me to bear witness to my life: I wasn't crazy, I wasn't friendless, I wasn't unlovable and I wasn't unworthy. All of the lies that I had been told began to unravel. I was writing my way out of shame. The shame of what others believed about me because I was black, poor, neglected, immigrant, female and, later, queer. I was writing my way out of all those lies. I could only get to the other side by going through, by sitting with the nausea, pain and memories and by tuning in to the low hum of anxiety. (Smith, 2008)*

Exemplary in both these words and the actions of Smith (in her founding of "A is for Orange," in her writing as activism) is her attention to locating the experiences of abjection, isolation, and "self-abnegation" at the crossroads of racist, classist, heterosexist, and heteronormative violence. Moreover, while she pays attention to "shame" as a reservoir for the affect that results from experiences of oppression, shame becomes a vehicle for self-and communal realization, as well as a platform for queering and interrogating the very structures and mechanisms that created the context for shame's (re)production in the first instance. What is being offered here, and I am imagining in the workshop at the Triangle Program, is a critique of a model of a liberal/male-white centric "coming out" process that presumes the following: first, that coming out is a personal journey of disclosure about sexual object choice that begins and ends "at the place of the self"; second, that this focus on individual journey is viewed as an adequate model for social transformation (Halberstam, 2005); third, that the model privileges sexuality to the exclusion of not only other experiences but also the ways in which experiences of racialization, poverty, citizenship, sexuality and gender are constituted through one another (in other words, in White's "coming out," experiences are understood as non-discrete and shifting, as opposed to markers of a fixed identity); fourth, that the model assumes a level of mobility—the freedom to move from a space of privacy ("the closet") to a space of freedom ("being out"). Finally, there is an assumption operating both within some trans spaces and certainly within larger LGB communities that "coming out as trans," necessitates a continuous declaration of the trans person's "non-normative"[10] and "not really real" identity. That is, coming out for trans people is deemed an ethical and authenticating process in which confession, justification and explanation of their "true, non natural" natures and their non conformance to a gender/biology/desire axis is required for authenticating legitimacy within LGBTQ space (Scheim, 2009).

As Hiram Perez and, certainly, Fanon remind us, there are a multitude of experiences of desire and identification that trouble these assumptions. Because of specific configurations of economic, familial, and cultural circumstances, the construction of private space as assumed by coming out discourses, cannot always be entertained. Moreover, racialised sexuality and gender expression is always already known through the interpreting lens and perverse fantasies of the white gaze. Freedom to disclose, and the freedom to possess a "privatized sexuality/gender," is thus, an assumed privilege for whiteness and a qualified/compromised or impossible experience for racialised queers and trans people (Perez, 2005, p. 177). Finally, Smith's "coming out" model mirrors Fanon's understanding that the experiences of racial oppression (as it inflects and is inflected by heteropatriarchy) cannot be construed as a discrete happening, but must be understood as a type of "constitutive social force in relation to" group and individual identification.

What I am curious about is how this critique is articulated within the space of the Triangle workshop, and if articulated, how it is able to sustain its energy in the face of the other resources that speak back to a politics of coming out that entertains and reinstates white, homo-normative privilege to the exclusion of other experiences. Moreover, I am interested to know whether in the workshop itself, in the Circle, or in discussion that ensues afterwards, the differential experiences of racism and heteropatriarchy as expressed by racialised and nonracialised students, trans and nontrans students are plumed for their insights into how colonialist/Eurocentric discourses and practices are reproduced and (re)integrated into the texture of everyday lives and interactions. Are these stories used as a site for critical reflection about privilege, access to subjective power, and the functioning of the local within global politics of Eurocentric domination, or is this site recolonised by the assumption of sameness ("a rainbow community"), a supposition that precludes the hard work of self/systemic inspection?

For Fanon, the creation of a "Nationalist culture" (and, here, we can affirm Triangle's desire to create "community") cannot be located in the past, but must be forged by a people "in their day to day struggle as they confront and overcome the ideology of colonialism and 'resume their own history" (Nursey-Bray, 1980, p. 139, quoted in Dei, 2008). This process of decolonization, and the reconstruction of a "we" (a nation, a community) we are reminded, involves both violent rupture, and a re-education, a re-orientation of identification and material practices away from the prescriptive logic of humanism and radical opposition between subject-Other. I would suggest that the coming out unit, by drawing on the critical work of queer activists like Smith, provides a model space in which to enact a Fanonian decolonization (and indeed serves as a reminder and example of how curriculum in general might operationalise this transformative practice). In other words, we might ask, in what pedagogical contexts can we as instructors enliven an opportunity to engage a sustained race/queer consciousness that has a critical eye to the ways in which whiteness and hetero-/homonormativity are mutually constituting? And in what ways will we allow for this form of coming together to story tell, a telling and exchange that refuses to domesticate and placate differences (differences that are articulate through and against the practices of colonization)? What I am urging is that we as educators craft dialogical/pedagogical spaces—like that enacted by Smith—that encourage "epistemic rupture" and that grant place to "violence." To be specific, violence, here within the school context, can be understood as the unapologetic expression—through voice, through text based and visual images—of pain, frustration, anger, and creativity in the face of the violence wrought by repressive and exclusionary practices. Violence and rupture, for Fanon, were what exposed the contingent limits of colonialist practice. Violence and rupture within the space of the Triangle Program's coming out unit (to name but one instance) has the possibility of exposing the contingent limits of homonormativity and its orientation towards the privileging of whiteness and sets the material and discursive "tone" for how queer community/queer pedagogy might be reconstructed anew. As Judith Butler reminds us, "importing this sort of violence into the hermeneutic scheme [a space of multicultural exchange] may well allow us to develop a view that prizes the 'we' as a condition and effect of dialogue without sacrificing the mobilizing force of difference" (Butler, 2001, p. 264). Opening up pedagogical practice to allow for an expansive and "internally fractious" notion of queerness, of difference, of togetherness to unfold, would be a liberating gesture along the lines that Fanon imagined.

Indeed, what Fanon so insightfully offers at the conclusion of the *Wretched of the Earth*, is as applicable as it was to newly emerging nations in the "postcolonial" period as it is to us today:

> *Moreover, if we want to respond to the expectations of the Europeans we must not send them back a reflection, however ideal, of their society, and their thought that periodically sickens even them. For Europe, for ourselves and for Humanity, comrades, we must make a new start, develop a new way of thinking, and endeavour to create a new humanity. (Fanon, 2004, p. 239)*

For Fanon, there was a tone of urgency that underlined his departing words. I imagine that for those of us teaching within queer/non queer spaces, and engaged in the queering of curriculum, inflecting our own queer pedagogical practices with a similar urgency is necessary at this historical juncture if we are to move beyond practices that colonize and eclipse the possibilites of our students, the communities to which they belong and indeed ourselves.

NOTES

1. LGBTQ (lesbian, gay, bisexual, transgender, queer) has become a standardized acronym used (at least) in North America to denote a spectrum of non-normative sexuality or gender identities. Other initials are often included in the acronym—T (Two-spirited—a North American First Nations' designation of a person who has received the gift of two spirits—one male, one female—from the Creator. Archeological and oral histories point to numerous nations' beliefs in multiple gender designations prior to colonization and Christian missionization); I (intersexed); T (transsexual); Q (questioning); A (asexual); O (omni sexual); p (pansexual or polymorphous); GQ (gender Queer). Cleo Manago, an African American writer and activist, coined the phrase "Black-men-who-love-men" and "same-gender-loving" to reposition sexual desire or expression within an Afro-centric, rather than Eurocentric, frame of reference.

2. "Queer theory" and political activism oriented under the label queer have often been sites for the reproduction of Eurocentric privilege and sites in which transgender/transsexual subjectivities have been "appropriated and subsequently erased" as a means of furthering a political project concerned myopically with desire and the expression of desire. Moreover, the term "queer" has often eclipsed or deemed as problematic the desire by some trans identifying people of claiming some form of essentialist comprehension of their gendered selves. Thus, one could argue that queer as a radical theoretical device has often been mobilized at the expense of racialised, two-spirited, and trans identities/experiences instead of embracing its own potential as transformative, inclusive, and productive practice. Many trans and two-spirited activists claim the impossibility of this project (Scheim, 2009). I will argue for its recuperative potential but with skepticism and attention to trans critique.

3. Fanon writes
   Let me write at once that I had no opportunity to establish the overt presence of Homosexuality in Martinique. This must be viewed as the result of the absence of the Oedipus complex in the Antilles. The schema of homosexuality is well known. We should not overlook, however, the existence of what are called there "men dressed like women" or "godmothers." Generally they wear shirts and skirts. But I am convinced that they lead normal sex lives. They can take a punch like any "he-man" and they are not impervious to the allures of women fish and vegetable merchants. In Europe, on the other hand, I have known several Martinicans who become homosexuals, always passive. But this was by no means a neurotic homosexuality: for them it was a means to a livelihood, as pimping is for others (Fanon, 1967, p. 18 ff44). Mercer (1996), Pellegrini (1997) and Walcott (2006) have offered critiques of this passage.

4. Of course, Fanon was emphatic in suggesting that this space of a socio-historically constituted difference and otherness as "inferior positionalities" within colonialism was "primarily" informed in and through the materiality of economic exploitation, its enforcement through technologies of physical violence and through inter and intra psychical mechanisms (Fanon, 1967, p. 13).

5. Within the negative dialectic posited by Western metaphysics, Self-actualization transpires within the dynamic of the interaction between Self and Other. Such interactions results first in confrontation, then in negation, and ultimately in the confirmation/conferring of sameness to both interlocutors (the moment of synthesis).

6. See note 5.
7. What appears in the mission statement might not be wholly reflective of what is being practiced in the classroom. For example, in a technology unit, the science teacher explores the wastage that is produced because of a North American/European obsession with newness and technological advancement in communications devices (including computers), and the myriad of ways in which this obsession is dependent on the countries of the South—as dumping ground for old technologies, as suppliers of raw material, as providers of cheap labour. He is also interested in exploring with his students the impact that this has on migration patterns to countries of the North. Moreover, in the Social Justice Unit, Peggy McIntosh's article is used as a vehicle for exploring different social locations and the impact that these locations have on accessing privilege and in articulating sexual identity. The unit also explores how these systems of oppression might be challenged (White 2009).
8. In written correspondence from one of the teachers, a description was offered of the way in which "they [the teachers] try to incorporate as many voices as possible, and the various intersections of the diverse and complex LGBTQ communities." Moreover, although this was not evident in the scheduling of the Modern Queer History Unit that was presented during this 2008/09 academic year, it was stated that guest speakers from Two-Spirited People's of the First Nations and speakers from "other marginalized LGBTQ communities" had been invited to speak in the classroom in the Social Justice and Homo-Equity Units.
9. Apart from the flag, there were only two other forms of visual representation on display in the main space—the piece that I will describe and another piece that consisted of a series of "mandalas" that had been painted onto the wall by students of the program. Each mandala, measuring the size of an American football had the first name of the person who had created the piece inscribed onto its centre. Most of the mandalas included some reference to popularized LGBTQ symbolism—triangles, interlocking gender signs, and rainbows. None transgressed into representation realms that would have disrupted the normativising force of these symbols or point in other directions towards other politics, other experience.
10. As Scheim elaborates, in other cultural (historical) contexts "it is quite possible that gender variance is simply an expected occurrence that does not demand explanation. (Scheim 2009)

REFERENCES

Ahmed, Sara (2007). *Queer Phenomenology: Orientations, Objects, Others.* Durham, NC, and London: Duke University Press

Alcoff, Linda Martin (2001). "Towards a Phenomenology of Embodiment." In Robert Bernasconi (ed.), *Race*, 267–283. Malden. MA: Blackwell Publishers.

Bhabha, Homi (1996). "Day by Day . . . with Frantz Fanon." In A. Read (Ed.), *The Fact of Blackness: Frantz Fanon and Visual Representation*, 186–205. Seattle, WA: Bay Press.

Bhabba, Homi (1986). "Remembering Fanon," foreword to Frantz Fanon, *Black Skin, White Masks.* London: Pluto Press.

Butler, Judith, & Martin, Biddy (1994). Cross-Identifications. *Diacritics*, 24 (2/3), Critical Crossings (Summer–Autumn p. 3).

Butler, Judith (2001). "Conversational Break: A Reply to Robert Gooding-Williams." In Robert Bernasconi (ed.), *Race*, 26–264. Malden, MA: Blackwell Publishers.

Dei, George. J. Sefa (2008). Lecture Notes on Reading Frantz Fanon for Pedagogy.
de Lauretis, Teresa (2002). "Difference Embodied: Reflections on *Black Skin, White Masks.*" *Parallax* 23, April-June Special Issue. 54–68.
Desai, Jina (2002). Homo on the Range: Mobile and Global Sexualities. *Social Text* 73, Vol 20 (4) 65–89.
Eng, David, (Halberstam, Judith) Estaban Munoz, Jose (2005). Introduction. "What's Queer About Queer Studies Now?" *Social Text,* Vol. 23 (3–4), 4–5.
Fanon, Frantz (2001). "The Lived Experience of the Black." In Robert Bernasconi (ed.), *Race*, 184–201. Malden, MA: Blackwell Publishers.
Fanon, Frantz (2004). *The Wretched of the Earth* (Trans. Richard Philcox). New York: Grove Press.
Fanon, Frantz (1967). *Black Skin, White Masks* (Trans. Charles Lam Markman). New York: Grove Press.
Ferguson, Roderick A. (2005). "Of Our Normative Striving. African American Studies and the Histories of Sexuality." *Social Text,* Vol. 23 (3–4), 85–101.
Fuss, Diana (1994). "Interior Colonies: Frantz Fanon and the Politics of Identification." *Diacritics,* Vol. 24, No. 2/3, Critical Crossings (Summer - Autumn, 1994), 20–42.
Grandy, Anthony (2009). Personal Correspondence. Triangle Program.
Halberstam, Judith (2005). "Shame and White Gay Masculinity." *Social Text,* Vol. 23 (3–4), 219–235.
Hall, Stewart (1996). "The Afterlife of Frantz Fanon: Why Fanon? Why Now? Why Black Skin, White Masks?" In A. Read (ed.), The Fact of Blackness: Frantz Fanon and Visual Representation, 12–37. Seattle, WA: Bay Press.
Jagose, Annamarie (1996). *Queer Theory: An Introduction.* New York: New York University Press.
Judy, R.A.T (1996). "Fanon's Body of Black Experience." In Lewis R. Gordon, T. Denean Sharpley-Whiting & Renee T. White (eds.). *Fanon: A Critical Reader.* Oxford: Blackwell Critical Reader Series. 53–73.
Kouri-Towe, Nathalie (2008). Queer Responses to the 2006 Lebanon War. Unpublished Manuscript
Kuntsman, Adi (2008). "The Soldier and the Terrorist: Sexy Nationalism, Queer Violence." *Sexualities* 11; 142–170.
Manalansan IV, Martin F. (2005). "Race, Violence, and Neoliberal Spatial Politics in the Global City." *Social Text*. 23 (3–4), 141–155.
Martin, Biddy (1994). "Sexualities without Genders and Other Queer Utopias." *Diacritics,* 24 (2/3), Critical Crossings (Summer - Autumn), 104–121.
Massad, Joseph A. (2007). *Desiring Arabs.* Chicago and London: The University of Chicago Press.
Mercer, Kobena (1996). "Decolonization and Disappointment: Reading Fanon's Sexual Politics." In A. Read (ed.), The Fact of Blackness: Frantz Fanon and Visual Representation 114–31. Seattle, WA: Bay Press.
Muñoz, José Esteban (1999). *Disidentifications: Queers of Color and the Performance of Politics.* Minneapolis: University of Minnesota Press.
Oswin, Natalie (2008). Critical Geographies and the Uses of Sexuality: Deconstructing Queer Space. *Progress in Human Geography* 32(1). 89–103.
Pellegrini, A. (1997). *Performance Anxieties: Staging Psychoanalysis, Staging Race.* New York: Routledge.

Perez, Hiram (2005). "You Can Have My Brown Body and Eat It, Too!" *Social Text*, 23 (3–4) 171–191.

Puar, Jasbir K. (2005). "Queer Times, Queer Assemblages" in *Social Text*, 23:3–4, Fall-Winter, 121–140.

Scheim, Ayden (2009). Personal correspondence.

Schneider, Margaret (1998). Response. *Harvard Educational Review*, Spring. Accessed Jan 02, 2009: http://www.hepg.org/her/abstract/174.

Smith, Dinah (2008). "And In This Corner: Writing through Trauma." *Shameless Magazine*. Fall. http://www.shamelessmag.com/issues/2008/fall/and-in-this-corner-writing-through-trauma/.

Thobani, Sunera (2007). *Exalted Subjects: Studies in the Making of Race and Nation in Canada*. Toronto: University of Toronto Press

Triangle Program Mission Statement, 2007 (unpublished).

Triangle Program Website: schools.tdsb.on.ca/triangle/.

Villarejo, Amy (2005). "Tarrying with the Normative. Queer Theory and Black History" *Social Text*. 23 (3–4), 69–84.

Waites, Matthew (2008). "Analysing Sexualities in the Shadow of War: Islam in Iran, the West, and the Work of Reimagining Human Rights." *Sexualities* 11(1/2), 64–73.

Waites, M. (2005). "The Fixity of Sexual Identities in the Public Sphere: Biomedical Knowledge, Liberalism and the Heterosexual/Homosexual Binary in Late Modernity." *Sexualities* 8(5), 539–569.

Walcott, Rinaldo (2006). "Black Men in Frocks: Sexing Race in a Gay Ghetto" (Toronto). In C. Teelucksingh (ed.). *Claiming Space: Racialization in Canadian Cities*, 121–134. Waterloo, ON: Wilfred Laurier University Press.

White, Jeffrey (2009). Written Correspondence, Triangle Program.

CHAPTER SEVEN

Strategic In/Visibility and Undocumented Migrants

FRANCISCO J. VILLEGAS

INTRODUCTION

Throughout his writings, Frantz Fanon discussed the relationship between visibility and power as well as invisibility and powerlessness. Through these relationships, the colonizer is made visible and thereby attributed power. At the same time, the colonized are deemed inhuman and their claims considered illegitimate, effectively invisibilizing them. While not clear-cut, the linkages between in/visibility and power/lessness provide an important understanding of colonial relations, whereby markers including race and gender connote or deny power and knowledge. However, as Fanon stressed, the relegation of the colonized to powerlessness is met with modes of resistance, including strategies where the colonized may access spaces of visibility and invisibility to avoid discipline and surveillance and to further their own goals or political agendas.[1] In this paper I intend to analyze the ways undocumented migrants in the U.S. strategically enter spaces of visibility and invisibility in their everyday life, as well as the physical and psychological costs attached to the avoidance of suspicions about their immigration status. Therefore, my goal is to map out the types of knowledge produced by discursive and material realities of undocumented status in the U.S. Such knowledge appears in the news, in the classroom, in the workplace etc. and is then taken up by audiences who learn to identify undocumented migrants accordingly-through ideas about race, gender, class and legitimacy to citizenship. Included in such audiences are undocumented migrants themselves, who experience the violence of being depicted as undocumented and are therefore liable to deportation and exclusion, but who also resist such impositions in their day to day lives. Of special significance are the lived experiences of undocumented university students and the ways these students negotiate stressors linked to their immigration status and age-related expectations.

Although undocumented migrants do not live in the same conditions as those experienced in 1950 Algeria, it is important to recognize that because of neocolonial endeavors large numbers of peoples from across the globe are displaced from their homes and forced to migrate. These individuals, along with those living with oppression in the context of reception (whether through birth or earlier migration) must contend with the daily experiences of colonial processes. Not only is the U.S. engaged in neocolonial activities abroad, but it is still a colonial space where the rightful owners of the land are denied self-actualization. Therefore, a major theme of this paper is what happens to particular colonized peoples who migrate to the heart of empire and are constructed as undocumented.

The works of Fanon are useful in examining the daily life of undocumented migrants in the U.S. today. His careful analysis of the many ways in which the everyday resistance of colonized peoples takes shape provides avenues to understand the complexities of visibility and invisibility. Furthermore, showing the effects of Manicheanisms on the deployment of racist discourse enables an understanding of the process through which entire populations are invisibilized. Finally, Fanon also discusses at length the effects of colonialism and by extension, the consequences of the visibilization and invisibilization of particular bodies on people's psyches.

Processes of visibility and invisibility are steeped with notions of power and as Fanon has shown in his writing, the colonized have utilized this knowledge in their resistance. He argues that by knowing the ways in which they can be perceived, as well as their options to make salient different facets of their identities, the colonized can strategically enter different levels of visibility and invisibility in order to further their goals.[2] An example of Fanon operationalizing these concepts is his discussion of the role the veil played in the Algerian revolution. During the Algerian revolution, women in the resistance strategically utilized the veil and strategically unveiled in order to avoid surveillance and suspicion. As I will argue, Fanon's anticolonial framework, and his insights into invisibility and visibility are useful in analyzing the current conditions that produce undocumented status today.

This paper will begin by exploring the concepts of visibility and invisibility in relation to the daily experiences of undocumented migrants. To aid in my analysis I will also draw on David Theo Goldberg's interpretation of Fanon's work on visibility and invisibility.[3] I explain the linkages between visibility and invisibility to power as well as their purpose and the ways in which they are constructed on an everyday basis. Following that, I present a discussion on the role Manicheanisms play in the deployment of racist, classist and gendered discourse in the everyday life of undocumented migrants. I argue that this discourse actively attempts to dehumanize and invisibilize undocumented migrants. I then move the discussion to the ways in which undocumented migrants can use both the concepts of strategic visibility and strategic invisibility in order to further broader political agendas as well as for their personal wellbeing. I conceptualize both of these endeavors as an attempt by undocumented migrants to reclaim their humanity. Finally, I look at the personal costs of strategically using these concepts in everyday life, including possible psychological consequences and violence. The last two sections incorporate excerpts from undocumented university students who narrate their experiences of invisibility and visibility and their use of strategic visibility and strategic invisibility. These excerpts come from a study I conducted in 2006 regarding the experiences of undocumented Latina/o students in a California university through a migrant rights campus organization.[4] My role within the group grew from supporter/observer in meetings, to active participant with a personal stake in the organization's political goals.

VISIBILITY AND INVISIBILIZATION

According to Goldberg, "visibility carries with it connotations that tend to be appealing-access, opportunity, ability—in short, power; and invisibility has tended to connote absence, lack, incapacity—in short, powerlessness."[5] In the colonial condition, visibility manifests itself when the knowledges and claims of the colonizer are upheld as universal truths, as well as when particular peoples fit within national paradigms and are constructed as legitimate and worthy subjects. Invisibility, in contrast, implies an erasure or dismissal of knowledges and experiences, resulting in powerlessness. Visibility and invisibility operate through a variety of markers including race, gender, sexuality, ability, and immigration status. For example, George Dei explains that "race continues to gain in social currency because of its utility in distributing unequal power, privilege, and social prestige."[6] These markers serve to legitimize and delegitimize the daily experiences of individuals as unimportant or socially irrelevant. Extending this analysis, however, scholars have argued how whiteness, as a racialized category, tends to be taken for granted and attempts to become invisible through claims to universality. There are no markers necessary, for it is the norm. As Kerstin Roger states, "the failure to research whiteness (even by whites) threatens to entrench its invisible centrality, revealing practices within supposedly reified relations of race, class and gender so that those practices that maintain the invisibility of whiteness cannot be named or explored."[7]

Undocumented migrants experience colonialism through processes of exploitation and dispossession in their contexts of departure, often mediated by American imperialism and exceptionalism. In addition, upon arrival to the U.S. they enter into a new but similar colonial experience. Therefore colonialism works transnationally and colonial relations affect the migratory patterns of displaced individuals. This section will examine the material benefits accrued by colonizers' invisibilization of entire populations as well as provide examples of the ways in which undocumented migrants are excluded from society.

Leo Chavez has described the forced invisibility experienced by undocmented migrants, which results in their leading "shadowed lives." [8] By shadowed lives, Chavez suggests that due to the racist, gendered, and legal discourses that construct and discipline undocumented migrants, they are often forced to "hide" by working under the table or by trying not to be too "visible" at public events.[9] These imperatives for invisibilization are part of what theorists identify as social processes through which people become "illegalized," or the production of "illegality." [10] Illegalization operates through a number of social and legal institutions as well as in the level of discourse.

For instance, the production of "illegality" necessitates discourses of race.[11] Particular bodies spark questioning and suspicion regarding status while other bodies do not because they are normalized within the national stereotype of citizenship. Such stereotypes have far-reaching effects, where people marked as suspicious may also associate parallel discourses, such as those of criminality, to undocumented status, thus exhibiting a form of internalized racism.[12] While migrants arrive with their own ideas of race and racism, these ideas are also affected by the context of reception, which may include popular notions of criminality and racism transmitted though the media and personal networks.[13] Race becomes a marker of difference and deficiency in colonial contexts. In order to maintain colonial relations, the colonized, constructed as racially different, are dehumanized through complex systems of oppression.

Given the relationship of visibility and invisibility to power we must think about whose interests are served when undocumented migrants are invisibilized. Because the colonizer and colonized are socially constructed categories, it is important to remember that as Fanon states, "it is the colonist who fabricated and continues to fabricate the colonized subject. The colonist derives his validity, i.e., his wealth, from the colonial system [emphasis in original]."[14] Similarly, Goldberg explains that, "the colonized are dehumanized, their humanity effaced, not simply for the sake of the colonizer's ego satisfaction but for the purpose of the colonized's exploitation."[15] In order for the dominant to remain in power, it must invisibilize the humanity of the colonized and construct their claims as illegitimate and unimportant. However, it must do so under the guise of equal opportunity and a meritocratic system. This process has been increasingly relevant since the liberalization of immigration policy in the mid-twentieth century, which removed among others, race-based exclusions. It also works to promote and mask a system of privilege based on social factors including race, gender, and immigration status. The false belief in the existence of a fair and equitable immigration system is then used to further the production of "illegality" by juxtaposing the good migrant who "fairly" applied for immigration authorization with the undocumented migrant who "cheated" or is attempting to "cheat" the system by jumping the proverbial immigration queue. In this discourse the many excluding factors present in immigration policy are overlooked and there is only room for the sensationalized criminalization of the undocumented. As Lina Newton states

> *immigration laws define a broad class of people 'immigrants,' and then redefine the component parts to justify differentiated policy treatments. In this process, race signals people who are undeserving. The racialized imagery of immigration restriction assuages: it communicates that the freeloaders, the threats, the people unwilling to conform to the standards and values prized in the polity are being denied or entry or access on arrival.* [16]

This system thus also naturalizes the dominant as legitimately holding positions of power without regard to social systems privileging them and affecting such outcomes.

In addition to the beliefs regarding the immigration system are claims to innocence regarding events happening throughout the world. Such events, often operating under the trope of globalization, work to displace communities from their land. Accordingly, George Dei states that "globalization is the new justification used by Euro-Canadian/American society for asserting its political and economic dominance over indigenous and colonized peoples." [17] These globalizing forces are often depicted in amorphous forms where the blame cannot be placed on anyone but rather it is thought to occur as a consequence of an economic system. Given such depersonalized global economic forces, citizens of those nations benefitting from the plight of the colonized can make claims to innocence as well as distance themselves from any responsibility.

According to Fanon, "because it is a systematized negation of the other, a frenzied determination to deny the other any attribute of humanity, colonialism forces the colonized to constantly ask the question 'who am I in reality?'" [18] This questioning of the self may not be purely an existential question for the colonized, but also a contextual question where one must think strategically about power and the aims of an interaction and assume only the particular facets of one's identity that provide the best possible result. As I will show later, this active strategizing becomes part of the everyday lived experiences of undocumented migrants.

The exploitation of undocumented migrants arises largely from knowledge about their immigration status and the possibility of deportation. Thus, exploitative practices can include the withholding of payment or payment of lesser wages, the forcing of undesired actions, and the deterrence or exclusion from accessing social services such as health care, education, and workers' benefits. These actions benefit the dominant since particular populations are relegated to a reserve pool of highly exploitable labor with little to no opportunity for legal recourse. Additionally, while unable to access many social services or voting rights, undocumented migrants provide large amounts of capital to the state through the taxing of daily purchases, property taxes, and income taxes through tax identification numbers and paycheck withholdings. In this way, while being paid minimal wages and paying taxes, undocumented migrants face a large number of barriers to, if not complete exclusion from, the social services paid for by those taxes.

Exploitation, be it in terms of labor or the exclusion from social services, has often been invisibilized through sensationalized claims of undocumented migrants' criminality and nativist ideals about legitimate subjects deserving of social services. [19] Goldberg, states that "what colonialism seeks to hide from view, to render invisible about itself, is the grounding fact of its possibility: that colonialism is predicated only on force and fraud." [20] The exclusion of undocumented migrants from services available to the general populace, as well as the fraud experienced when unable to access the benefits of tax monies paid to the government, is forced through threats of violence and deportation by the state. One instance of this process is undocumented migrants' exclusion of services being written into American law, thus standardizing exclusion for such migrants and creating more barriers to their regularization.

More specifically, exploitation through labor practices is a major theme in this discussion. Such exploitation operates both materially and discursively. As Goldberg explains, colonialism invisibilizes the colonized to "minimize the costs of economic reproduction and labor enforcement." [21] In other words, the colonial power does not need to provide people with education and training or basic labor rights based on their lack of status and therefore legitimacy as humans or members of society. The capitalist need for the colonizer to find a cheap, recyclable and deportable workforce enables the enactment of laws that exclude colonized populations from the full benefits of citizenship. This allows the segmentation of the workforce and the creation of a reserve army of labor that is forced to work under poor conditions while it is also brought under the realm of "illegality" and criminality.

Undocumented migrants experience supervision and discipline through the constant threat of deportation while at the same time being actively recruited by employers due to this exploitability. [22] The threat of deportability operates not by large numbers of deportations in relation to the population of undocumented migrants, though recently the forced removal of migrants has increased dramatically, but through highly publicized immigration raids. [23] It is the threat of deportation and detention that affects migrants, the possibility of being caught in a raid, of being stopped by the police at a random stop, or for many racialized migrants, of experiencing racial profiling. This is one example of the push for invisibility described by Chavez in *Shadowed Lives*. [24]

An important way in which colonialism has invisibilized itself is though the enactment of law. To facilitate the exploitation of undocumented migrants, laws have been enacted that actively produce "illegality." As De Genova explains, "everyday life for the undocumented has become more and more saturated by the regimes that receiving states impose through immigration laws." [25] The law, as a social construction considered to be impartial, is crafted with specific agendas in mind; agendas that often do not benefit the marginalized. For example, in 1996, the Illegal Immigration Reform and Immigrant Responsibility Act (IIRIRA) limited the number of social services available to all noncitizens including permanent residents, and instituted harsher penalties for undocumented migration. Policies such as this, in conjunction with the walls built on the U.S. southern border, have caused undocumented migrants to remain in the U.S. for longer periods of time. This prolonged stay is directly affected by the increasingly dangerous terrain some people are forced to cross in order to enter the U.S. as well as the possible legal repercussions of being caught if attempting to return. [26]

Laws and institutional policies keep undocumented migrants living under constant stress about the possibility of deportation of themselves and their loved ones. These policies also often shift the level of enforcement from national authorities to local police forces and individuals, either of whom can report suspicions of undocumented status. Such individuals can include disgruntled employers who may be unhappy with undocumented workers standing up for their rights, or who may have finished a job and may want to deport their workforce rather than pay them. The invisibility of the law detailed here is prevalent in many contexts including academic literature examining the undocumented experience. According to De Genova, "across an extensive, multidisciplinary, social science literature, one encounters a remarkable visibility of 'illegal immigrants' swirling enigmatically around the stunning invisibility of the law." [27]

However, De Genova also argues that the law is not always intentional, unified or anticipatory, but is instead constituted over time as a series of tactics implemented to manage particular historical moments. He explains that these tactics

> *that aim to make a disciplined and manageable object of any given social group are conjunctural and can never be assured of the certainty of their realization. These tactics are ensnared in a struggle to subordinate the intractability that is intrinsic to the constitutive role of labor within capital.* [28]

The law thus needs to be crafted in a flexible manner, so that it can adjust according to new 'crises.' For instance in the example outlined above, the IIRIRA emerged out of lawmakers' beliefs that previous immigration laws did not sufficiently enforce the denial of rights in relation to access to state-funded services, higher education, etc. Thus, as previous laws, IIRIRA visibilized the imposed "illegality" ascribed onto undocumented migrants and further intensified it. Another example is the Patriot Act, which emerged out of a sensationalized focus on national security which impeded the passage of comprehensive immigration reform backed by both President George W. Bush and powerful labor unions. [29]

While the law may attempt to mask colonialism at the same time that it dehumanizes undocumented migrants, undocumented migrants are not passive subjects. At the national level, through massive collective efforts, undocumented migrants and their allies have been successful at derailing some of the most punitive legal proposals. For instance, Proposition 187 in California in 1994 would have excluded undocumented migrants from all essential services including emergency health assistance and education. Similarly, in 2006 House Resolution 4437 at the U.S. national level would have categorized undocumented status as a felony as well as any action considered to aid or abet an undocumented migrant. At an individual level, some undocumented migrants have utilized the strategic practice of invisibilizing their immigration status in order to avoid suspicion and at times circumvent negative policies. However, Manicheanisms presenting particular racialized bodies as deficient provide an additional complexity to consider in conceptualizing the agency and resistance of migrants.

MANICHEANISMS

Manicheanisms are a prevalent theme in Fanon's writings. They describe how characteristics that come to be located as positive and powerful are attributed to the dominant while characteristics positioned as negative and powerless are relegated to the colonized. These characteristics are clearly divided along racial and color lines where the closer an individual is considered to have approached whiteness, the more positive their characterization. The Manicheanism regarding visibility and invisibility works along these ideas, and as quoted above, according to Goldberg,

> *Whiteness has long been characterized in terms of light and learning, blackness in terms of darkness and degeneration. Accordingly, visibility carries with it connotations that tend to be appealing—access, opportunity, ability-in short, power; and invisibility has tended to connote absence, lack, incapacity-in short, powerlessness.* [30]

Manicheanisms work with visibility and invisibility in so far as they invisibilize the colonized-including undocumented migrants, their experiences and their knowledges-using negative characterizations, while the dominant are visibilized through claims of universality as well as the ascription of positive characteristics and perspectives. These Manicheanisms, situated at the discursive level, have material effects. They are prevalent in the daily life of undocumented migrants where the media, political figures, and the law relegate them to the margins of society. In discussing how migrant "illegality" is produced, De Genova, among others, has discussed how this process necessitates discourses of race, gender, and class. [31] The bodies of undocumented migrants are ascribed negative stereotypes that stand in contrast to the markers of legality and legitimacy of dominant, normalized bodies. Ultimately this serves to effectively negate and invisibilize all claims to their humanity.

Sensationalized claims to criminal behavior and abuse of social services, as well as fears regarding the reproduction of bodies of color, serve to further the exclusion and marginalization of undocumented migrants from society. In *Wretched of the Earth*, Fanon explains that, "the colonist is not content with stating that the colonized world has lost its values or worse never possessed any. The 'native' is declared impervious to ethics, representing not only the absence of values but also the negation of values." [32] According to this logic, society structures its institutions to include and exclude bodies based on the ascriptions of these negative moral characteristics. It is no coincidence that when attempting to cut back services, people of color, particularly migrants, are blamed or scapegoated as causing an overextension of resources. In the case of undocumented migrants this is evident in the discourses of crime and abuse utilized to put forward Proposition 187 in California and U.S. House Resolution 4437. Such political discourses are frequently facilitated by the juxtaposition of citizens as legitimate subjects who pay for social services through financial contributions to the tax system, and undocumented migrants as illegitimate recipients of social benefits and abusive of the rule of law. These discourses also often speak to a differential value being given to human lives depending on the body where the citizen's life, whose body is constructed as white and male, is considered more valuable than that of the migrant. Such was the case for Operation Gatekeeper, which in 1994, saw the building of a wall on the U.S.-Mexico border along prominent crossing routes for undocumented migrants and as a stated goal attempted to force undocumented migration to more dangerous areas. [33] This has directly resulted in over one thousand deaths along the Arizona border. [34]

The media, through the use of Manicheanisms also play a pivotal part in the production of "illegality." As Goldberg states, "radio and television are technologies that can promote invisibility and produce depersonalization." [35] For undocumented migrants, nativism and xenophobia have generated careers for on-air personalities whose main task it is to scapegoat undocumented migrants for all social problems. Examples include the daily rants of shock jocks and news celebrities such as Lou Dobbs and Bill O'Reilly. These individuals provide a forum for racist and xenophobic rhetoric. Additionally, anti-immigrant rhetoric is not solely relegated to radio and television. Leo Chavez, through his work examining mainstream magazine covers depicting themes of immigration, has shown that anxieties regarding the "darkening" of the nation have resulted in the constant and continuous negative depiction of undocumented migrants.[36] Such media outlets mirror nativist anxieties and exacerbate fears regarding migrants' perceived criminality and the potential abuse of social services. Furthermore, the use of race, gender and presumed class of undocumented migrants are prevalent themes. These discourses target racialized groups as menacing and capable of threatening the white nation-state and specific geographic regions, such as the U.S.-Mexico border, as danger zones. At the same time, women are depicted as a large threat due to their ability to reproduce racialized bodies.[37]

According to Fanon, "sometimes this manicheanism reaches its logical conclusion and dehumanizes the colonized subject. In plain talk, he is reduced to the state of an animal."[38] This discursive pattern is prevalent in the context of reception where undocumented migrants' "arrival" is discussed in terms of mindless intrusion such as flows, or national disasters like floods and swarms.[39] In addition to the catastrophe metaphor, undocumented migrants are also frequently animalized, further dehumanizing them. As Otto Santa Ana has shown,

> *The connotations of IMMIGRANT AS ANIMAL should be abundantly clear. In Western European culture a purported natural hierarchy has been articulated since the time of Thomas Aquinas to justify social inequity. In its full extension, it subordinates other living creatures to human beings, and ranks the inherent quality of humans from base to noble [emphasis in original].*[40]

The connotations linking migrants to animals speak to the way in which certain migrant groups are racialized and considered as lesser beings. Through the discursive dehumanization of undocumented migrants in political discourse and media coverage, it is possible to facilitate the production of "illegality" that constructs migrants as disposable. Such dehumanizing practices devalue the worth of migrants' lives and allow for the possibility of collective violence. As Griffin states,

> *The use of metaphors which suggest an undifferentiated mass ('flood', 'wave' etc.), and indeed the use of abstract nouns such as immigration, lead to a depersonalization, one might argue a de-humanization of those involved which deflects from the fact that we are using people, and people who are classed, gendered, raced, endowed with a whole range of traits that constitute them as complex entities, both individually and as groups.*[41]

Materially, this dehumanization results in the creation of policies that exclude migrants from a myriad of essential services and enable the creation of violent vigilante groups such as the minutemen who consider it their patriotic responsibility to police specific bodies near the U.S.-Mexico border. Overall, this invisibilization results in the discursive and material denial of undocumented migrants' humanity.

Furthermore, the fact that particular migrants are dehumanized is especially interesting in a colonized territory where the colonizer claims the colony as home or begins to believe him/herself as "native." They begin to fear the possible "recoloring" of the nation such as the browning or yellowing of the nation and develop nativist ideals based on the exclusion of particular bodies that do not fit the imagined construction of the national identity.

STRATEGIC IN/VISIBILITY

Although contemporary power relations serve to discursively and materially invisibilize the colonized, instances of visibility and invisibility can also be strategically used to further their own needs. Therefore, visibility and invisibility are of vital importance to the wellbeing of undocumented migrants. This section examines different ways in which undocumented migrants utilize strategic visibility and invisibility in order to further a political agenda. According to Goldberg,

> *the value of in/visibility are contextually determined. There are moments, for example, when those working for dramatic social transformation want their struggle to remain invisible, unseen though not unfelt; there are other times when its impact is registered fully only when openly conducted and witnessed, where its effects are witnessed, visible, and registered in the media.* [42]

For undocumented migrants, broad, strategic, and collective actions visibilizing the power of undocumented migrants are employed "for dramatic social transformation," mainly, the reclamation of their humanity. At the same time, strategic invisibility may mask their immigration status from the many possible supervising bodies that may disclose this information to immigration authorities. It must be said that regardless of the strategy used by the migrants, suspicions about immigration status will arise when they bear markers or signifiers that accord with the current discourse regarding undocumented migrants. Migrants cannot always control how they are perceived in relation to class, gender, sexuality and/or race and as such, depending on time and space, they may fit the stereotypes regarding undocumented migrants including the way they look, dress, as well as the presence of an accent.

Despite such modes of categorization, undocumented migrants use a variety of coping and resistance strategies to facilitate their everyday mobility and decrease their status-related anxieties. Similar to Goldberg, Bailey, Wright, Mountz, & Miyares explain their concept of "strategic visibility" as a method used by Salvadoran migrants in their study so that society members and government officials recognize their presence. [43] This visibility became strategic because in a neighborhood where few Salvadoran cultural icons existed, the migrants decided when to visibilize their presence. For Bailey and company, examples of "strategic visibility" included "the timing and circumstances of marriage, the nature of intergenerational aspirations, and the circumstances of political mobilization." [44] Other examples of strategic visibility used by undocumented migrants include the decision by an individual or family to publicize their deportation orders in order to rally public support, or large scale demonstrations such as those that occurred in the U.S. in 2006 in response to anti-immigrant legislation known as H.R. 4437. [45] In these rallies migrants visibly resisted their prescribed criminality and engaged in the demand for justice and recognition.

Strategic visibility in this context should not be seen as simply the visibilizing of undocumented migrants' immigration status. Rather, it should also be understood as a strategic mechanism where part of the strategy in visibilizing oneself is deciding which facets of their identity one wishes to visibilize. For example, in a demonstration against police brutality, individuals may wish to visibilize their membership in a panethnic Latina/o community but not necessarily their immigration status. Similarly, depending on the context, individuals may purposefully visibilize their identities as workers, students, or residents of a particular community, while masking or not finding it strategically beneficial to display other facets of their identity, including their immigration status.

As previously discussed, the media has been widely used to demonize undocumented migrants. However, some media outlets can also become sites of strategic visibility. As witnessed in the May Day marches across the U.S. in 2006, some media outlets took an active role in their promotion and organization. [46] In particular, DJs of Spanish-language radio aided in the organizing of communities to demand the rejection of House Resolution 4437 as well as a regularization program to provide all undocumented migrants with status. Through these media undocumented migrants and their allies were able to visibilize their presence as a political and economic force that would engage in organizing to dispel negative stereotypes about them and would actively reclaim their humanity. These events go a long way towards proving Goldberg's claim that "radio and television can make the invisible visible via explication, obviating, reporting, renewing," and to a large extent mirror Fanon's explanation of the way in which "The Voice of Algeria" visibilized the resistance of the colonized. [47] As I have shown, the media can have an invisibilizing or visibilizing effect depending on the source and the purpose underlying the portrayal or representation. It is nevertheless important to remember that as Goldberg warns, *technology offers a medium for the dissemination of information but at once mediates the message. To inform is to give form to the empirical, to make visible the hidden, and audible the silent or silenced, just as it makes invisible the seen and inaudible the spoken.* [48]

Similar to strategic visibility, migrants can also attempt to strategically invisibilize their immigration status.[49] Because of increasingly punitive responses to undocumented status by the state, many migrants are forced to find ways in which to alleviate suspicions regarding their immigration status. Therefore, for undocumented migrants, their visibility as undocumented poses a significant threat, including the potential of deportation. According to Ruggiero, anti-immigrant laws in France resulted in "the increasing thrust towards the criminalization [of undocumented migrants] and thus towards invisibility." [50] Strategic invisibility may include a wider political agenda, but it is also a daily mechanism to ensure their wellbeing.

There are many ways in which people can invisibilize their immigration status. Often, this strategic invisibility works directly through certain forms of strategic visibility such as those discussed above. In regards to strategic invisibility, the identity visibilized is one that works counter to prevalent beliefs of undocumented migrants. Such identities can be linked to union membership, entrepreneurship, and being a university student, because the prevalent beliefs may center on the inability of undocumented migrants to belong to such groups or partake in particular activities.

In 2006, I conducted a study focusing on the experiences of undocumented Latina/o students at a California university. As part of this study I worked with a university organization whose mission statement focused on advancing the higher educational opportunities of undocumented students and activism concerning undocumented immigrant rights. Data for this paper consist of field notes taken during meetings and seven semi-structured interviews. Collection of data took place during the 2005-2006 school year. Because of the sensitive nature of the project, pseudonyms were used to protect the identity of the participants. All but one participant were members of the student organization and recruited through the meetings. The only participant not part of the group was referred by a member. In order to participate in the interviews, participants had to fulfill two criteria: enrollment in higher education at the time of the study and undocumented status at any time during enrollment.

At the time of this study, this organization was mainly made up of undocumented students. However, because of ideas regarding the inability for undocumented migrants to access the university, they could at times invisibilize their immigration status by using their university student status. This allowed them to engage in political work including holding workshops in high schools regarding their ability to access higher education in California and attending political rallies.

The effectiveness of this strategy was affected by their racialization and the conflation of Latina/os with undocumented status. When speaking about this conflation, particularly for my participants who were all Mexican, there is a history of prejudice that further affects undocumented migrants. In the case of Mexico, this collection of prejudices and the employment of deficiency theories on Mexicans predate the annexation of what is now the American Southwest.[51] According to Fanon the collective ascription of attitudes and prejudices must be understood not as abstract and possibly innocent cognitive functions, such as the collective unconscious, but instead as a consequence of colonial relations.[52] For Fanon, the use of theories naturalizing prejudices forget history and the longevity of colonial impositions, including those that ascribe deficiency or superiority. Specifically, when speaking about Jung's concept of the collective unconscious Fanon states that "the collective unconscious is not dependent on cerebral heredity; it is the result of what I shall call the unreflected imposition of a culture."[53] To Fanon, the collective unconscious "is purely and simply the sum of prejudices, myths, collective attitudes of a given group."[54] Whether speaking of a collective unconscious or another reified set of ascriptions regarding social groups, the effect is the same. For undocumented Latina/os, this means the imposition of deficiency ideologies based on their racialization and "illegalization." In addition to how race invokes suspicions of undocumented status, gender plays an important role in the way those bodies are further marked. This can include ideas about the "dangerous man of color" principally relating to the possibility of gang membership, or the angry woman of color illegitimately relying on social services. These physical markers could at times be negotiated by attempting to make particular facets of their identity more easily recognizable in order to avoid suspicion.

Strategic invisibility does not only consist of strategically accentuating, enacting or visibilizing one identity in order to invisibilize another deemed contradictory to the first. It also entails other strategic forms of invisibilizing oneself including the way one looks and sounds in order to blend into the mainstream. Because of the discrimination experienced by many migrants, there is a long history of parents refusing to teach their children their "native language" due to fears that their children will also receive similar discriminatory treatment. This practice has a long history and became a coping strategy for individuals contending with institutions based on the devaluing of minoritized peoples' cultures and preaching "success" as assimilation. In situations where assimilation is considered the best strategy, children may be only allowed to speak in the language considered dominant in their current nation of residence. In such instances, the loss of an accent may also be deemed the best possible outcome.

Practices to appear as part of the mainstream and not stand out could also include learning the current modes of dress among peers. In my study, one student reminisced about his high school experience and his need to fit in by stating that "high school is the time to be popular you don't want to feel embarrassed you don't want people to make fun of you, you don't want people to call you wetback or whatever."[55] Invisibilizing strategies associated with modes of dress can also include wearing clothing or buttons with American references including "U.S." sweatshirts and other nationalist or popular icons.

In order to avoid suspicion, undocumented migrants can also strategically invisibilize their status through providing rationalizations for not being able to partake in activities from which they are barred. These rationalizations can involve playing up counter-mainstream identities that appear to have nothing or little to do with immigration status. Rationalizing reasons for not engaging in activities considered to be important to peers can be a strategic form of minimizing or dismissing suspicions regarding an individual's immigration status. Examples of this can include the student who is of "voting age" but tells her/his friends that she/he will not vote because they don't like the candidates, are not interested in politics, or doesn't think a vote will make a difference. Again, drawing on my 2006 study, one student who was considered to be a radical and political hippie told his peers that he was not interested in receiving financial aid because he did not want the government's help in receiving an education.[56] He strategically expressed a rationalization that was believable due to his persona and that would not arise any suspicions about his immigration status.

It is important to not confuse strategic invisibility with assimilation. This means that migrants utilizing this method do not dispose of their cultural beliefs and replace them with dominant ideas. Instead, strategic invisibility is a method for undocumented migrants to circumvent the oppressive forces exercised upon them through the production of illegality. The purpose of strategically invisibilizing oneself is merely to appear as part of the mainstream in order to deflect suspicions about their immigration status. Therefore, the act of strategically invisibilizing oneself may be considered as a form of counter-acculturation. According to Fanon, "the phenomena of counter-acculturation must be understood as the organic impossibility of a culture to modify any one of its customs without at the same time re-evaluating its deepest values, its most stable models."[57] I do not claim that migrants do not assimilate or that assimilative pressures can be lessened through the practice of strategic invisibility. Instead, I recognize that the constant assimilative pressures experienced by undocumented migrants have a significant effect upon them. There are also costs attached to the practice of appearing mainstream or assimilated including exclusion from one's own group because of perceptions of rejecting of one's culture.

VIOLENCE AND THE COST OF STRATEGIC IN/VISIBILITY

One of the predominant themes in the discussions above is how the myriad forms of violence affect the daily lives of undocumented migrants. These forms of violence can have psychological as well as physical effects on each individual. At perhaps a more basic level, the threat of violence, that is, the knowledge that violence can occur, can have deep psychological impacts. It can deter individuals from engaging in community activities, forging new networks, obtaining better employment, and accessing education or training programs as well as medical and mental health services.

Violence from the state can include social barriers, detention, deportation, obstruction at the border and death directly or indirectly arising from interaction with immigration enforcement. As Fanon states, "in colonial relations ... the proximity and frequent, direct intervention by the police and the military ensure the colonized are kept under close scrutiny, and contained by rifle butts and napalm."[58] Examples of such interventions for undocumented migrants include the increased militarization of borders, the continuous and increased spending on immigration enforcement, and the high profile immigration raids that have become more prevalent. These overt practices that attempt to discipline have a ripple effect since they are intended to incite the fear of state violence in all other undocumented migrants who could become targets themselves.

Violence is also transgressed through the exclusion from essential services. As Fanon states,

> *the colonized world is a world divided in two. The dividing line, the border, is represented by the barracks and the police stations. In the colonies, the official, legitimate agent, the spokesperson for the colonizer and the regime of oppression, is the police officer or the soldier.*[59]

For undocumented migrants the dividing line may be the service provider or administrator when attempting to access a social service as well as the police or immigration officer, or simply any individual willing to disclose their immigration status to the authorities. As Anzaldúa reminds us, borders, at all levels, serve a specific purpose in colonial relations. She states "borders are set up to define the places that are safe and unsafe, to distinguish *us* from *them* [emphasis in original].[60] Such instances of exclusion experienced by undocumented migrants are referred to as "boundaries" by Cunningham and Heyman.[61] They explain how such boundaries, "along with other lines of spatial enclosure provide a crucial vantage point on otherwise seemingly natural definitions of spaces, peoples, and commodities."[62] The boundary is often the request for proof of citizenship or permanent residence by service providers. These boundaries result in experiences of violence for migrants including the denial of health services except for emergency services, the ineligibility for drivers' licenses, and the possibility that a service provider may divulge information to immigration authorities. As Cunningham and Heyman explain, "as the role of states has grown in the reproduction of society and in education, health care, urban services, the environment, and political debates that surround those roles, boundaries rise in importance as a means of regulatory enclosure." [63] In Fanonian terms, the myriad borders, barriers, and boundaries undocumented migrants experience must be considered colonial encounters where migrants are ascribed a particular subjugated subjectivity according to their immigration status. As such, boundaries are often depicted in zero-sum discourses where the gain of one is to the detriment of another. In this way, access for undocumented migrants is often presented as a burden on everyone else. In addition, given the dehumanizing way in which undocumented migrants are presented to the public, the exclusion from essential services is seen as a natural course of action given the ways their lives are often devalued. It is imperative that race and the racialization of undocumented migrants be considered as having an important effect on their everyday life and the barriers they face. According to Newton "race plays a role in solidifying popular conceptions of who deserves and who does not deserve public benefits and that's why race cannot be sidelined." [64] In this way, the racialization of undocumented migrants works to further dehumanize them and invisibilized the violence transgressed upon them.

Oppression is not relegated solely to colonized-colonizer relations but can also include relations between the colonized. As Zlolniski has shown, the community or family can also employ oppressive practices towards undocumented migrants.[65] At times taking the role that Fanon discussed as "intermediaries," some individuals become an oppressive link between employers and their family members.[66] Zlolniski found that these oppressive relations include taking a cut from or withholding migrants' wages, imposing deplorable housing conditions, or determining their working conditions.[67] These forms of violence are made possible through the invisibilization migrants are forced to live under. Those living "shadowed lives" understand their limited recourse to protection from the law as well as their vulnerability if someone were to contact immigration enforcement.[68] This understanding of their social position in the context of reception is reminiscent of Fanon's statement that "the colonial subject is a man penned in; apartheid is but one method of compartmentalizing the colonial world. The first thing the colonial subject learns is to remain in his place and not overstep its limits." [69] The limits forced upon undocumented migrants are transgressed to an extent through a number of strategies, however these strategies can carry a physical and psychological cost as well.

While earlier sections of this paper have shown a number of strategies that undocumented migrants employ to resist the violences inherent in their immigration status, it is important to recognize the possibility of violence entwined in their use. For undocumented migrants this means having prepared responses to suspicions regarding their immigration status. These responses, while strategically utilized, come at a cost. Undocumented migrants must constantly think about how to switch particular conversations to steer clear of questions about their immigration status or have already prepared answers in case questions arise.[70] Psychologically, the cost of such a strategy includes, as stated above, possible negative sanctions from within one's own community, as well as the stress of having prepared responses available at all times. Furthermore there are the possible effects to self-esteem internalizing how undocumented migrants are perceived in today's society and the need to mask such an important part of their everyday life. According to Fanon,

> *The defensive positions born of this violent confrontation between the colonized and the colonial constitute a structure which then reveals the colonized personality. In order to understand this 'sensibility' we need only to study and appreciate the scope and depth of the wounds inflicted on the colonized during a single day under a colonial regime.*[71]

A potential consequence to the psychological impact of being undocumented includes depression and a loss of self-esteem.[72] For instance, two participants in my study described the effect undocumented status had on their everyday life. A third year university female student stated, "You make your own mental situations of what could happen to you and it kind of like creates this like psychological mindset that you know, like you're less than everybody else."[73] Similarly, a second year female student at the same university who had also sought a university psychologist stated,

> *I just feel that people are going to look down upon me because I'm undocumented, I don't have the same rights that they do . . . I see people and I talk to them and I tell them yeah I'm undocumented and then I like right away when I tell them that I feel like my level went down you know? As long as they don't know they see me as anyone else but I feel that if they know that I'm undocumented like my self-esteem goes low.*[74]

These excerpts from the interviews describe the psychological impacts of undocumented migrants who must continuously invisibilize their immigration status, as well as the internalization of the negative ways in which undocumented migrants are portrayed.

Another facet of an individual's strategic invisibilization of their immigration status may include the physical avoidance of social interactions that carry the danger of disclosing their immigration status. These interactions may include what today are considered vital services, such as attempting to access health clinics and schools, as well as contacting the police, should the need arise. It is important to recognize that in many localities the fears of disclosing undocumented status to social service providers, teachers, or police are well founded and come from a collective experience. Finally, locations where migrants may develop community may also become unavailable when threatened by rumors of immigration round-ups or when policing is increased.

Although the potential for violence is high, as I have discussed, this does not mean that the colonized will internalize its effects or that they will not resist. As Fanon reminds us,

> *Confronted with a world configured by the colonizer, the colonized subject is always presumed guilty. The colonized does not accept his guilt, but rather considers it a kind of curse, a sword of Damocles. But deep down the colonized subject acknowledges no authority. He is dominated but not domesticated. He is made to feel inferior, but by no means convinced of his inferiority.* [75]

Violence is an intrinsic facet of the production of "illegality." It invisibilizes undocumented migrants through the use of dehumanizing rhetoric and by instituting policies that devalue the worth of their life.

CONCLUSION

Through the use of various concepts advanced by Fanon, I have examined the ways in which visibility and invisibility affect undocumented migrants, as well as some strategies migrants use in order to navigate between periods of visibility and invisibility. In the U.S. and other imperialist nations today, capitalist growth depends on the exploitation of labor, and racist colonial ideas that position particular undocumented migrants as disposable and deportable labor. As a result, nativist and xenophobic violence (at all levels and in all its forms) will continue to increase. However, the strategic use of resistance at the individual and collective levels will enable the colonized to continue to resist the constant attempts to strip them of their humanity. Similar to Fanon's reports of Algerian society at the time of the Algerian revolution, undocumented migrants know of the importance of strategically visibilizing and invisibilizing themselves in order to avoid suspicion and surveillance. In addition, migrants and their allies have also engaged with mediums of communication to mobilize around important issues as well as combat attacks on their communities.

NOTES

1. Frantz Fanon, *The Wretched of the Earth* (New York: Grove Press, 1963), 183; Frantz Fanon, *A Dying Colonialism* (New York: Grove Press, 1965).
2. Fanon, *A Dying Colonialism*.
3. D. T. Goldberg, "In/Visibility and Super/Vision: Fanon on Race, Veils, and Discourses of Resistance," in *Fanon: A Critical Reader*, ed. Lewis R. Gordon, T. Denean Sharpley-Whiting, and Renee T. White (Oxford: Blackwell Critical Readers Series, 1996).
4. F. J. Villegas, "Challenging Educational Barriers: Undocumented Immigrant Student Advocates" (Thesis, San Jose State University, 2006).
5. Goldberg, "In/Visibility and Super/Vision: Fanon on Race, Veils, and Discourses of Resistance," 179.
6. George Jerry Sefa Dei, *Anti-Racism Education: Theory and Practice* (Halifax, N.S.: Fernwood Pub., 1996), 41.
7. Kerstin Roger, "("Making") White Women through the Privatization of Education on Health and Well-Being in the Context of Psychotherapy," in *Anti-Racist Feminism*, ed. Agnes Calliste and George J. Sefa Dei (Halifax, Nova Scotia: Fernwood Publishing, 2000), 125.
8. Leo R. Chavez, *Shadowed Lives : Undocumented Immigrants in American Society, Case Studies in Cultural Anthropology*. (Fort Worth, TX: Harcourt Brace Jovanovich College Publishers, 1992).
9. Leo R. Chavez et al., "Undocumented Latina Immigrants in Orange County, California: A Comparative Analysis," *International Migration Review* 31, no. 1 (1997); Chavez, *Shadowed Lives : Undocumented Immigrants in American Society*; Leo R. Chavez, "A Glass Half Empty: Latina Reproduction and Public Discourse," in *Women and Migration in the U.S.-Mexico Borderlands : A Reader*, eds. Denise A. Segura and Patricia Zavella (Durham, NC: Duke University Press, 2007).
10. Nicholas De Genova, *Working the Boundaries : Race, Space, and "Illegality" in Mexican Chicago* (Durham, NC: Duke University Press, 2005).
11. Ibid.
12. Frantz Fanon, *Black Skin, White Masks* (New York: Grove Press, 1967).
13. De Genova, *Working the Boundaries : Race, Space, and "Illegality" in Mexican Chicago*.
14. Fanon, *The Wretched of the Earth*, 2.
15. Goldberg, "In/Visibility and Super/Vision: Fanon on Race, Veils, and Discourses of Resistance," 183.
16. Lina Newton, *Illegal, Alien, or Immigrant: The Politics of Immigration Reform* (New York and London: New York University Press, 2008), 153.
17. Dei, *Anti-Racism Education : Theory and Practice*, 68.
18. Fanon, *The Wretched of the Earth*, 182.
19. Ruben Rumbaut and Walter Ewing, "The Myth of Immigrant Criminality and the Paradox of Assimilation: Incarceration Rates among Native and Foreign-Born Men," (Washington, DC: Immigration Policy Center, 2007); Kent A. Ono and John M. Sloop, *Shifting Borders: Rhetoric, Immigration, and California's Proposition 187* (Philadelphia: Temple University Press, 2002).

20. Goldberg, "In/Visibility and Super/Vision: Fanon on Race, Veils, and Discourses of Resistance," 183.
21. Ibid., 184.
22. De Genova, *Working the Boundaries : Race, Space, and "Illegality" in Mexican Chicago;* Gilbert G. Gonzalez and Raul A. Fernandez, *A Century of Chicano History : Empire, Nations, and Migration* (New York: Routledge, 2003).
23. Luis Gutierrez and Joe Baca, "Mr. President, Stop Your Raids on Our Communities," *Chicago Tribune*, http://archives.chicagotribune.com/2008/aug/06/opinion/chi-oped0806raidaug06.
24. Chavez, *Shadowed Lives : Undocumented Immigrants in American Society*.
25. Nicholas De Genova, "Migrant 'Illegality' and Deportability in Everyday Life," *Annual Review of Anthropology* 31 (2002): 431.
26. Joseph Nevins, *Operation Gatekeeper: The Rise of The "Illegal Alien" and the Making of the U.S.-Mexico Boundary* (New York: Routledge, 2002).
27. De Genova, "Migrant 'Illegality' and Deportability in Everyday Life," 432.
28. Ibid., 425.
29. Steven Greenhouse, "Labor Urges Amnesty for Illegal Immigrants," *New York Times,* Feb 17 2000; Ginger Thompson, "U.S. And Mexico to Open Talks on Freer Migration for Workers: Bush Signaling New Focus on Immigration Issues," *New York Times,* Feb 16 2001.
30. Goldberg, "In/Visibility and Super/Vision: Fanon on Race, Veils, and Discourses of Resistance," 179.
31. De Genova, *Working the Boundaries : Race, Space, and "Illegality" in Mexican Chicago*.
32. Fanon, *The Wretched of the Earth,* 6.
33. Nevins, *Operation Gatekeeper: The Rise of The "Illegal Alien" and the Making of the U.S.-Mexico Boundary*.
34. *Arizona Daily Star,* "Death at the Border," http://regulus.azstarnet.com/borderdeaths/search.php.
35. Goldberg, "In/Visibility and Super/Vision: Fanon on Race, Veils, and Discourses of Resistance," 190.
36. Leo R. Chavez, *Covering Immigration : Popular Images and the Politics of the Nation* (Berkeley: University of California Press, 2001).
37. Ono and Sloop, *Shifting Borders: Rhetoric, Immigration, and California's Proposition 187;* Newton, *Illegal, Alien, or Immigrant: The Politics of Immigration Reform*.
38. Fanon, *The Wretched of the Earth,* 7.
39. Chavez, *Covering Immigration : Popular Images and the Politics of the Nation*.
40. Otto Santa Ana, *Brown Tide Rising: Metaphors of Latinos in Contemporary American Public Discourse* (Austin: University of Texas Press, 2002), 84.
41. Gabriele Griffin, "The Uses of Discourse Analysis in the Study of Gender and Migration," The University of York, http://www.york.ac.uk/res/researchintegration/Integrative_Research_Methods/Griffin%20Discourse%20Analysis%20April%202007.pdf.
42. Goldberg, "In/Visibility and Super/Vision: Fanon on Race, Veils, and Discourses of Resistance,"

43. Ibid.; Adrian J. Bailey et al., "(Re)Producing Salvadoran Transnational Geographies," Annals of the Association of American Geographers 92 (2002).
44. Ibid., 137.
45. Anthony Reinhart, "Good Enough for a Federal Scholarship..." *The Globe and Mail* 2008; Leo R. Chavez, *The Latino Threat : Constructing Immigrants, Citizens, and the Nation* (Stanford, CA.: Stanford University Press, 2008).
46. Ibid.
47. Goldberg, "In/Visibility and Super/Vision: Fanon on Race, Veils, and Discourses of Resistance," 190; Fanon, *A Dying Colonialism*.
48. Goldberg, "In/Visibility and Super/Vision: Fanon on Race, Veils, and Discourses of Resistance," 191.
49. F. J. Villegas, "Visibility/Invisibility: A Catch-22 for Undocumented College Students," in *"Displacements: Borders, Mobility and Statelessness." The 2008 John Douglass Taylor Conference* (McMaster University, Hamilton ON: 2008).
50. Vincenzo Ruggiero, "The Fight to Reappear," *Social Justice* 27, no. 2 (2000): 53.
51. Gilbert G. Gonzalez, *Culture of Empire: American Writers, Mexico, and Mexican Immigrants, 1880-1930* (Austin: University of Texas Press, 2003).
52. Fanon, *Black Skin, White Masks*.
53. Ibid., 191.
54. Ibid., 188.
55. Villegas, "Challenging Educational Barriers: Undocumented Immigrant Student Advocates," 75.
56. Ibid.
57. Fanon, *A Dying Colonialism*, 41-42.
58. Ibid.
59. Ibid., 3.
60. Gloria Anzaldúa, *Borderlands/La Frontera : The New Mestiza*, Second ed. (San Francisco: Aunt Lute Books, 1999), 25.
61. Hillary Cunningham and Josiah M. Heyman, "Introduction: Mobilities and Enclosures at Borders," *Identities* 11, no. 3 (2004).
62. Ibid., 294.
63. Ibid., 293.
64. Newton, *Illegal, Alien, or Immigrant: The Politics of Immigration Reform*, 138.
65. Christian Zlolniski, *Janitors, Street Vendors, and Activists : The Lives of Mexican Immigrants in Silicon Valley* (Berkeley: University of California Press, 2006).
66. Fanon, *A Dying Colonialism*.
67. Zlolniski, *Janitors, Street Vendors, and Activists : The Lives of Mexican Immigrants in Silicon Valley*.
68. Chavez, *Shadowed Lives : Undocumented Immigrants in American Society*.
69. Fanon, *The Wretched of the Earth*, 14.
70. Villegas, "Visibility/Invisibility: A Catch-22 for Undocumented College Students."
71. Fanon, *The Wretched of the Earth*, 182.
72. Villegas, "Challenging Educational Barriers: Undocumented Immigrant Student Advocates."
73. Ibid., 74.

74. Ibid., 77.
75. Fanon, *The Wretched of the Earth*, 16.

REFERENCES

Anzaldúa, Gloria. *Borderlands/La Frontera : The New Mestiza*. Second ed. San Francisco: Aunt Lute Books, 1999.
Arizona Daily Star. "Death at the Border." http://regulus.azstarnet.com/borderdeaths/search.php.
Bailey, Adrian J., Richard A. Wright, Alison Mountz, and Ines M. Miyares. "(Re)Producing Salvadoran Transnational Geographies." *Annals of the Association of American Geographers* 92 (2002): 125-44.
Chavez, Leo R. *Covering Immigration : Popular Images and the Politics of the Nation*. Berkeley: University of California Press, 2001.
——— "A Glass Half Empty: Latina Reproduction and Public Discourse." In *Women and Migration in the U.S.-Mexico Borderlands: A Reader*, edited by Denise A. Segura and Patricia Zavella, 67-91. Durham, N.C.: Duke University Press, 2007.
——— *The Latino Threat : Constructing Immigrants, Citizens, and the Nation*. Stanford, CA: Stanford University Press, 2008.
——— *Shadowed Lives : Undocumented Immigrants in American Society, Case Studies in Cultural Anthropology*. Fort Worth, TX: Harcourt Brace Jovanovich College Publishers, 1992.
Chavez, Leo R., Allan Hubbell, Shiraz I. Mishra, and Burciaga R. Valdez. "Undocumented Latina Immigrants in Orange County, California: A Comparative Analysis." *International Migration Review* 31, no. 1 (1997): 88-107.
Cunningham, Hillary, and Josiah M. Heyman. "Introduction: Mobilities and Enclosures at Borders." *Identities* 11, no. 3 (2004): 289-302.
De Genova, Nicholas. "Migrant 'Illegality' and Deportability in Everyday Life." *Annual Review of Anthropology* 31 (2002): 419-47.
——— *Working the Boundaries : Race, Space, And "Illegality" in Mexican Chicago*. Durham, NC: Duke University Press, 2005.
Dei, George Jerry Sefa. *Anti-Racism Education : Theory and Practice*. Halifax, N.S.: Fernwood Pub., 1996.
Fanon, Frantz. *Black Skin, White Masks*. New York: Grove Press, 1967.
——— *A Dying Colonialism*. New York: Grove Press, 1965.
——— *The Wretched of the Earth*. New York: Grove Press, 1963.
Goldberg, D. T. "In/Visibility and Super/Vision: Fanon on Race, Veils, and Discourses of Resistance." In *Fanon: A Critical Reader*, edited by Lewis R. Gordon, T. Denean Sharpley-Whiting and Renee T. White, 179-202. Oxford: Blackwell Critical Readers Series, 1996.
Gonzalez, Gilbert G. *Culture of Empire: American Writers, Mexico, and Mexican Immigrants, 1880-1930*. Austin: University of Texas Press, 2003.
Gonzalez, Gilbert G., and Raul A. Fernandez. *A Century of Chicano History : Empire, Nations, and Migration*. New York: Routledge, 2003.

Greenhouse, Steven. "Labor Urges Amnesty for Illegal Immigrants." *New York Times,* Feb 17 2000, 26.

Griffin, Gabriele. "The Uses of Discourse Analysis in the Study of Gender and Migration." The University of York, http://www.york.ac.uk/res/researchintegration/Integrative_Research_Methods/Griffin%20Discourse%20Analysis%20April%202007.pdf.

Gutierrez, Luis, and Joe Baca. "Mr. President, Stop Your Raids on Our Communities." *Chicago Tribune,* http://archives.chicagotribune.com/2008/aug/06/opinion/chi-oped0806raidaug06.

Nevins, Joseph. *Operation Gatekeeper: The Rise of the "Illegal Alien" and the Making of the U.S.-Mexico Boundary.* New York: Routledge, 2002.

Newton, Lina. *Illegal, Alien, or Immigrant: The Politics of Immigration Reform.* New York and London: New York University Press, 2008.

Ono, Kent A., and John M. Sloop. *Shifting Borders: Rhetoric, Immigration, and California's Proposition 187.* Philadelphia: Temple University Press, 2002.

Reinhart, Anthony. "Good Enough for a Federal Scholarship . . ." *The Globe and Mail* 2008.

Roger, Kerstin. ("Making") White Women through the Privatization of Education on Health and Well-Being in the Context of Psychotherapy." In *Anti-Racist Feminism,* edited by Agnes Calliste and George J. Sefa Dei, 123-42. Halifax, Nova Scotia: Fernwood Publishing, 2000.

Ruggiero, Vincenzo. "The Fight to Reappear." *Social Justice* 27, no. 2 (2000): 45-60.

Rumbaut, Ruben, and Walter Ewing. "The Myth of Immigrant Criminality and the Paradox of Assimilation: Incarceration Rates among Native and Foreign-Born Men." 20. Washington DC: Immigration Policy Center, 2007.

Santa Ana, Otto. *Brown Tide Rising: Metaphors of Latinos in Contemporary American Public Discourse.* Austin: University of Texas Press, 2002.

Thompson, Ginger. "U.S. And Mexico to Open Talks on Freer Migration for Workers: Bush Signaling New Focus on Immigration Issues." *New York Times,* Feb 16 2001, 1.

Villegas, Francisco J. "Challenging Educational Barriers: Undocumented Immigrant Student Advocates." Thesis, San Jose State University, 2006.

——— "Visibility/Invisibility: A Catch-22 for Undocumented College Students." In "Displacements: Borders, Mobility and Statelessness." The 2008 John Douglass Taylor Conference. McMaster University, Hamilton, ON. 2008.

Zlolniski, Christian. *Janitors, Street Vendors, and Activists: The Lives of Mexican Immigrants in Silicon Valley.* Berkeley: University of California Press, 2006.

CHAPTER EIGHT

Concerning Modernity, the Caribbean Diaspora and Embodied Alienation
Dialoguing with Fanon to Approach an Anticolonial Politic

MARLON SIMMONS

Somewhere within the humanism of Euromodernity resides the Diasporic constellation. One being formed through bodies of time and space, as of having its contours shaped through the congeries of unsettling geographies, cultural landscapes, difference, cosmopolitanism, as being co-existing constituents of the Enlightenment public sphere, one marked through transcendental relations. How might we begin to understand the poetics of Diasporic life? As the title suggests, I am concerned with how and by what means the Caribbean Diaspora come to make meaning of its everyday social interactions? Increasingly, I have been thinking about how Fanon could help me to better understand this experience. Fanon too, experienced a Diasporic way of being, having moved from his place of birth, Martinique, to study clinical psychiatry in France. Arriving in the heart of France, at the center of modernity, he bumped into racism in a particular way that differentiated itself from his Caribbean experience in Martinique. The propensity of racism as was practiced in France, conjured many distinct moments to his racial experience of Martinique. In Martinique as Fanon would say, he was a "West-Indian," a distinct coterminous category to that of the African. Being well educated, as he was, allowed his body to maneuver through, in Fanon's terms, the "historical racial schema" as embedded in Martinique through plantation life. He found that his body, as deeply entrenched within the corporeal schema of colonization, to be closer to the body of Euromodernity, a proximity that brought a refreshing distancing to the nearby plantation enclave. Moreover, this plantation life was already pre-reserved for the body of the African. But in coming to France the experience taught him otherwise, he found his 'blackness' rooted to the African, buttressed to the plantation. How was Fanon then, in his newly found Diasporic environment to now work with this archetype human condition of plantation life? Keeping Fanon in mind, I would like to grasp the way in which the Caribbean Diasporic body comes to know itself through the governance of hue. I am more interested in how the Caribbean Diasporic body is discursively formed and at the same time positioned and regulated by a Eurocentric discursive field. I want to sift out the way in which the morals of colonialism come to be internalized, and simultaneously produce a particular docility (Foucault 1995) on the Diasporic body. From the location of the Caribbean Diaspora, how then I ask, does one come to experience and make sense of modernity? How do Diasporic peoples understand their lived public sphere? How does culture as a way of knowing form integrative spaces for Diasporic bodies? By what means do race, culture, Diasporic experiences organize the human condition of blackness? How do Diasporic peoples build a working cultural registrar to strategically engage their everyday lived social existence? And how do Caribbean Diasporic peoples come to understand the need to wittingly or to strategically de-race themselves to maneuver through their everyday socio-political terrain? (Dei 2008 a,b).

One cannot discuss these questions without talking about issues of colonialism, such as, by what means does the colonial re-present itself within contemporary public sphere? What are the ways in which the human conditions of Diasporic peoples materialize themselves through hue? What does Fanon give us by way of an anti-colonial politic to earnestly engage these contemporary issues? Questions concerning violence, identity, race, subjectivity, culture, liberation, gender, sexuality and the able-body are all relevant to the everyday social. But how can we read Fanon to think through these everyday issues of the social? Fanon has come to be placed on the margins of academia, and some have said that his language comes across as out of context at times, some have said that Fanon condones violence, that the hetero-patriarchal masculinist overtones are way to saturated in his writing. Not to dismiss or sweep aside these critiques, Sekyi-Otu's (1996) reading is important, if we are taking up Fanon as an interpretative framework to help us understand our present political terrain. Sekyi-Otu suggests reading Fanon as "one dramatic dialectic narrative." That is, within the colonial context, to think of these questions in relation to each other, rather than to isolate or to say individualize in some linear format. Yet Sekyi-Otu's reading of Fanon as "one dramatic dialectic narrative" can be limiting, that is, to seek to theorize Fanon on an intellectual level from the academic halls as anachronistic determinants, and not as a voice from within the violent encounter. We always need to remind ourselves of the colonizing experience that centered his writing, that Fanon spoke from the trenches, he spoke from his lived

CONCERNING MODERNITY | 173

experience with white colonial forces, be it from Martinique, Algeria or France, the experience was already imbued in and through racism. With this discussion then, I am not focusing on an in-depth examination of Fanon's intellectual contribution, the intention is more to think through Fanon's oeuvre in order to build on an anticolonial politic. The purpose here is to extricate the Diasporic body of difference from a homogenous socialization of Euro-modernity by engaging in what I am thinking of as selective communicative practices, which come to self-determine Diasporic citizenship. I am not though attempting to come up with a prescription or the ideal set of solutions. I am however trying to invoke "pedagogic thoughtfulness" (Van Manen 1997), more of a sense of critical discernment on day-to-day Diasporic life in order to understand how one's Diasporic experience might come to be accepted performative norms.

In what follows, I speak about hue and the way it forms itself into a material currency for the Diaspora. With this I am concerned about how hue comes to embody time and space, that is, how does a particular space come to be suggestive of a certain form of hue? I am thinking about what does this mean for Diasporic bodies to have to engage these spaces through these already permanent suggestions? I bring attention to the moment whereby Diasporic peoples come to know, as Foster (2007) puts it, one's ethnoracial register. I am interested in how this ethnoracial register comes to provide the tacit knowledge needed to form communicative strategies that allows for temporary 'extrication' from what Fanon frames as the epidermal regions of inferiority, that is, the locus of the Diasporic domain, what we come to know as the Caribbean. I ask some pointed questions concerning this nomenclature of the Caribbean, that is, to consider the historical origins and implications for the Diasporic body. I then consider the popular 'black' body within contemporary public sphere, that of Presidency, in particular some complexities concerning limitations and possibilities of the fact of blackness. I also discuss what Fanon locates as the alienation of blackness, the conversation here concerns itself with how alienation embodies the ethical and moral conditions of Diasporic 'Truths'. I then move to the intricacies of the Diasporic experience, through Fanon's discussion on particular acts of assimilation, integration, acculturization and simultaneous deculturization. I am concerned here with, to what extent do these acts constitute forms of strategic distancing to local Diasporic cultures? This conversation spills over into the nuances of Diasporic peoples as of having a sense of national consciousness. I try to tease the way Indigenous ways of knowing come to re-present themselves, in order to engage the public sphere of Euromodernity. I want to better understand how Diasporic bodies come to lactify certain communicative processes, which in of itself constitutes a particular geo-denegryfication. I ground the discussion by contemplating Caribbean identity, the possibilities for Diasporic intersubjectivity, the unfreedoms of a post-humanism and the potentiality for education.

MATERIAL EMBODIMENT OF HUE: WHAT IS THIS CARIBBEAN?

Before we set out, I think it is important to talk about the material conditions of Diasporic peoples, in particular, the body, as it constitutes the material. We need to note also, the relationship through enslavement and plantation life where the colonizer's epistemological imposition of hue come to form the raw resources for present day 'Truth' systems. We cannot discount the question of time and space, and we cannot neglect the way in which, historical meanings resonate in our daily interactions, we cannot simply trumpet the notion of democracy and say access for all regardless of ableism, race, class, gender, and sexuality. We cannot continue to talk about issues of oppression and domination through a de-raced lens that cries out to a neo-liberal humanitarian ideology (Dei 2008 a, b). We cannot sweep the issue of hue and the co-present currency under the rug. If we were to speak to these pressing issues, then concerning the matter of hue, for the moment I would like to position 'blackness' as the base of material conditions. Firstly let me say from the front, that I am thinking of 'blackness' as a colonial discursive formation that organizes and inscribes particular meanings onto the said body. I am thinking of 'blackness' as an already formative occasion that brings a classificatory system of "Truth' on the said body. That through 'blackness' one comes into an already disciplined way of understanding humanity. Concerning the 'already formative occasion,' I am thinking of the ontological. Egon G. Guba and Yvonna S. Lincoln talk about ontology:

> *As a reality which was shaped over time by the congeries of social, political, cultural, economic, ethnic, and gender factors, and then crystallized (reified into a series of structures that are now inappropriately) taken as "real," that is, natural and immutable. For all practical purposes the structures as "real," a virtual or historical reality. (Guba and Lincoln 1994: 110)*

The ontological question then is, " what is the form and nature of reality" that governs the Caribbean Diasporic body? Concerning the Caribbean, Glissant's question is important here, that of, "What is the Caribbean in fact?" (Glissant 1999: 39). Glissant speaks about the Caribbean as being a "multiple series of relationships." Yet, immanent to these relationships are denigrating colonial constructed categories of knowledge which come to represent Indigeousness, need we be reminded of Carib, Arawak, and Amerindian. Here devalued meanings are colonially ascribed to not only a peoplehood, but in a totalizing way, to bodies, geographies, time and space, which then come to be deemed as "uncivilized, barbaric, bestial, ugly" (Fanon 1967). I want to historically trace the origins of these colonially engendered formations to the discourse of 'blackness.' So in thinking about the Caribbean through the matter of hue, it is not my position then, to come across in a totalizing way to say that every body that emerges from the Caribbean in a permanent way is constructed as 'black.' I am saying though that the Caribbean, which was historically framed through the trope of barbarism, through the trope of primitivism, that the archipelago, which has come to be governed through this accepted title of Caribbean, was discursively organized and inscribed through grand colonial narratives, that the Caribbean, the archetype for plantation life, had as its base, the material human condition of 'blackness,' that this geography known as the Caribbean comes to be constituted, as Fanon would say, as the epidermalization of inferiority. In a sense through Euromodernity, the Caribbean was formed as this historical abject. What we ought to understand is that what emerged with modernity is the dialectic discursive field of "whiteness/blackness" (Goldberg 1993:43). Whiteness then is in relation to 'blackness' (Fanon 1967: 110). Hence in talking about modernity, the Caribbean Diaspora embodied alienation, I do not think we can afford to discard the dialectical material embodiment immanent in 'black.' I think we also have to guard here against slippage in interpreting hue as a sum homogeneous schema of the Caribbean. So with this understanding of the Caribbean as being constituted through hue, I am now then, thinking of hue as this shifting constitutive paradigm that endows modernity with a particular mode of orientation. I am more thinking how time, place, bodies and geographies in a very totalizing way come to be discursively scripted through hue and come to form a mode of organizing relations for Diasporic peoples. I am also mindful that within contemporary public sphere life we have no certainty that this discursive has some said definite locus, instead what is experienced is this shifting spatio-temporal terrain onto the body. I think we ought to spend some time here and talk about the ethical and moral implications of speaking of this thing of 'blackness' in way that strategically acknowledges the dominant historic paradigm. What are the consequences and implications to let us say strategically essentialize, to work with what Fanon calls 'the epidermalization of inferiority,' to posit this 'black' as abject, as denigrating? And what about essentializing? Mind you, regarding essentializing, I am thinking about the constitutive process which accords permanent negating knowledges onto the said body. So we have to be careful here in already scripting the 'limits of possibilities' onto the said 'black' body, this is not to negate the human conditions of plantation life, that of master-slave dialectic as void of the contemporary public. I think the question that is pushing out here is, How is it that colonial moments re-present themselves in our every day lives? If we are to acknowledge this shifting spatio-temporal terrain of the 'black' body then what does it mean here to strategically essentialize?

What does it mean for the 'black' body to be cognizant of this designated public sphere reading of self? What does it mean for the 'black' body to understand the fluid discursive rules of 'blackness'? The question coming up here, which to me seems to be permeating throughout Fanon's text, is that of, how do we extricate ourselves from 'blackness'? (Fanon 1967: 10). More so, how does the Diasporic body come to understand which discursive rule to embody and simultaneously reify as some material good? And what knowledge counts to inform everyday communicative practices, which are utilized to engage strategically, the contemporary public sphere of Euro-modernity? So if we are thinking about our contemporary public sphere, how do we understand this presidency as it emerged through 'blackness.'

PRESIDENCY—THE EXTRICATION OF BLACKNESS?

I remember November 4, 11ish pm, 2008. I was glued to my computer screen, checking out the elections. I don't know if I was more in shock or awe that Barack Obama won the elections, or was it the global attention the elections received, the fact that millions were watching/listening/paying attention in some way? But what was the interest? Was it that the world was curious/interested in political science/electoral politics or let's say issues pertaining to contemporary America? Or was it that a 'black' body won the presidency? What about this 'black' body left the world whispering? Is it that, at that moment there was this universalized perception/understanding of, what does it mean to be 'black'? Is it that, at that moment 'black' was in a global way understood, as Fanon would say as the 'wretched of the earth'? What does it mean then for that which is classified as the 'wretched of the earth,' for the body designated for plantation life to emerge to the position of presidential life? To what extent does this experience provide the conditions for (and to borrow Fanon's term) 'the extrication of blackness'? Is it that this moment ought to be interpreted as a moment of "ontological security"? (Giddens 1990). And within contemporary public sphere does it work to condition pedagogic trust among different bodies? There was a lot of shoo-shooing around Obama's identity. American, African-American, Black, African were all tossed around. I think though, that throughout the campaign, Obama's politics was more centred through a totalizing discourse of American. What are the implications here for Diasporic communities? What does it mean for "the fact of blackness" to be part and parcel, that is centre of White House operations? How does this speak to the moment Obama appeared hand in hand with the family for the token victory speech? I think we ought to talk about how do we understand "the fact of blackness" as an organizing principle of White House operations. Historically we come to know this location as organized/inscribed in and through modernity, that of presidential subjectivity. What then does this mean for modernity and the Diaspora when presidential subjectivity is now occasioned/attended to by the raw material of plantation? Is this representative of this "new humanism" Fanon spoke about? What does this moment mean for countries that have been underdeveloped? What then does it mean for imperial America to be governed by the 'black' body? Another important conversation I think we ought to have, though I think it is too much for this discussion, is to consider the role of plantation life, in inscribing spiritual principles and ethical procedures onto the Diasporic body.

ALIENATION AS A HUMAN CONDITION

I want to point to what Fanon calls the "alienation of blackness" (Fanon 1967:11) as a material good. I am more or less thinking about the ways in which this material good becomes the interpretive framework for the said Diasporic body to make meaning of its lived socioeconomic public sphere. What are some of the limits and possibilities here and "how do we extricate ourselves?" (Fanon 1967:10). What are some of the communicative attitudes developed to mold Diasporic identity? And how is it that this "alienation of blackness," embodies the ethical and moral conditions of 'Truth,' which at the same time, accords a certain governance on the everyday lives of Diasporic bodies?

In the context of the Caribbean Diaspora, what we have here, is a way of engaging; it is more so a particular experience whereby the Diasporic body, through day-to-day negotiating, interacts with its newly found terrain, a sort of pick and choose if you will. This is not to say this negotiating is done in some formal sense. What it is, is that the Diasporic body goes through this unyielding self-dialogue where the goal is always already to fit in, acceptance or to say mobilize itself within the broader community. One could imagine that in coming to a new place these goals would pose some challenges. For me, I am more concerned with how and by what means do Diasporic peoples take up some of these challenges. With alienation as experienced from within, that is, this internalized inferiority, as a material good, as a starting point, and as alienated politically and socioeconomically, Diasporic peoples then as poised through what I am thinking of as a liminal constant, come to interact, form itself as this subjugated counterpublic (Fraser 1992: 123), which hereby, operates itself not necessarily with the will to subvert dominant paradigms, but more so in a way to strategically acculturize itself to the existing conditions of the present public sphere. This process can become quite complex, needless to say problematic, for to have to discursively interface with dominant paridgms, it seems to me it ensconces what Fanon speaks of as the need "to dissimulate, to deculturize and at the same time acculturize" (Fanon 1964: 40, 41, 42). Maybe we ought to open up the conversation here, to speak about dissimulation, deculturization, and acculturization, these important experiential moments for Diasporic peoples, what I think make for possible pedagogical moments which come to be imbued through this 'alienation of blackness.'

EPISTEMIC SALIENCE OF THE DIASPORIC EXPERIENCE: DISSIMULATION, DECULTURIZATION, AND ACCULTURIZATION

Concerning deculturization, I am more thinking of how the Diaspora through time and space, distances itself from continental lands, which then materializes itself through cultural modes of communicative exchange. Now, if as wa Thiong'o talks about, that "culture is a product of a peoples' history, and that it also reflects that history and embodies a whole set of values by which people view themselves and their place in time and space" (wa Thiong'o 1993: 42), mind you, here I am cognizant of the danger of bringing a particular monolith, fixed, homogenous reading of culture. So by no means am I trying to peg culture to such a position, I recognize the fluidity, flux and heterogeneity of culture, where I am going though, is to suggest that wa Thiong'o's reading is one of the possible ways of coming to understand culture and Diasporic peoples. So if we were to think of culture as it reflects history and as of embodying the values of Diasporic peoples, we can drum up some sort of communicative discursive interface, which ought to insulate Diasporic subjectivities from governing cultural practices. Yet this discursive interface more works to distance the Diasporic self from homegrown cultural dispositions, so be it "metaphysical guilt or be it the obsession with purity"(Fanon 1964: 18) the Diaspora then, comes to exude particular attitudes, whereby one of the experiences as Fanon succinctly puts it, is to "judge, condemn, to abandon language, food habits, sexual behavior, way of sitting down, resting, and laughing as such" (Fanon 1964: 39). What reveals itself in myriad ways is more of a dissimulated Diaspora where, dispositions, attitudes, expressions and behavioral ways are specifically re-shaped in order to be recognized by the popularized dominant culture. But dissimulation requires experiential knowledge, it requires an inter-intra cultural understanding of the lived social.

Aptly, Fanon refers to this particular experiential knowledge as "technical knowledge" (Fanon 1964). What we have with this everyday technical knowledge, is in a sense a form of purposive reasoning which always already has its mode of orientation steeped within the historical paradigms of colonial Euro modernity. It is more a mode of orientation whereby the governing locus emerges through plantation origins, which to me constitutes liminality, in that, plantation life provides for the Diaspora that consciousness, that spirit if you will, that cannot readily be felt or let us say be experienced by the dominant culture. If one of the problems coming out here is the capacity to communicate, then we ought to remember, and as Fanon reminds us, that well sketched within the Diaspora is this "historical racial schema" (Fanon 1967:111) a schema that comes to codify and let us say govern communicative and Diasporic interactions. If we were for the moment to think of the Diaspora as this "racial epidermal schema" then of concern here is the way in which the Diasporic body becomes a site of cultural exchange, through which communicative practices are informed by a particular mode of reasoning, whereby one's understanding of culture becomes a technical knowledge (Fanon 1964). There is a question of surveillance here, where the saliency of hue becomes the crucible for knowledge and makes possible a re-inscribed self-regulating way of knowing for the Diasporic body. This way of knowing is not to be confused with that of having epistemological authority (Dei 2008c). It is more an epistemic salience (Dei 2005) where the location of hue is historically shackled to colonial knowledging, which in a disciplined way work to position and re-position the domain of Diasporic interactions. As the Diaspora continues the never ending quest for the better life in the West, and as this Diasporic life becomes more and more entrenched with the push and pull of colonial positioning, with the push and pull of Euromodernity, communicative strategies then become very important. Indigenous peoples speak about the urgent need for "survival, recovery, development and self-determination" (Smith 1999). But how is it that the Diaspora takes up these moments? Is it through the process of assimilation? And if one were to assimilate with the governing culture, to what extent then is this integrative process a procedure of deracialization? What does it mean to say as a communicative pragmatic, the Diaspora to some extent has strategically de-raced language? To have self-determination, recovery, survival, and development to be all governed in and through this particular deracialization process, allows for totalizing deculturalized relations. See assimilation accords integration in a particular way that obtains in a sense a permanent dismissal of Diasporic culture. If we are talking integration then we ought to ask on whose terms. For how then, does the public sphere of Euromodernity integrate itself with Diasporic communities and take up its multiple centers? To speak of the integration of multiple public spheres, multiple communities, multiple centers is to be open to interactions of cultural difference. Problems pop up when these interactions come to exist through a one-way, fixed direction, whereby the compass becomes navigated through this universalized homogeneous scripting of Euro modernity. The economic outcome is real here for the Diaspora, resulting in assimilation becoming more and more the Diasporic companion. But what ought to take up more than a companion like position to Diasporic relationships is the experience of decolonization. In fact if we remember that colonial is not only foreign imposition but also as imposed from local positions (Dei & Kempf, 2006), we can then begin to discuss decolonization for all, rather than for a particular body that has its genealogy located within the colonized experience. With decolonization Diasporic peoples can work with embodied ways of knowing; Diasporic peoples can work with experiential knowledge as a cultural raw resource. Importantly here, the Diasporic body ought to be centered within their experience rather than being determined through some tangential existence. But what does it mean for the Caribbean Diaspora to work with the memory of local Indigenous histories?

MODERNITY, DIASPORIC DICTION, LACTIFICATION, AND THE EMBODIMENT OF CULTURAL CURRENCY: WHAT DOES IT MEAN FOR DIASPORIC PEOPLES TO HAVE A SENSE OF NATIONAL CONSCIOUSNESS?

While in France, Fanon's Diasporic experience was quite influenced by the Negritude movement, which allowed him to think of "the fact of blackness" more as a cultural raw resource than as some denigrating source. Leopold Senghor invites us to not only think of Negritude as a form of humanism, but also to think of the humanism of Negritude, in relation to the humanism as engendered through Euromodernity. He tells us that Negritude is "a will to return into oneself, that it is a will to take on the values of the black world, to live them oneself, that one has to make descent into a series of negations to retrieve the meaning of blackness, that Negritude is a humanism with a universal scope" (Senghor 2001). But this humanism with a universal scope, I think ought to be queried. Giddens asks us to think about modernity "beyond an epoch or an era, to think of modernity as an attitude, as a mode of organizing the social that emerged in Europe, To think then of modernity as set of political/institutional/economical/cultural/social processes located at a certain point in the development of Europe that universalized its way of knowing, as knowledge for all" (Giddens 1990, 1991). To some extent then, we are all historically determined through modernity. So when Senghor speaks of a humanism with a universal scope, I think too that this universality was always already discursively encoded through Eurocentric ways of knowing, and it is this said universal that provided the conditions of possibility and at the same time the limitations for the Negritude movement. Foucault reminds us of a certain humanism as revealed through Euromodernity, which was preoccupied with a set of themes, and as preserving by particular values, that was prominent in European societies (Foucault 2007: 111). Some of these themes were racism, masculinity/femininity, sexuality, whiteness, violence, aesthetics, ableism and religion. One of these themes that Fanon confronted was racism. A theme, in effect, legitimized whiteness as a Eurocentric aesthetic body of knowledge, and as being the only material means to humanism, a theme in fact, Negritude left well in place. So in a sense then, Negritude as a form of humanism was already ethically and morally constituted through the values of the cultural register of Euromodernity. Fanon, in wanting the wretched of the earth to extricate themselves from blackness, moved beyond the movement of Negritude. Fanon more so, troubled the humanism of Negritude, in doing so he centered the white-black dialectic, that is, the location of his blackness in relation to white, that black was constructed in relation to white, as the abject, as that of negation. Fanon spoke about:

> *The dialectic that brings necessity into the foundation of my freedom drives me out of myself. It shatters my unreflected position. Still in terms of consciousness, black consciousness is immanent in its own eyes. I am not a potentiality of something, I am wholly what I am. I do not have to look for the universal. No probability has any place inside me. My Negro consciousness does not hold itself out as a lack. It is. It is its own follower (Fanon 1967: 135).*

At the same time, Fanon challenged modernity as this Eurocentric body of knowledge, which determines this singular mode of humanism. and then proceeded to counter "epistemic salience" of modernity, by coming to understand how the black body make meaning of their lived experience in a white colonial public sphere and at the same time challenging the domain of white colonial, which in of itself is an anti-colonial politic, point of departure from the movement of Negritude, where Fanon seemed not to be convinced that Negritude was working to counter modernity as a master narrative, but more so, Negritude thought through Euro-paradigms to retrieve and shape its cultural histories. This is not so to say in a totalizing way we ought to dismiss the project of Negritude, no. In fact Sartre is correct when he speaks not of Negritude as anti-racist racism, but of Negritude being as a "dialectical progressive." The question coming out here then is, To what extent then did Negritude challenge or leave modernity intact as a form of humanism? Or to what extent did Negritude bring ontological security (Giddens 1991: 36; 1990: 92), to 'blackness'?

With the colonization of time the question of modernity has been bursting. Be it a particular period, a particular epoch, be it the way of organizing life and the ensuing behavioral expressions, be it the classification of the social. We ought to remember the historically trajectory of modernity, wherein the interests concern itself with a particular geo-humanity. More so to, we ought to think through how this humanism has come to be universalized as a mode of knowing in our everyday life. Familiarity with this text has governed contemporary norms, becoming in a sense, one's tacit go to sociocultural registrar. Navigating through these complex and yet sophisticated contours of public sphere life could be come quite challenging for Diasporic peoples. Given this text of modernity, what does it mean then for Diasporic peoples to work with a sense of national consciousness? Though some have argued for a cultural supermarket, that we live in a multicultural society, where we can participate in the myriad spaces that culture offers. Choice more often comes through this selective process of experiential understanding. What one comes to know innately, is in a sense, the value of the moment, the currency of the exchange, the currency of the interaction where the registrar makes its count in relation to Euromodernity. Cultural supermarket more so becomes the spatio-temporal meeting point, whereby expressions, behavioral ways and modes of thinking come to be socially organized at the site of the body. The body though comes to be inscribed in and through what Fanon talks about as the "historical racial schema" (Fanon 1967: 111). Challenging here is to understand how the Diasporic body comes to be discursively scripted and simultaneously becomes the occasion for the "corporeal malediction"(Fanon 1967: 111). That is, how do these sociohistorical discursivities of the "corporeal schema" mould the perceptions of Diasporic spaces? How do Diasporic spaces come to be preconditioned with the interpretive faculties to make meaning of the embodiment of cultural currency? What then are some of the attitudes that are formed through this understanding? If we are thinking about the embodiment of cultural currency and the ensuing attitudes within Diasporic spaces, then we ought to talk about the "Manicheism delirium" (Fanon 1967: 183). Firstly, where does this cultural currency (Bourdieu 1991) reside as distinctive of its embodiment? What constitutes this cultural currency? How does the Diaspora come to know this material good of race? What are some of the socio-historic discourses that come to form this knowledge of cultural currency? And what about this thing of a Diasporic spirit? How does this Diasporic spirit come to be fecund? What is the condition of the Diasporic spirit as it comes to be determined through these communicatives exchanges?

As society becomes more and more bound through Diasporic difference, and as the determinants of modernity work to re-codify social categories, the public sphere now quickly adapts itself by re-configuring its mode of orientation, difference that is, to the tune of Euromodernity. So, how is it then, that Diasporic difference learns to adapt or to what extent is Diasporic difference equipped for the challenges of the public sphere as governed through a Euro modernity mode of orientation? Is it through as Itwaru (1994) speaks about, an imitative intellectuality? In a sense then, this experience begs the question of the quality of humanism within the Diaspora. Concerning the quality of humanism here, Sylvia Wynter on reading Fanon, poses seemingly simple questions, that of, "What it is like to be human? and What it is like to be black?" (Wynter 2001: 31). We ought to note too, that there are different modes of the lived experience of blackness, as it circumscribes and forms constitutive elements within the constellation of the Diasporic difference. That immanent to the "lived experience of blackness" there is the sense of the liminal other (Wynter 2001: 57, 58), more of an anachronistic consciousness within Diasporic difference. For the lived experience of blackness to come into a particular humanism, to engage with "what it is like to be human?" the socializing process as determined through the Diaspora, takes up different modes of organizing itself. Let us take for instance language and the way perceptions, behavioral patterns, culture, communicative exchanges are shaped through this medium. For the Caribbean Diaspora, language is always already the moment of engaging with the liminality of the 'self/other' (Fanon 1967: 17: Wynter 2001: 57, 58). It is a moment of exchange whereby Diasporic diction comes to be an appreciated/depreciated material good in which hue constitutes its historical base. Be it to strategically distance self from Diasporic encodings, or be it to resist the dominant culture, or be it to assimilate/integrate with the dominant encodings of the Western public sphere, Diasporic diction comes into being through moments of selective performative practices. These selective practices come to circumscribe a certain experience of the peoples of the Diaspora, which Fanon amplifies when he speaks about:

> *Every colonized people—in other words, every people in whose soul an inferiority complex has been created by the death and burial of its local cultural originality—finds itself face to face with the language of the civilizing nation; that is, with the culture of the mother country. The colonized is elevated above his jungle status in proportion to his adoption of the mother country's cultural standards. He becomes whiter as he renounces his blackness, his jungle (Fanon 1967: 18).*

So if we were to take language for example, where the idealized language of the colonizer comes to form itself as the imperial sacrosanct, as being the language of the colonized, and to say that within the archipelago known as the Caribbean there exist a particular way in which difference is situated on the diction or, if I can say on the 'vernacular.' To what extent then through language, does the Diaspora come to "lactify" its communicative practices? In fact, is it that for the most part, Diasporic exchanges come to lactify itself, in order to present a manner that is non-inchoate? What I am concerned with, is how language, that is, Diasporic diction as a lactifying procedure, comes to form itself as an archetype humanism. I am interested in how the Diaspora comes to understand the moment of recognition in which lactifying procedures ought to be taken up in order to meaningfully socialize. I am interested in the different moments or to say, different pictures where as Fanon tells us, of talking like a book or scorning the dialect (Fanon 1967: 21). I want to better understand how Diasporic lactifying performatives become a disciplinary way of life, a humanism in of itself, how this performative comes to embody Diasporic culture, how this performative comes to be the identity for bodies of difference. I am thinking about the inter/intra socializing processes, that of, the communicative exchange between the Diaspora and Euromodernity and at the same time communicative exchanges through bodies of difference as it contains and confines itself to the geography of its Diasporic constellation. To what extent is this socializing behavior constituted through a "neurotic orientation" (Fanon 1967:60). Is the diction of the Diaspora as lactified and as the performative formation of identity an expression of what Fanon calls, Manicheism delirium (Fanon 1967:183). How then does the Caribbean Diaspora utilize language as a communicative pragmatic, to cogently engage with the public sphere of Euro-modernity? Is it that this language of the Caribbean Diaspora, this language immanent to plantation life, has its alterity as tangential to the paradigms of Euromodernity?

With its rhythms reverberating through colonized territories, Diasporic citizenry and the co-present protean, come to take up this sense of a historic belonging within the framework of nation-state. Yet to strategically engage with this sense of belonging calls for selected communicative practices, selected communicative practices that ought to have the capacity to dialogue with this naturalized universal way of reasoning. If then, these communicative practices are selected, how does the Diasporic subject then come to understand what knowledge come into play with this selection process? How then do Caribbean Diasporic peoples make meaning of their lived experience in the Western public sphere? So if this sense of nationalism that one takes up as his or her own is entrenched colonially to subhuman status, what Fanon would call "epidermal regions of inferiority." Is it then to dismiss, or maybe perhaps to rename all colonial categories? Is this part and parcel of the decolonizing project? How would this renaming project shape or rupture the Caribbean experience? Given cultural difference, given cultural heterogeneity, what does it mean for the Diaspora in an Indigenous way to have a sense of national consciousness? Would it make for possible different discursive contours of the Diasporic body? Is it that the Diaspora, in of itself, in a totalizing way, as it emerged through the reservoir of plantation life, as it comes to exist, constituted through 'blackness,' as Euromodernity's 'other'? Fanon tells us, "alterity for the black man is not the black but the white man" (Fanon 1967: 97), that "the black soul is a white man's artifact" (Fanon 1967: 14), that "it is not I (the black body) who make meaning for myself, but it is the meaning that was already there, pre-existing waiting for me" (Fanon 1967: 134), that "I am overdetermined from without. I am the slave not of the "(idea)" that others have of me but of my own appearance" (Fanon 1967: 116). To what extent then is it that every 'body' that comes through this Diaspora wittingly or unwittingly perform acts of 'denegryfication'? (Fanon 1967: 111). What then are the moments when the Caribbean Diaspora comes to recognize its "Negritude"? We cannot help but notice how the language of the Caribbean has come to exist as the "ontological alienation" of Diasporic peoples. If as wa Thiong'o (1993) mentions, language is this crucible for culture, that language in of itself is Indigenous to identity. It seems to me, that the language of the Diaspora, more so then, comes to be experienced as the embodiment of its own alienation. It is not as simple to take up Fanon's ways, that is, to "extricate ourselves" or to rid ourselves from this Indigenous way of knowing, from an Indigenous way of communicating. To turn a new leaf and pick up some new found way to enunciate is to rid the self of particular histories, is to rid the self of insulating memories. But with the myriad permutations and arrangements of culture, it is not to say the Diaspora ought not work with different cultural practices, be it language, food, religion, dance, and what have you. But to willingly disengage from Indigenous ways, to communicate, that is, to strategically practice a way of life as distinct from one's Indigeneity, to interact in a totalizing way through practices, which unilaterally converge to historical and contemporary dominant paradigms of Euromodernity, is to engage in what I am thinking of, as epidermal displacement practices. It is to engage in particular practices where one local Indigenous sociocultural way of coming to understand becomes silenced and it is this silence that comes to write the history of Diasporic possibilities, it is this said silence which provides a platform of meaning for Diasporic experiences. If silence, then becomes one of the possible modes to organize relations between the Diaspora and public sphere of Euromodernity, how then does the Diaspora come to interface with itself? How do Diasporic communities come to organize themselves, considering the inter-intra relations of cultural difference? By what means do Diasporic bodies as "epistemologically limited" (Gordon 1995) through its embodied alienation, engage Diasporic spaces by being cognizant of the proximity and distancing from its historic-cultural artifacts? How does the Diaspora come to understand the experience of the lived public, when spaces as the "town hall, institutions, school administration offices, the school, sports arenas, administrative places come to be strategic places of alienation" (Glissant 1999: 36).

What I am hoping to come out of this conversation is for us to bring to the surface, the everyday or taken-for-granted embodied 'Truth' talk that organizes communicative principles of colonial modernity. So be it the morals of colonialism, or colonial logic, how is this as a mantra taken up as one's own and at the same time work to position the lived black? If as Fanon requests we were to de-ontologize the lived 'black,' then as a starting point we can introduce colonial historic specificities. I am more concerned here with colonial constituents some of which are to say, the temporal, space, violence, anachronism, dialectic of hue, racism, geographies, civilization, Euro-intelligentsia and plantation life. Notably, there is a danger here in discarding these constituents as relic, as some irrelevant distant artifact, instead maybe we ought to think about how these constituents come to be re-shaped, re-organize and regulate our present day social. So as our daily conversations become mediated through these colonial constituents we can begin to wonder how certain knowledges come to be centered within different sociocultural sites. We can come to understand what embodied knowledge is selected as a communicative procedure to form some sort of working harmonious union. Be it a performative procedure or not, the Diasporic subject wittingly or unwittingly makes meaning through integrating viable 'Truth' systems. It is not necessarily in the Fanonian sense that the Diasporic subject is undergoing and "inferiority complex." I think it is more of having a working understanding of the socio-economic-cultural registrar of modernity and how it plays out in time space, that is, the consequences of practicing a certain reading of the body at particular social sites.

CONCLUSION

With this discussion I hoped to have enhanced the potentiality for education by invoking "pedagogic thoughtfulness." I wanted to think through certain sites that operationalized the centre of Fanon's colonial experience, such as race, hue, culture and alienation. My learning objective was to bring awareness to certain discontinuities, in particular, how hue as embodied, self-regulates different Diasporic spaces. I wanted to accord cognition to Diasporic socio-historical conditions. With the hope of transforming our social reality, I wanted us to come to be critically reflexive on our experiences, in order to think about some pragmatic communicative possibilities. In doing so, I think it is pertinent we continue to remind ourselves that this embodied alienation we are speaking about, has its mode of orientation well rooted within the interstices and aesthetics of the colonial index. As Fanon reminds us, we have a Diasporic self then experiencing alienation of the body from within. We also have a self here that experiences alienation from historic ways of knowing, from customs, from values, from habitual practices. I am also concerned about the ahistoric ways of coming to know Diasporic self. Be it that self comes to make sense of its social field as Fanon framed, through lactification practices, or be it a self imbued as (Du Bois 1989) mentions, through the "eyes of the other," or be it a self experiencing what (Asante 2007) calls a "tortured consciousness" that results in the body being "magnetized by white privilege," there is, in a sense, an incommensurable loss (Butler 1997; Oliver 2004) being experienced here. For me, I am more interested in how this sense of an incommensurable loss, comes to seduce the Diasporic self through a mode of thinking that brings a self-regulating surveillance on the body, which materializes itself in the production of a particular geo-subject. I am left here contemplating, how then does this incommensurable loss endow the socialization process where self has to integrate different socio-cognitive interests to form cogent communicative strategies of the lived social, as organized through the classificatory system of Euromodernity? So if we were to talk about the Caribbean Diasporic, if we were to speak about Diasporic intersubjectivity and Caribbean identity, then we cannot forget to speak about the link with colonial alienation, we cannot forget, that as a starting point and as (Gordon 1995) reminds us, "ontology must be suspended"(Gordon 1995:14), that the Caribbean Diaspora, experiences "absolute ontological rigidity" (Gordon 1995: 43). What then are some of the properties of this "absolute ontological rigidity," which circumscribes the everyday Diasporic experience? Is this absolute ontological rigidity race? How do we decolonize beyond the text, this illiberal ontological rigidity of the Diaspora? How does Fanon's colonial experience diverge and converge to the contemporary Diasporic experience? By way of decolonizing pedagogies, what does Fanon offer us to subvert the homogeneity of Euromodernity's humanism? If we were to think of lactification as it is reified through time and space, what does it mean for the body of difference to lactify beyond the epidermal schema? What does it mean for everyday sites of interaction, to say, from the choice of food, to the way one speaks, to the conversation on religion that is tacitly encoded through bodies of distinct geographies, to the choice of clothes, to schooling and education, to the institutions of work, to be aesthetically and epistemologically oriented to the humanism of Euromodernity? What are the unfreedoms for the Diaspora when this humanism of Euromodernity becomes the only way out for bodies of difference? In the search for a different humanism, Fanon pushes us to think of the ontological underpinnings of our experience. Fanon leaves us pondering the form and nature of our reality, the protean elements concerning race, class, gender, sexuality, ableism, religion, which mold and shape our existence. More so we are left thinking about the underlying bodies of knowledge that worked to conceptualize our participatory form of humanism, we are left contemplating the ethical and moral implications of socializing through particular communicative practices. Frantz Fanon's oeuvre provides us with possible decolonizing pedagogies to understand different Diasporic experiences. Moreover, Fanon gives us the means to understand local colonial encounters and compels us to unconditionally question the colonial archetype and its ensuing humanism.

REFERENCES

Asante, K. M. 2007. *An Afrocentirc Manifesto*. Cambridge: Polity Press.
Bourdieu, P. 1991. *Language and Symbolic Power*. Trans. G. Raymond and M. Adamson, Edited & Introduced Thompson, B. John. Cambridge,MA:Harvard University Press
Butler, J. 1997. *The Psychic Life of Power: Theories in Subjection*. Stanford, CA: Stanford University Press.

Cesaire, A. 1972. *Discourse on Colonialism.* New York: Monthly Review Press.
Dei, G. J. S., Karumanchery. L. L., & Karumanchery-Luik, N. 2004. *Playing the Race Card: Exposing White Power and Privilege.* New York: Peter Lang.
Dei, G. J. S. 2005. "Critical Issues in Anti-Racist Research Methodologies: An Introduction." In G. J. S. Dei, and G. Johal (eds). 2005. *Critical Issues in Anti-Racist Research Methodology.* New York: Peter Lang. pp. 1-27.
Dei, G. J. S. 2006. "Introduction: Mapping the Terrain-Towards a New Politics of Resistance." In G. J. S. Dei, and A. Kempf, (eds.) *Anti-Colonialism and Education: The Politics of Resistance.* Rotterdam: Sense Publishers. pp. 1-23.
Dei, G. J. S. 2008a. "Crash and the Relevance of an Anti-Racism Analytical Lens." In G. J. S. Dei, and S.S. Howard, (eds.) *Crash Politics and Antiracism: Interrogations of Liberal Race Discourse.* New York: Peter Lang. pp 13-23.
Dei, G. J. S. 2008b. *Racists Beware: Uncovering Racial Politics in Contemporary Society.* Rotterdam: Sense Publishers.
Du Bois, W. E. B. 1989. *The Souls of Black Folk.* New York: Penguin Books.
Fanon, F. 1967. *Black Skin, White Masks.* New York: Grove Press.
Fanon, F. 1965. *A Dying Colonialism.* New York: Grove Press.
Fanon, F. 1964. *Towards the African Revolution.* New York: Grove Press.
Fanon, F. 1963. *The Wretched of the Earth.* New York: Grove Press.
Foster, C. 2007. *Blackness & Modernity: The Colour of Humanity and the Quest for Freedom.* Montreal & Kingston, London, Ithaca: McGill-Queen's University Press.
Foucault, M. 2007. *The Politics of Truth.* LosAngeles: Semiotext(e).
Foucault, M. 1995. *Discipline and Punish: The Birth of the Prison.* New York: Vintage Books.
Fraser, N. 1992. "Rethinking the Public Sphere: A Contribution to the Critique of Actually Existing Democracy." In Calhoun, C. (ed.) *Habermas and the Public Sphere.* Cambridge, MA: and London, England: MIT Press.
Giddens, A. 1991. *Modernity and Self-Identity: Self and Society in the Late Modern Age.* Stanford, CA: University Press.
Giddens, A. 1990. *The Consequences of Modernity.* Stanford, CA: Stanford University Press.
Glissant, E. 1989. *Caribbean Discourse: Selected Essays.* Charlottesville: University Press of Virginia.
Goldberg, D.T. 1993. *Racist Culture: Philosophy and the Politics of Meaning.* Oxford. Blackwell.
Gordon, R. L. 1995. *Fanon and the Crisis of European Man: An Essay on Philosophy and the Human Sciences.* New York: Routledge.
Guba, E. G., and Lincoln, Y. S. 1994. "Competing Paradigms in Qualitative Research." In N. K. Denzin and Y. S. Lincoln (eds.), *Handbook of Qualitative Research.* Thousand Oaks, CA: Sage. pp. 105-117.
Habermas, J. 1991. *The Structural Transformation of the Public Sphere: An Inquiry into a Category of Bourgeois Society.* Cambridge, MA: MIT Press.
Itwaru, A. H. and Ksonzek, N. 1994. *Closed Entrances: Canadian culture and Imperialism.* Toronto, Cardiff: TSAR.
Ladson-Billings, G. "Racialized Discourses and Ethnic Epistemologies." In N.K. Denzin and Y. S. Lincoln, (Second Ed) *Handbook of Qualitative Research.* 2000. pp 257- 277) Thousand Oaks, CA: Sage Publications.

McKittrick, K. 2006. *Demonic Grounds: Black Women and the Cartographies of Struggle.* Minneapolis, London: University of Minnesota Press.

Oliver, K. 2004. *The Colonization of Psychic Space.* Minneapolis: University of Minnesota Press.

Sartre, J-P. 2001. "Black Orpheus." In Robert Bernasconi (ed.), *Race.* Malden, MA: Blackwell Publishers. pp. 115-142.

Sekyi-Otu, A. 1996. *Fanon's Dialectic of Experience.* Cambridge, MA: Harvard University Press.

Senghor L. 2001. "Negritude and Modernity or Negritude as a Humanism for the Twentieth Century." In Robert Bernasconi (ed.), *Race.* Malden, MA: Blackwell Publishers. pp. 143-166.

Smith Tuhiwai, L. 1999. *Decolonizing Methodologies: Research and Indigenous Peoples.* London: Zed Books and University of Otago Press.

Van Manen, M. 1997. *Researching Lived Experience: Human Science for an Action Sensitive Pedagogy.* Winnipeg, Manitoba: The Althouse Press.

wa Thiong'o, N. 1993. *Moving the Centre: The Struggle for Cultural Freedoms.* James Currey, Oxford. EAEP, Nairobi. Heinemann, Portsmouth, NH.

wa Thiong'o, N. 1986. *Decolonising the Mind: The Politics of Language in African Literature.* Oxford. EAEP, Nairobi. Heinemann, Portsmouth, NH.

Wynter, S. 2001. "Towards the Sociogenic Principle: Fanon, Identity, the Puzzle of Conscious Experience, and What It Is Like to Be 'Black.'" In Mercedes F. Duran-Cogan and Antoni Gomez-Moriana, eds., *National Identities and Socio-Political Changes in Latin America,* 30-66. New York: Routledge.

Notes on Contributors

PAUL BANAHENE ADJEI is a Ph.D. candidate at the Ontario Institute for Studies in Education (OISE), University of Toronto, and a sessional lecturer to the course *New 444H1: Social change and Non-violence* at New College, University of Toronto. His publications include: "Decolonising knowledge production: The pedagogic relevance of Gandhian Satyagraha to schooling and education in Ghana," *Canadian Journal of Education (2007)* and "Unmapping the tapestry of *Crash*," in P. Howard and G. Dei (Ed.), *Crash politics and antiracism: Interrogations of liberal race discourse (2008)*.

KATIE AUBRECHT is a Ph.D. candidate in Sociology and Equity Studies in Education at the Ontario Institute for Studies in Education, University of Toronto. Using a Critical Disability Studies perspective, her Ph.D. research questions the ordinary and commonplace ways embodied responses to the violence of prevailing discourses of power are assimilated under colonial knowledge regimes. Her publications include "The Power of Anguish: Re-Mapping Mental Diversity with an Anti-Colonial Compass" with Tanya Titchkosky in *Breaching the Colonial Contract: Anti-Colonialism in the US and Canada*, edited by Arlo Kempf, and "CTOs: A New Order of Terror?" in *Engaging Terror: A Critical and Interdisciplinary Approach*.

RORY CRATH is a second-year Ph.D. student at the Faculty of Social Work, University of Toronto. His research interests centre around arts-based research that explores how social work practitioners and community agencies negotiate and articulate issues of space, racialised difference, and self-determination of "the client" both historically and within current contexts. Rory has 15 years of community- and arts-based experience working with street-involved youth and second-generation and immigrant youth and young adults.

GEORGE J. SEFA DEI is professor (and immediate past Chair) of the Department of Sociology and Equity Studies, Ontario Institute for Studies in Education of the University of Toronto (OISE/UT). His teaching and research interests are in the areas of antiracism, minority schooling, international development, and anticolonial thought. He has published extensively on race, antiracism, minority youth schooling, and anticolonial thought. In 2008 he published *Racists Beware: Uncovering Racial Politics in Contemporary Society* and *"Crash" Politics and*

Anti-Racism: Interrogating Liberal Race Discourse (coedited with Philip Howard). His forthcoming book is *Teaching Africa: Towards a Transgressive Pedagogy*.

CAMILLE LOGAN is a doctoral candidate at the Ontario Institute for Studies in Education of the University of Toronto. As an elementary school administrator, her research centres on educational leadership and inclusive education. She is particularly interested in implementation and ways to subvert resistance to transforming education.

DONNA M. OUTERBRIDGE is an Ed.D. candidate at the Ontario Institute for Studies in Education/University of Toronto in the Department of Sociology and Equity Studies in Education. Her research interests include anticolonialism, antiracism, black feminism, indigenous knowledge, and Afrocentricity.

MARLON SIMMONS is a Ph.D. candidate in the Department of Sociology and Equity Studies at the Ontario Institute for Studies in Education, University of Toronto. His current research interests include anticolonial thought, issues of governance and self in the context of schooling, and educational reform. The focus of his thesis is on modernity and colonialism, with a particular attention to diasporic experiences and the interplay in the context of the West. He recently coauthored *The Indigenous as a Site of Decolonizing Knowledge for Conventional Development and the Link with Education: The African Case* (2009) with George J. Sefa Dei, edited by Jonathan Langdon.

FRANCISCO J. VILLEGAS is a doctoral student in the department of Sociology and Equity Studies in Education at the Ontario Institute for Studies in Education at the University of Toronto. His research focuses on immigration and schooling and his proposed dissertation will look at the experiences of families with undocumented children in Toronto schools. He received his MA in Mexican American Studies from San Jose State University and completed a thesis examining the experiences of undocumented students at a California university.

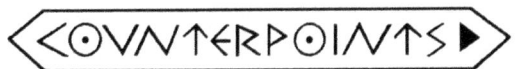

Studies in the Postmodern Theory of Education

General Editors
Joe L. Kincheloe & Shirley R. Steinberg

Counterpoints publishes the most compelling and imaginative books being written in education today. Grounded on the theoretical advances in criticalism, feminism, and postmodernism in the last two decades of the twentieth century, Counterpoints engages the meaning of these innovations in various forms of educational expression. Committed to the proposition that theoretical literature should be accessible to a variety of audiences, the series insists that its authors avoid esoteric and jargonistic languages that transform educational scholarship into an elite discourse for the initiated. Scholarly work matters only to the degree it affects consciousness and practice at multiple sites. Counterpoints' editorial policy is based on these principles and the ability of scholars to break new ground, to open new conversations, to go where educators have never gone before.

For additional information about this series or for the submission of manuscripts, please contact:

> Joe L. Kincheloe & Shirley R. Steinberg
> c/o Peter Lang Publishing, Inc.
> 29 Broadway, 18th floor
> New York, New York 10006

To order other books in this series, please contact our Customer Service Department:

> (800) 770-LANG (within the U.S.)
> (212) 647-7706 (outside the U.S.)
> (212) 647-7707 FAX

Or browse online by series:
> www.peterlang.com

www.ingramcontent.com/pod-product-compliance
Ingram Content Group UK Ltd.
Pitfield, Milton Keynes, MK11 3LW, UK
UKHW022231230426
12048UKWH00016BA/1185